Marketing Culture and the Arts

Third Edition

D0621708

Cover artwork:

En coulisse, l'hôtel du libre échange

Painting by **Jeannette Perreault**

Jeannette Perreault was born in Montreal in 1958. In 1976, she became interested in the visual arts and began to study drawing and ink on paper. In 1984 she began to participate in numerous live-model workshops and to explore the medium of oil on canvas.

Perreault emphasizes the vitality of forms and has developed a brush-stroke technique that allows colour and line to interact freely. She refines the form and uses colours for their intrinsic expressiveness and luminosity. People are the centre of her themes.

Since 1993 she has frequented the Théâtre du Nouveau Monde to sketch actors and scenes, particularly in the dressing rooms and backstage. From these sketches on paper, she creates paintings that evoke the intimacy and ambience of the theatre.

Represented by galleries since 1986, Perreault has participated in several group and solo exhibitions. Her works are shown at the Galerie Jean-Pierre Valentin in Montreal, Roberts Gallery in Toronto, and Winchester Galleries in Victoria.

FRANÇOIS COLBERT

with the collaboration of Suzanne Bilodeau, Johanne Brunet, Jacques Nantel, and J. Dennis Rich
and with the participation of Philippe Ravanas and Yannik St-James
Foreword by Dan J. Martin

Marketing Culture and the Arts

Third Edition

HEC MONTRÉAL

Carmelle and Rémi Marcoux
CHAIR IN ARTS MANAGEMENT

Library and Archives Canada Cataloguing in Publication
Colbert, François
Marketing culture and the arts / François Colbert; with the
collaboration of Suzanne Bilodeau, Johanne Brunet, Jacques Nantel
and J. Dennis Rich; and with the participation of Philippe Ravanas
and Yannik St-James; foreword by Dan J. Martin. – 3rd ed.
Translation of: Le marketing des arts et de la culture.
Includes bibliographical references and index.
ISBN 978-2-9808602-1-8

1. Arts–Marketing. 2. Arts–Management. 3. Cultural industries–Management.
4. Culture diffusion. 5. Marketing. I. École des hautes études commerciales (Montréal,
Québec). Carmelle and Rémi Marcoux Chair in Arts Management II. Title.

NX634.C6413 2007   700.68'8   C2006-906642-6

Several trademarks are mentioned in this book. The publisher has not provided a list of these
trademarks and their owners and has not inserted the relevant symbol next to each, because they
are mentioned for information purposes only and to the benefit of the trademark owner, with no
intention to infringe on the rights relating to these trademarks.

Printed in Canada

Translated from *Le marketing des arts et de la culture*
© 2007 Les Éditions de la Chenelière inc.
© 1993, 2000, Gaëtan Morin Éditeur ltée
All rights reserved.

First English Edition:
© Gaëtan Morin Éditeur ltée, 1994

No part of this work may be reproduced or copied in any form or by any means without the
prior consent of the publisher. Illegal reproduction is an infringement of copyright law.

Publishing assistant: Louise St-Pierre
Copy editing: Jane Broderick
Head translator: Andrea Neuhofer
Cover design: Stéphane Lortie, Atelier de graphisme, HEC Montréal
Layout: Rolande Trudeau, Atelier de graphisme, HEC Montréal

© 2007 Carmelle and Rémi Marcoux Chair in Arts Management, HEC Montréal.
All rights reserved for all countries.
Distributed by the Carmelle and Rémi Marcoux Chair in Arts Management, HEC Montréal,
3000, chemin de la Côte-Sainte-Catherine, Montréal (Québec), Canada, H3T 2A7,
tel.: 514 340-5629, www.gestiondesarts.com/index.php?id=717

Legal Deposit – Bibliothèque nationale du Québec – National Library of Canada, 2007

To Maxime, Simon and Julien

Acknowledgements

The author would like to thank his collaborators, Suzanne Bilodeau, Johanne Brunet, Jacques Nantel, and Dennis Rich; and Dan J. Martin for writing the Foreword; as well as acknowledging the contributions of Yannik St-James and Philippe Ravanas and the participation of Nathalie Courville. He also would like to aknowledge the excellent contribution of his research assistant, Véronique Lafleur.

Professor Colbert extends his thanks to all the colleagues from different countries who graciously agreed to provide examples of good marketing practices (in alphabetical order):

Stephen Boyle
University of South Australia
Australia

Alessandro Bollo
Fitzcarraldo Foundation
Italy

Antonella Carù
SDA Bocconi School of Management
Bocconi University
Italy

Craig Cooper
Sydney Opera House
Australia

François H. Courvoisier
Haute École de Gestion Arc
Neuchâtel Business School
Switzerland

Véronique Cova
Laboratoire GREFI-Faculté
d'Economie Appliquée
France

Patricia Dewey
University of Oregon
USA

Jane Frank
Queensland University of Technology
Australia

Rose Ginther
Grant MacEwan College
Canada

Harmon Greenblatt
University of New Orleans
USA

Tad Janes
Maryland Ensemble Theatre
USA

Bronwyn Klepp
Queensland Theatre Company
Australia

Juan D. Montoro
Universitat de València
Spain

Steven Morrison
University of Cincinnati College
– Conservatory of Music
USA

Jorge Cerveira Pinto
Evcom Lda
Portugal

William D. Poole
University of Waterloo
Canada

Manual Cuadrado
Universitat de València
Spain

Michael Quine
City University
United Kingdom

Jennifer Radbourne
Deakin University
Australia

Ruth Rentschler
Deakin University
Australia

Michelle Richards
Adelaide Symphony Orchestra
Australia

Simon Roodhouse
Bolton Institute of Higher Education
United Kingdom

Fabiana Sciarelli
University of Naples "Federico II"
and University of Perugia
Italy

Anne W. Smith
Arts Management and Education
Services
USA

Ludovico Solima
Università degli Studi di Napoli,
Federico II
Italy

Zannie G. Voss
Duke University
USA

Foreword

"Marketing is evil!" How many times have you heard that from a colleague? How many times might you have said it yourself?

This point of view is understandable if one's experience of marketing reflects only market-driven industries where the product is created solely in response to the demands of the market, where marketing professionals force changes to an established product in order to meet consumer desires or expectations, or where unscrupulous marketers misrepresent the product in order to make a quick sale. Culture, heritage and the arts – the not-for-profit variety – is a *product-driven* industry. Our artists envision and create their work with little if any regard for how the market might embrace it; they create in response to their own passions and inspirations.

Successful marketing professionals in cultural enterprises recognize that their work is carried out within an industry that is "product driven but market sensitive and customer oriented." *Product driven:* cultural marketers understand the creative product and know why it merits as large an audience as possible. *Market sensitive but customer oriented:* cultural marketers identify the appropriate target market segments for the work, then design and implement communications campaigns that grab attention, develop interest, and move the targets to take action. The best cultural marketers go even further; they facilitate appreciation for the creative work – not demystifying it but positioning it within the consumers' interests, experiences and expectations – and they strive to build consumer trust and loyalty, which results in repeat business.

Developing, nurturing, and expanding loyal and active audiences for our arts, culture, and heritage centres is a formidable challenge. How is it done? Painstakingly, with a thorough understanding of marketing theories and practices, careful market research, and a strategic and comprehensive marketing plan. All of this will help us to achieve our goal of a theatre or exhibition space full of informed, engaged and loyal patrons eager to experience all that our artists have to offer.

"Marketing is *evil*"? Soon, with the right principles and practices in place, you may be hearing, "Marketing is *vital*"!

François Colbert's *Marketing Culture and Arts* is an important step forward in achieving that goal. This book explains and contextualizes complex and sophisticated marketing principles in a clear, straightforward manner using examples from the cultural sector; it offers readers – both first-year students and working professionals – the critical foundation upon which effective and efficient communications programs are built.

Dan J. Martin
Associate Dean, H. John Heinz III School
   of Public Policy and Management
Director, Institute for the Management
   of Creative Enterprises
Carnegie Mellon University
Pittsburgh, Pennsylvania, USA

Contents

2   THE PRODUCT

3   THE MARKET

4   CONSUMER BEHAVIOURS   *by Jacques Nantel*

5   THE PRIVATE SECTOR MARKET   *by J. Dennis Rich*

6   SEGMENTATION AND POSITIONING   *by Jacques Nantel*

7   THE PRICE VARIABLE

8   THE DISTRIBUTION VARIABLE

9   THE PROMOTION VARIABLE

10   MARKETING INFORMATION SYSTEMS

11 PLANNING AND CONTROLLING THE MARKETING PROCESS

PLAN

Chapter 1

Cultural Enterprises and Marketing

OBJECTIVES

- Understand the specificity of cultural enterprises
- Pinpoint the artist's role in a cultural enterprise
- Make the distinction between the arts sector and cultural industries
- Understand the evolution of marketing
- Distinguish between traditional marketing and the marketing of culture and the arts

INTRODUCTION

This chapter sets out those characteristics of the marketing of culture and the arts that distinguish it from traditional marketing. In the first section, we define the notion of marketing and then go on to review the history of marketing, from its humble beginnings to the rise of specializations – in particular, the marketing of culture and the arts. In the second section, we consider cultural enterprises as a whole by examining their place in our society, the artist's role within them, and their mission in terms of a product. We then determine what sets different cultural enterprises apart and, more specifically, what differentiates cultural industries from those attached, by definition, to the arts sector. We then define this specialization by comparing the traditional model of marketing with one adapted to the reality of an artistic product.

Lastly, we provide a broad overview describing each component of the marketing model used in later chapters.

1.1 MARKETING

1.1.1 A Definition of Marketing

The goal of marketing is optimization of the relationship between companies and customers and maximization of their mutual satisfaction.

The notion of marketing implies essentially four elements: a consumer need, satisfaction of this need, a link between the company and the consumer, and optimization of profits. The distinction between optimization and maximization is important. The maximization process attempts to generate the highest profits possible. Optimization seeks to obtain the highest possible profits while taking into account organizational or environmental elements, such as ensuring employee welfare, creating a solid corporate image, satisfying the customer, or getting the company involved in its community.

Marketing is thus a tool at the service of an organization – whether not-for-profit or for-profit – in the corporate or the cultural sector. It is the job of the organization's managers to use this tool in a way that fulfils the organization's mission.

It is important to remember that marketing, while considered a science, is also an art. Three points should be kept in mind.

First of all, since the market is made up of human beings, and since people are by nature complex beings, nothing is ever black and white. One of the characteristics of marketing is that managers are frequently required to work in a climate of uncertainty, without access to all the information they need, and therefore are forced to rely as much on instinct as on any systematic analysis of their environment.

Secondly, to succeed in marketing, marketers must be able to put themselves "in the consumer's shoes." To strike a chord with the target group, the manager must know what consumers are thinking and how they make their decisions.

Finally, consumers typically base their decisions on perceptions. The perception of the message conveyed or the product offered by a firm thus becomes reality in the mind of the customer. Even if this perception is false, customers will nonetheless base their decisions on a reality that they perceive as true.

These three characteristics are what make marketing such a difficult task for those responsible for this function within organizations. That is why it is essential they have a full grasp of all the different facets of marketing.

1.1.2 The Birth and Development of Marketing

Marketing as a science developed in parallel with improved material well-being in the industrialized world and as a result of the development of trade.

During the nineteenth century, supply clearly created the demand. At this time, the average consumer did not have much of an income and manufacturers could barely satisfy the basic needs of the population. The distribution system for goods was made up of small manufacturers on the one hand and small shopkeepers on the other. Wholesalers and various intermediaries served to link the two extremes. It was definitely a seller's market as opposed to a buyer's market.

Industrialization dramatically changed these conditions. At the beginning of the twentieth century, manufacturing costs were lowered through assembly-line procedures. As a result, the size of manufacturers and stores grew. Clusters of firms developed in certain industries. Competition intensified on both the local and international level. At the same time, firms broke with the custom of pricing a product based on its manufacturing costs. Manufacturers realized that consumers with increased spending capacity wanted goods that would satisfy not only their needs but also their tastes and desires. They were no longer necessarily ready to buy the lowest-priced product on the market.

Economists were the first to reflect upon the problems related to market and demand. In the early days, marketing actually borrowed a great deal from economics. According to Bartels in *The History of Marketing Thought*,[1] the term "marketing" began to mean something more than distribution or trade around 1910, and it was not until the 1920s that the first marketing studies and textbooks were published. At that time, other publications came out on retail, sales, and advertising techniques.

Sometime during the 1950s, the focus shifted from product and sales – the view that a product sells if promoted well – to a marketing view based on the consumer. This shift heralded the advent of modern marketing.

Between 1945 and 1960, the postwar baby boom and the swelling middle class encouraged marketing specialists to survey the needs and desires of potential consumers, who now had enormous purchasing power. With a view to knowing the clientele better, marketing experts delved into such social sciences as psychology and sociology in their quest to understand individual and collective consumer behaviour. This vast subject generated a great deal of data which, during the 1960s, started to be generated according to the latest quantitative and computerized methods. Thus, although marketing may have started with the application of economic theory, it was later enriched by knowledge gleaned from other sciences and then applied to create a separate discipline.

During the 1970s, marketing went from fairly general and standardized to specialized. Reference material now dealt with marketing in small and medium-sized businesses, hospital settings, service industries, and not-for-profit organizations, as well as industrial sectors. This period also marked the beginning of philanthropic marketing and the first attempts at integrating these concepts into the arts sector.

After a slow start in the 1960s, the number of academic programs in arts administration began to increase rapidly in the early to mid-1970s. The Master's in Fine Arts (MFA) program with a concentration in arts administration established by Yale University in the United States in 1966 is widely viewed as the first university program in arts management. Other programs soon followed, including those established at City University in England in 1967, St. Petersburg Theatre Arts Academy in Russia in 1968, and York University in Canada in 1969. While there were only about 30 such programs worldwide in 1980, and 100 in 1990, today there are over 400.[2]

1.2 CULTURE AND THE ARTS

1.2.1 The Position Held by Cultural Enterprises within Society

It is important to remember that the artist (or the artists' collective) plays a key role in any cultural enterprise. Indeed, all cultural products are dependent on this highly specialized labour force. Without the artist, there would be no cultural enterprise to begin with.

The notion of a cultural enterprise may be viewed narrowly or broadly. In the narrow view, it represents production and distribution companies specializing in the performing arts, such as theatre, music, opera, or dance, in the visual arts found in galleries and museums, and in libraries and heritage sites. In a broader point of view, the notion of a cultural enterprise expands to include the cultural industries (films, sound recording, publishing, crafts) and the media (radio, television, newspapers, periodicals).

Cultural enterprises also play a key role in society. They reflect the cultural identity of a country insofar as the products they produce reflect the people of that country – their customs, values, contradictions, and aspirations – while the artists who create the works are firmly rooted in their cultural traditions. Cultural enterprises also open a window on the world for citizens by presenting the reality of other cultures. In addition, cultural enterprises constitute an important economic force by virtue of the jobs they create and their contribution to a country's GNP (gross national product).

1.2.2 The Artist's Role within the Cultural Enterprise

Obviously, without artists there could be no cultural enterprise. Moreover, the artist is indispensable to other industries that fall outside the traditional definition of cultural activities. In advertising, for example, the artist is the basic resource used in creating an advertising product. In fact, filming a commercial involves a producer, musicians, actors, set designers, and so on. Often, the actors are the same ones seen on stage, television, or the big screen.

1.2.3 The Mandate of Cultural Enterprises in Terms of Product

All cultural enterprises share two characteristics: they give the artist an important role, and they deal with the product of a creative act. Often, this artistic act is independent of any organization or firm, especially in disciplines such as the visual arts or literature, where the artist usually works alone. As well, if products vary substantially from one discipline to the next, cultural enterprises may play quite different roles vis-à-vis the product. Roles may range from designing, producing, and reproducing, to distributing or preserving the product (see Figure 1.1). Depending on the mission of the cultural enterprise, it may perform one or several of these functions. Various combinations are possible, but the organization's mission determines the number of functions performed.

In the performing arts, some theatre companies create, produce, and distribute their works themselves, while others count on a specialist to distribute the product that they create and produce. Touring companies are an example of this distinction. Thus, an enterprise may have a mandate to handle only the distribution of a play without any participation in its creation or staging. The same pattern can be seen in the visual arts, where exhibition halls simply show works, while museums also conserve them.

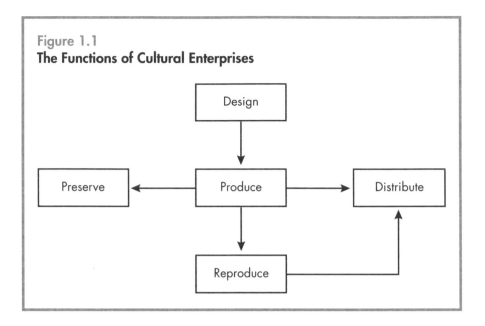

Figure 1.1
The Functions of Cultural Enterprises

This is also how things work in the cultural industries. For example, a television production company develops and produces documentaries or drama series that are then broadcast on a television network. Similarly, a company that produces a feature film typically hands over to a distributor the responsibility for distributing it in the local, national, and international markets.

1.2.4 Distinctions among Cultural Enterprises

Cultural enterprises vary considerably in size, structure, discipline, and function. It would therefore be difficult to speak of a national museum, a record company exporting abroad, and a small modern-dance troupe in the same breath, even though they are all cultural enterprises. Perhaps the best way to proceed is to differentiate and then recategorize cultural enterprises according to specific criteria.

The first criterion concerns the orientation of the enterprise's mission, which can be positioned on a continuum that has product focus and market focus as its extremes. An enterprise oriented toward (or centred on) the product would focus on the product as its *raison d'être*. Examples include a chamber-music ensemble, a children's-theatre festival, or a contemporary art museum. At the other end of the continuum is the market-oriented or market-centred enterprise, which concentrates on the market that supports it. Between these two extremes lie a vast range of different possibilities.

The second criterion applies to the way works of art are produced. The production of an artistic work is analogous to the building of a model or prototype. There is no recipe or set of instructions to guarantee the outcome. Consequently, there is a healthy dose of mystery in the assembly of each product, be it a show, a painting, or a sculpture.

On the other hand, for some disciplines and product types, the prototype is specifically designed to be mass produced in order to have many copies simultaneously. This is the case for films, records, and books.

Obviously, for any product to be reproduced, there must be an original – a manuscript, master, prototype, or model. The task of producing or reproducing may be handled by one company or several companies. This second criterion clearly distinguishes between unique products not designed to be reproduced (a prototype industry) and products manufactured in runs or batches using a prototype so that many copies appear at the same time.

By combining these two criteria, as shown in Figure 1.2, it is easier to distinguish between cultural industries and enterprises in the arts sector.

Quadrant 1 of Figure 1.2 represents product-centred enterprises whose *raison d'être* is the unique product or prototype. As a group, these enterprises form what is commonly called the "arts sector." Usually, they are small not-for-profit groups; however, there may be significant exceptions.

In the diagonally opposite corner, quadrant 3, are the market-centred enterprises, which reproduce a product. Of course, these are the profit-

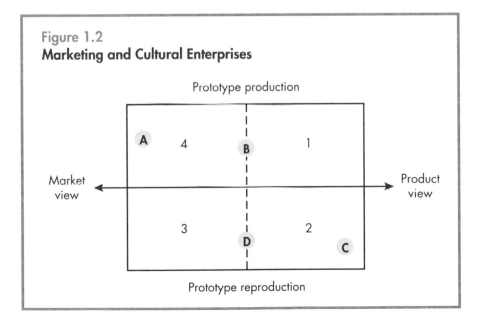

Figure 1.2
Marketing and Cultural Enterprises

Prototype production

A 4 B 1

Market view ← → Product view

3 D 2 C

Prototype reproduction

generating firms, which include most cultural industries. They include the producers, broadcasters, and distributors of these works.

Quadrants 2 and 4 represent mixed cases. Quadrant 4 includes Broadway productions like *Dracula* or *Phantom of the Opera*. Although these companies do produce unique works similar to a prototype, they are first and foremost market-centred companies. These are the cultural industries. In quadrant 2 is the product-centred enterprise, which nevertheless produces many copies of a work. A not-for-profit publisher printing a volume of poetry would fit into quadrant 2. This type of firm, though considered a cultural industry, often has more in common with the arts sector.

The other two criteria used here provide some interesting nuances; they are the size and the legal status of the enterprise.

The legal status of the enterprise quite often confirms whether it is market- or product-centred. Naturally, this is a general rule that does have its share of exceptions. Take as an example a cultural centre whose mission is to serve a linguistic minority through an entertainment program. This centre could very well be both a not-for-profit organization and market-centred. This criterion no longer distinguishes but certainly adds a nuance relevant to the description of the organization.

Size is the last criterion. Obviously, multinational firms are typical in the cultural industries. The legal status and, most of all, the mission of an enterprise in the arts sector are incompatible with the expansion of activities implied by the very concept of a multinational enterprise. The average size of firms in the arts sector is, therefore, much smaller than that of firms in the cultural industries.

This classification system will be useful in the chapters that follow, since the approach specific to marketing culture and the arts applies only to certain types of enterprises. Other types tend to use the traditional approach. Any detailed discussion of this distinction between traditional marketing and the marketing of culture and the arts should first put these approaches into perspective.

1.3 MARKETING CULTURE AND THE ARTS: DEFINITIONS

In 1967, for the first time, the question of marketing cultural enterprises was raised by an academic. Kotler,[3] in his introductory textbook, pointed out that cultural organizations, be they museums, concert halls, libraries, or universities, produce cultural goods. All of these organizations were now realizing that they had to compete for both the consumer's attention and their own share of national resources. In other words, they were facing a marketing problem.

The first books specializing in marketing culture soon followed, including works by Mokwa et al.,[4] Melillo,[5] Diggle,[6] and Reiss.[7] These texts, which focus on managing culture and the arts, offer a few definitions of marketing that diverge from the traditional ones. Diggle,[8] for example, states that "the primary aim of arts marketing is to bring an appropriate number of people into an appropriate form of contact with the artist, and in so doing to arrive at the best financial outcome that is compatible with the achievement of that aim."

Diggle's definition unequivocally places the artist, and hence the artistic product, in the foreground of any marketing strategy. The accent is on the contact between the artist's work and the consumer, and the idea is to bring as many people as possible to the point of making this contact. The initial goal is not to satisfy any consumer need, but to invite consumers to get to know and appreciate a work. This goal bears no secondary financial gain. According to Diggle, marketing culture and the arts essentially seeks to distribute or disseminate a work and generate the best possible financial results. The ultimate goal is artistic rather than financial. Unlike the commercial sector, which creates a product according to consumer needs, artistic concerns create a product first and then try to find the appropriate clientele. Evrard[9] describes this reality as "marketing the supply."

Based on the notion of satisfaction in the exchange between product and market, Hirschman[10] outlines three market segments, as illustrated in Figure 1.3. The three segments are defined according to the artist's creative orientation and goals. The first market segment is the artist or creator. In this case, creativity is said to be self-oriented and the artist's goal is simply to satisfy an individual's need to express oneself. The second segment comprises peers – other artists, critics, or other professionals in a particular discipline – and creativity is said to be peer-oriented – the artist seeks recognition in a particular milieu. The third segment, the public at large, can be divided into several sub-segments; hence, the artist's creativity is said to be commercial, or market-oriented. The primary objective in this case is most often financial gain. Artists may create in the hope of reaching one or another of these segments, or even all three at once. Even if artists are trying to reach all three segments, they should still find satisfaction in their work. In fact, one artist may choose to create different products for each segment.

Whenever the work produced stems from self-oriented creativity, the marketing process is product-centred and distinct from the traditional, market-centred process. In this case, the artistic organization must find consumers who are likely to appreciate the product.

We could combine the above definitions by saying that cultural marketing is

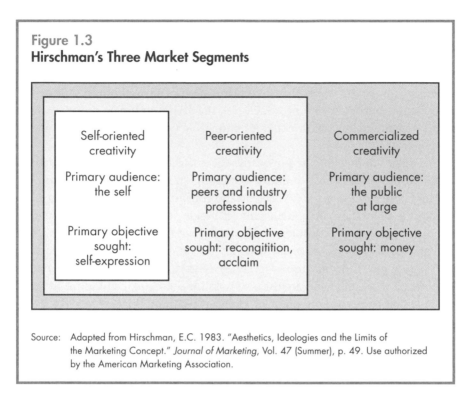

Figure 1.3
Hirschman's Three Market Segments

Self-oriented creativity	Peer-oriented creativity	Commercialized creativity
Primary audience: the self	Primary audience: peers and industry professionals	Primary audience: the public at large
Primary objective sought: self-expression	Primary objective sought: recongitition, acclaim	Primary objective sought: money

Source: Adapted from Hirschman, E.C. 1983. "Aesthetics, Ideologies and the Limits of the Marketing Concept." *Journal of Marketing*, Vol. 47 (Summer), p. 49. Use authorized by the American Marketing Association.

The art of making contact with market segments that are likely to be interested in the product by adapting the marketing variables – price, distribution and promotion – in order to put the product in contact with a sufficient number of consumers, thereby achieving the objectives that were set based on the company's mission.

1.4 THE MARKETING MODEL

Marketing theoreticians use a model to describe in simplified fashion how a company markets a product. Since the reality of the cultural or artistic milieu is different from that of commerce or industry, the marketing model must be adjusted accordingly.

1.4.1 The Traditional Marketing Model

In the traditional model, which describes the reality of commercial and industrial firms, the components must be considered a sequence that starts in the

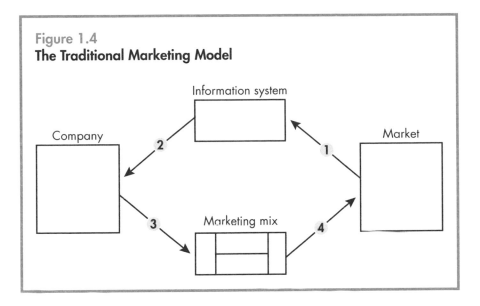

Figure 1.4
The Traditional Marketing Model

Information system

Company

Market

Marketing mix

"market" square (see Figure 1.4). This theory maintains that a company seeks to fulfil an existing need among consumers. Using data provided by the company's marketing-information system, the company evaluates the existing need and its capacity to meet that need, given current resources and the corporate mission. The company then takes the four elements of the marketing mix and adjusts them to produce the desired effect on the potential consumer. The sequence here is as follows: market – information system – company – marketing mix – market. The market is thus both the starting point and the finishing point for this process.

1.4.2 The Marketing Model for Culture and the Arts

Although this model contains the same components as the traditional marketing model, the marketing process for product-centred cultural enterprises is different. As a result, the traditional marketing model cannot adequately reflect the reality of the artistic milieu. As Figure 1.5 shows, the process starts within the enterprise, in the product itself, as stated in the definition adopted above. The enterprise tries to decide which part of the market is likely to be interested in its product. Once potential customers are identified, the company will decide on the other three elements – price, place, and promotion – for this clientele. In this type of company, the process order would be company (product) – information system – market – information system – company – marketing mix – market. The starting point is the product and the destination is the market.

Figure 1.5
The Marketing Culture and the Arts Model

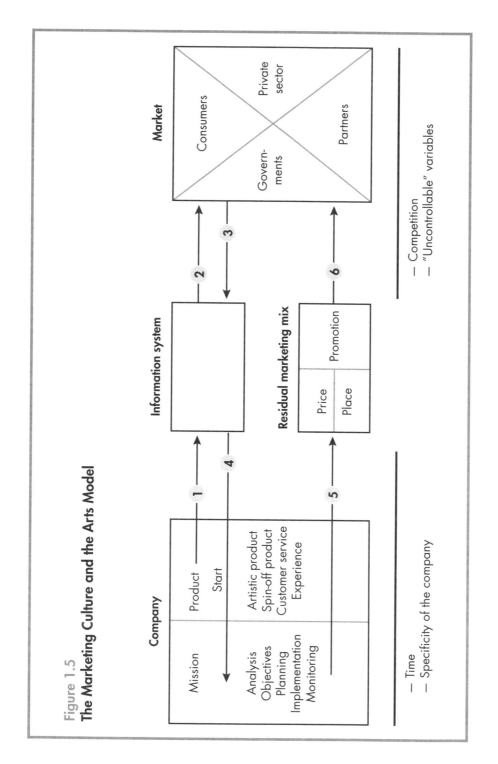

This model could also describe the reality for other types of companies. For example, in industry and commerce, the discovery of a new product or application leads to a search for a market where the product can be introduced. In this particular case, therefore, the point of departure lies in the company and its product, just as in a cultural venture. There is still, however, a considerable difference between the two situations. Essentially, the objectives are different: the commercial firm seeks a market where profit may be optimized, or it will abandon the market due to lack of consumer interest; the product-centred cultural enterprise has art rather than profit as its ultimate objective. Reaching the artistic goal is a truer measure of success for the company executing an artistic rather than a financial project.

As we have seen, some cultural enterprises are basically market-centred, with a financial rather than an artistic goal. In their case, the traditional marketing model would best describe the marketing process.

1.4.3 Marketing and Cultural Enterprises

Looking again at the model presented in section 1.2.4, we can not only distinguish between enterprises in the arts sector and those defined as cultural industries, but also clearly see in which instances traditional marketing or marketing of culture and the arts is appropriate (see Figure 1.2, Marketing and Cultural Enterprises).

Quadrants 3 and 4 in Figure 1.2 contain market-centred companies, whose marketing approach would be essentially traditional. On the other hand, in quadrants 1 and 2, where the companies are basically product-centred, the marketing approach would correspond to the marketing model for culture and the arts.

Beyond these two opposing situations, enterprises may shift, to various degrees, toward one approach or the other. For example, firm A would have a clear market orientation even if its product was unique, such as a Broadway type of show. Firm B would consider market conditions, but less rigidly than firm A. This difference would distinguish firm B from the companies in quadrant 1. Similarly, if we look at firms C and D, two companies reproducing artistic works, firm C has a clear-cut product orientation, while firm D has a less definite product orientation. This is also the difference between firm D and the companies in quadrant 3.

These examples reveal three different marketing situations: firms using a "pure" traditional marketing approach (quadrants 3 and 4), those with a "pure" approach to cultural marketing (quadrants 1 and 2), and a third category whose mixed approach allows for some compromises on product or adjustments to the product according to consumer preferences (situations B and D).

1.5 COMPONENTS OF THE MARKETING MODEL

1.5.1 The Market

A market is a group of economic agents (consumers or sponsors, for example) expressing desires and needs for products, services, or ideas. The notions of need and desire are the cornerstone of marketing and the key to any marketing strategy.

Thus, an economic agent expresses needs, which a company seeks to meet through a range of products and services. A commercial organization would study these needs before designing a product. A cultural enterprise, on the other hand, would seek out clients with needs likely to be met by the works produced. These could be either individuals or other organizations; in the case of a cultural enterprise, it could be consumers, a government (and, by extension, peers sitting on juries), the private sector (arts patrons, foundations, sponsors), or partners (distribution intermediaries, co-producers, distribution partners or presenters, media). Needs and desires, given their rather subjective nature, are not always as easily defined. Even at the movies, a consumer may distinguish among the broad categories (comedy, horror, and action) yet remain unaware of the countless nuances of potential benefit or interest.

By buying products or services, clients create what economists call "the demand," or the amount of a good or service that economic agents acquire in a given market.

A market may be divided into subgroups or segments according to tastes and needs. A commercial enterprise or organization designs a product with a clientele in mind. The product is shaped to meet the needs of those potential customers. The company thus sets itself apart from the competition, whose product offering is not marketed the same way. The company with a clear-cut advantage over its competitors thus consolidates its market position. By creating market segments, a cultural enterprise identifies a clientele made up of individuals likely to appreciate the features of its product. In the private-sector funding market, individual donors can be considered a separate segment – distinct from foundations, corporate donors, and even the sponsorships undertaken by corporate donors, since the needs, desires, and objectives of each are different.

1.5.2 The Environment

A marketing strategy cannot be drawn up in a vacuum; there are many external restrictions affecting the market and the firm. The environment, including both the company and the market, is composed of two elements which constantly influence all organizations: competition, over which the company has some control, and macro-environmental variables, also known as "uncontrollable variables."

Competition is often defined as a semi-controllable variable. That is, even if a competitor's strategy cannot be directly affected, there are various ways to react – for example, following the opponent's lead by lowering prices or matching a lively advertising campaign with an equally lively promotional campaign. A firm is not as powerless when confronted with semi-controllable variables as it is when facing macro-environmental variables.

Macro-environmental, or uncontrollable, variables constantly affect the life of any corporation, which may have to adapt to radical changes yet never have the chance to act upon the causes of these changes.

There are five main variables in the macro-environment: demographic, cultural, economic, political-legal, and technological. They will be described in detail in Chapter 3.

Example 1.1
The Sydney Opera House: Facing and Adapting to the Competition

A few years ago, managers at the Sydney Opera House (SOH) in Australia noticed that Thursday shows had mysteriously become those with the slowest pre-sales and the lowest attendance. Environmental analysis revealed that Thursday meant late-night shopping in the suburbs and that the trend of shopping-as-entertainment was growing. Thursday was also, apparently, becoming the "new Friday," with many workers heading out to socialize straight from work.

The SOH responded by scheduling opening nights on Thursdays whenever possible (a largely invited audience) and then, on subsequent Thursdays in the same season, making the performance an "early show" (6 pm). This gave audiences an immediate post-work entertainment option, which they could either substitute for shopping or combine with later activities.

The strategy has proven to be effective: Thursday is now one of the busiest weeknights at the SOH. As one comedian quipped upon finding his late-night cabaret performance rescheduled for early evening, "This is great, isn't it? Now you can see a show and then head out and buy some pants."

Source: Stephen Boyle, Associate Director, Arts and Cultural Management Program ,University of South Australia, Adelaide, Australia.

1.5.3 The Marketing Information System (MIS)

Marketing information systems rely on three key components: internal data, secondary data published by private firms or government agencies, and the data collected by the company itself.

"Internal data" means all information available from within the firm itself. The firm's accounting system actually provides more than financial analysis; it is a rich source of internal data for the marketing specialist.

The term "secondary data" is used to describe data published by public-sector agencies, such as statistics bureaus, arts councils, or ministries of culture, and private-sector firms that specialize in producing research reports; the term also applies to data drawn from other sources, such as the Internet.

Before a market study is initiated, the main sources of secondary data must be consulted – if only to ensure that the proposed study does not already exist!

If all the internal and secondary data do not provide the information required in the decision-making process, it may be useful to gather primary data. In other words, the consumer must be questioned directly. This is commonly called a market study. The goal may be to determine consumer purchasing habits, tastes, and preferences or to test public reaction to an advertising poster or different endings for a film.

1.5.4 The Marketing Mix

Every marketing strategy is composed of the same four components: price, product, place, and promotion. Together, the "four Ps" make up what is known as the marketing mix. Successful marketing depends on a skilful balance of these components. A great distribution network and a powerful promotional campaign will not sell a product that consumers do not want, no matter how cheap it may be! The same applies to a fine product badly priced or inadequately distributed because of an error in promotion strategy. These are the fundamentals of any marketing strategy, and all firms aim at creating synergy through the combined strengths of all four. Synergy exists when the overall effect of several elements is greater than the sum of the effect of the elements taken separately.

Although the four Ps form a whole, there is a logical order in defining them. Even in the commercial sector, marketers must first know the product being sold before pricing it or deciding on its distribution. Similarly, a promotional campaign would be impossible without knowledge of the product offering, the price, and the points of sale. Initially, decisions are made following this pre-established sequence. Later on, a firm or organization may learn by experience how to blend the components.

The components of the marketing mix are called "controllable variables," in contrast with competition, which is a semi-controllable variable, or the macro-environment, which is considered uncontrollable.

Mastering and optimizing controllable variables in order to minimize the harmful effects of uncontrollable variables, or using them for their leverage effect, is a crucial issue for all companies.

Product

The product is the centrepiece of any enterprise. This statement becomes particularly meaningful in the cultural sector, where the product constitutes the starting point of any marketing activity.

In this book, the term "product" is used in its broadest sense to mean a tangible good, a service, a cause, or an idea. "Product" is associated with any result of the creative act – for example, a performance, a festival event, an exhibition, a CD, a book, or a television program.

The term "product," which includes artistic products, encompasses three additional elements, which are examined in detail in Chapters 2 and 4. These are spin-off products, customer service, and the experience of the person who comes into contact with a work of art.

Price

Every product has a price, which is normally expressed as the monetary value attributed to it. Price also includes the various expenses related to its consumption (transportation, restaurant, babysitter, etc.), the effort a consumer must expend in the act of buying the product, the time spent consuming it, and the perceived risk that the product will be inadequate. Thus, there is always a price to pay for a product, even when it is free.

The amount paid for a product is not necessarily proportionate to its manufacturing cost. The same may be said of the value attributed to it. The admission fee for a movie has nothing to do with a film's production costs. In fact, the uniqueness, fame, and symbolic value of an object may increase the price consumers are willing to pay. A work of art could, for instance, fetch a very high price that has nothing to do with the cost of creating it.

The fairest price is, therefore, the one that the consumer is prepared to pay. It is this price that a company should use to develop its strategies.

Place

Place comprises several elements. The main ones are distribution channels, physical distribution, and commercial location. Any distribution network (or channel) must be managed, which means overseeing the relationship between the various intermediaries in the network and, more specifically, between the artists, producers, and distributors. Physical distribution includes the logistics involved in distributing a product, organizing a tour, moving a book from the publisher to the end consumer, or distributing a film in theatres. Lastly, location is an important factor in the success or failure of companies selling directly to the consumer. The location of a bookshop, movie theatre, hall, museum, or even a traditional business must be carefully selected.

Promotion

Promotion comes last in the first sequence of this definition of the marketing mix. In the pre-preparation stage of a promotional campaign, a company must know which product is offered at which price and where. It must know beforehand the main characteristics of the targeted consumers and, in particular, the most convincing selling arguments for those consumers.

Since the same consumers are targeted by advertising, promotional, and marketing campaigns, these three areas are often confused. They are inclusive, since promotion is made up of four distinct components – advertising, personal selling, sales promotions, and public relations – and since marketing includes promotion.

1.5.5 Two Influential Elements

Two other elements must be considered in any marketing analysis: time, and the specificity of the firm.

Time

All companies must work within a changing environment. Market conditions evolve over time, as do economic agents, needs, and tastes. The variables of the macro-environment may be modified and the competition may adjust its strategies. An excellent marketing strategy may seem outdated after a few years, or even a few months. The marketing professional must constantly review the current strategy. Time is also important to the company's own growth, since corporate objectives – and hence marketing policies – may be altered. Marketing should be considered an evolving process, and any strategy must be periodically reviewed and adjusted according to the environment and corporate priorities.

Specificity of the Firm

Every organization has its own personality and acts as an individual entity. What may be an excellent marketing strategy for firm A may prove hopelessly inadequate for firm B. Neither their products nor their market shares are necessarily the same. Their corporate images may also vary. It would therefore be risky to try to transplant a strategy from one firm to another. In some instances, however, a successful competitor's strategy may serve as inspiration. Many small companies successfully imitate the products and marketing policies of their competitors and manage to save enormous sums on marketing studies. Rarely, however, can all the elements of a strategy be borrowed from a competitor.

1.5.6 The Company and Its Marketing Management

Decisions on marketing strategies must always conform to the company's mission and objectives. These decisions must also take into account the organization's human, financial, and technical resources.

The marketing management process may be broken down into five key steps: analysis, setting of objectives, planning, implementation, and monitoring. First, marketers analyze the situation by looking at the relevant market and at the company's objectives and resources. This analysis enables them to set marketing goals that are compatible with the current situation. At the planning stage, marketers focus on both the strategic aspects (product positioning, competitor's predicted reaction, most suitable distribution channel) and the more operational aspects (sales-force meetings, distribution of advertising material at the right time and place, etc.).

Implementation of a marketing plan requires the skilful co-ordination of all parties involved and the participation of all corporate sectors. For example, production must be included to ensure that resources are available. Finance must be on board to make funding available. Personnel must be advised in case additional staff is needed. As soon as a strategy is set up, corporate executives must be kept up to date on the operation. Monitoring allows the company to compare results with objectives and, if need be, address any discrepancies through corrective measures.

1.5.7 The Interdependence of the Elements

Although the various elements of the marketing model have been presented individually, they are interdependent. In fact, they form a whole in which one or all may influence the others.

Marketing managers must be well acquainted with the market and the variables likely to influence it. They must correctly determine consumers' needs, measure the level and development of the demand for a particular good, and divide the larger market into sub-markets or segments in order to take advantage of opportunities and gain a distinct advantage over the competition. They must also study the different variables within the macro-environment. Competition in any form may affect product sales. Demographics, culture, economics, laws and regulations, and technology constantly change the rules of the game. As a result, marketing professionals must use their information system wisely and know how to juggle the variables of the marketing mix.

1.6 ETHICS IN MARKETING

As consumers become increasingly concerned about issues of corporate ethics, corporations have every reason to adopt a code of conduct and to make it known to every member of the organization. While the cultural sector is sensitive to the issue of marketing ethics and ethics in general, the importance of the principle of ethics in marketing cannot be emphasized enough.

In response to several high-profile financial scandals, as well as numerous consumer complaints concerning practices perceived as fraudulent or unethical, the American Marketing Association (AMA) has established a comprehensive code of ethics for its members; many advertisers have also adopted a code of conduct administered by Advertising Standards Canada.[11]

The rules of ethical conduct in marketing cover each of the variables contained in the marketing mix. Products must be safe, pricing practices must be fair, and marketers must not engage in price fixing. Distributors, producers, and retailers must not take advantage of their position of strength to impose overly restrictive conditions on the rest of the network. Advertisers must refrain from making false, misleading, or deceptive claims. Finally, all customers must receive the same quality of service, without discrimination.

Example 1.2
The Edmonton Folk Music Festival: A Case Study in Success

In recent years, folk music has captured the hearts and ears of many Canadians, but the success of the Edmonton Folk Music Festival (EFMF) sets this folk event apart from others across the country. See www.edmontonfolkfest.org

The EFMF started from humble beginnings in 1980 but has grown and matured into a formidable event. It is attended by nearly 85,000 people over four days, and in 2006 it completely sold out of festival passes and single-night tickets.

Close examination of the marketing approach used by the organization, led by Executive Director/Producer Terry Wickham since 1988, provides a near-perfect case study of marketing success.

In true "marketing philosophy" form, the EFMF has a clear organizational vision with measurable goals and objectives; it has a thorough understanding of the audience and audience needs, and it undertakes to address these needs each year through the execution of its marketing plan.

(continued)

Example 1.2 (continued)

A key difference between the EFMF and other festivals and not-for-profit organizations is that at the EFMF all aspects of the marketing mix are examined and re-energized each year. While many organizations are product-focused, the EFMF recognizes that the **product** is not just what is on stage but includes the entire experience. From the port-a-potties to the food vendors to the children's play area, each part of the festival is "new and improved" each year. The sound quality and sight lines for the main stage and each of the seven ancillary stages are examined and refined. Core product spans folk, blues, roots, world, rock, pop, country, ska, bluegrass, and just about every possible combination of these genres.

When it comes to **place**, the EFMF takes advantage of the natural amphitheatre provided by Gallagher Park. An urban ski hill in the winter, Gallagher Park is the ideal downtown, river valley site for the event, affording excellent sight lines, grassy inclines, and a terrific view.

Price is another key aspect of the festival's success. Although organizers acknowledge that folk festival aficionados could likely afford much higher prices, in 2006 a four-day non-transferable pass was only $119 (less than $30 per day). Children under 12 and seniors 65 and over are still admitted free.

The EFMF's actual **promotion** is low key. Promotion is kicked off by a well-attended media conference in May, but very little paid advertising or sales promotion is needed, as the festival usually sells out well in advance of the start date. Anyone who is interested in the festival knows that tickets go on sale the 1st of June every year, and word of mouth and e-mail newsletters provide updates to ticket buyers in the first few days of June.

Finally, the EFMF's success is a result of not only the organization's attention to the four marketing staples, but the efforts of the many people involved in their execution. With more than 2,000 volunteers and a small but dedicated staff and board, every aspect of the experience is planned, nurtured, and evaluated annually. Volunteers are entrusted with managing the stages, security, gates, hospitality, and almost every aspect of the festival. As the years pass, the children who once attended the festival for free with their parents become the adult volunteers and patrons, attending with their own children. Many people proclaim that they plan their vacation around the EFMF dates each year.

Source: Rose Ginther, Chair, Arts and Cultural Management Program, Grant MacEwan College, Edmonton, Canada.

SUMMARY

Cultural enterprises play an important role in society. Their products or activities revolve around or stem from an act of artistic creation. The artist thus holds a pivotal position in such an enterprise and can be found at the many different stages of production, creation, and diffusion.

There are many differences among cultural enterprises, which are usually divided into two sectors: the arts, and the cultural industries.

Cultural companies can be further divided by their mission, which may be market- or product-oriented, and the nature of their product, which may be unique (a prototype) or mass produced. Their orientation obviously affects their size and legal status.

The approach specific to marketing culture and the arts concerns enterprises in the arts sector in particular, although certain firms in the cultural industries also have a product-oriented approach. For others, the traditional approach is adequate.

The traditional marketing model must be adjusted to reflect the reality of companies in the arts sector. Although the components are the same, their sequence may be different. The product is more than a simple variable in the marketing mix, since it is the company's *raison d'être*, regardless of market needs.

Marketing, as a discipline within the management curriculum, emerged at the beginning of the twentieth century. It now comprises a mixed body of knowledge separate from any other science. Marketing knowledge expands constantly and has an increasing number of applications in specific sectors, as is the case in marketing culture and the arts.

Overall, marketing must be seen as a set of activities designed to draw company and consumer together. The four components of marketing are the market, the marketing information system, the company, and the marketing mix.

QUESTIONS

1. What do we mean by "optimization of profits"?
2. Give some highlights from the history of marketing.
3. What does "seller's market" mean?
4. Why is the artist the cornerstone of the marketing strategy of any cultural enterprise?
5. What are the four criteria that enable us to distinguish between the arts sector and the cultural industries?
6. What is the difference between traditional marketing and marketing in the arts? Between traditional marketing and marketing in the cultural industries?
7. According to Hirschman, how can artists themselves form a market segment?
8. Can you find examples of companies in the arts sector that are obviously market-oriented? Companies in the cultural industries that are clearly product-oriented?
9. Why do people who are not in the field often confuse marketing and advertising?
10. Why do we call each of the four elements of the marketing mix "controllable"?
11. Why do we put the product and the company in the same box in the marketing model for the cultural sector?
12. Why do we call competition a "semi-controllable" variable?

Notes

1. Bartels, R. 1976. *The History of Marketing Thought*, 2nded. Columbus, Ohio: Grid.
2. Evrard, Y., and F. Colbert. 2000. "Arts Management: A New Discipline Entering the Millennium?" *International Journal of Arts Management*, Vol. 2, n° 2 (Winter), p. 4–13.
3. Kotler, P. 1967. *Marketing Management: Analysis, Planning and Control*. Englewood Cliffs, New Jersey: Prentice-Hall.
4. Mokwa, M.P., W.M. Dawson and E.A. Prieve. 1980. *Marketing the Arts*. New York: Praeger.
5. Melillo, J.V. 1983. *Market the Arts*. New York: Foundation for the Extension and Development of the American Professional Theater.
6. Diggle, K. 1986. *Guide to Arts Marketing: The Principles and Practice of Marketing as They Apply to the Arts*. London: Rhinegold.
7. Reiss, A.H. 1974. *The Arts Management Handbook*, 2nd ed. New York: Law-Arts Publishers (1st ed. 1979).

8. Diggle, K. 1986. *Guide to Arts Marketing: The Principles and Practice of Marketing as They Apply to the Arts*. London: Rhinegold.

9. Evrard, Y. 1991. "Culture et marketing : incompatibilité ou réconciliation?" In *Proceedings of the First International Conference on Arts Management*, F. Colbert and C. Mitchell, eds. Montreal: Chaire de gestion des arts, HEC Montréal (August), p. 37–50.

10. Hirschman, E.C. 1983. "Aesthetics, Ideologies and the Limits of the Marketing Concept." *Journal of Marketing*, Vol. 47 (Summer), p. 40–55.

11. *The Canadian Code of Advertising Standards*. http://www.adstandards.com/en/

For Further Reference

Agid, P., and J.-C. Tarondeau. 2003. "Manager les activités culturelles." *Revue française de gestion*, Vol. 29, n° 142, January/February, p. 103–112.

Bendixen, P. 2000. "Skills and Roles: An Essay on Concepts of Modern Arts Management." *International Journal of Arts Management*, Vol. 2, n° 3 (Spring), p. 4–13.

Botti, S. 2000. "What Role for Marketing the Arts? An Analysis of Art Consumption and Artistic Value." *International Journal of Arts Management*, Vol. 2, n° 3 (Spring), p. 14–27.

Evrard, Y. 1993. *Le management des entreprises artis-tiques et culturelles*. Paris: Economica.

Killacky, J.R. 1998. "Corporate Research and Venture Capital Models for the Arts." *International Journal of Arts Management*, Vol. 1, n° 1 (Fall), p. 4–8.

PLAN

Chapter 2

The Product

OBJECTIVES

- Define "cultural product"
- Set out the main characteristics of a cultural product
- Explore the idea of a product life cycle
- Apply the life-cycle concept to cultural products
- Understand the risks that cultural organizations face

INTRODUCTION

The product is the cornerstone of every cultural enterprise, and hence of every marketing strategy. In the first section of this chapter, we look at the product from various vantage points and propose a definition. We also discuss the specific characteristics of the cultural product.

In the second section, we introduce an important concept in managing products: the product life cycle. This model, which describes the different stages in the life cycle according to how the market and corporate environment develop, enables marketing professionals to create various corporate survival strategies.

In the third and last section, we look at the specific type of risk that cultural companies face, by examining the way in which new products are designed – in particular, cultural products vis-à-vis mass consumer products.

2.1 PRODUCT

2.1.1 Defining the Term "Product"

In order to develop effective marketing strategies, companies would be wise to consider and use the point of view of the consumer – in other words, put themselves "in the customer's shoes." This is particularly true in the case of the product variable. If we were to adopt the point of view of a marketing specialist, we might define a product as *the set of benefits as they are perceived by the consumer.*

A product may be described by its technical dimension or its symbolic value, yet, in the end, what the client buys is a set of benefits, real or imaginary. Clients agree to invest money and effort in obtaining the product according to the importance of their needs and the resources available to them.

This behaviour also applies to the cultural sector. A reader does not buy a book for its physical aspect – bound sheets of paper containing printed words – but, rather, for the pleasure or intellectual stimulation to be gained from reading it. A music lover purchases not merely a ticket to the New York Philharmonic but also the prospect of spending a pleasant evening either alone or with a companion. A television viewer acquires not merely a TV set but also moments of relaxation and entertainment after a hard day's work. Similarly, a sponsor does not invest in the mission of a performing arts company, but, rather, seeks a promotional vehicle – such as a performance or a festival – through which to reach consumers; the sponsor's reasons for choosing one company over another have to do with the perceived benefits of the association. The same can be said of the economic agents in the other markets of a cultural enterprise.

2.1.2 The Different Components of a Product

The notion of product involves several additional elements that are important to the consumer. Most products have the following main components:

1) the central product or object itself;
2) related services;
3) the value, be it symbolic, affective, or other, that consumers attach to the product.

In buying a car, the consumer acquires a means of transportation (central product), but also certain services, such as a warranty and a service contract. There is also, of course, a symbolic value, which may be prestige, power, or the fulfilment of a dream.

The reasons behind choosing a particular brand or product may vary from one consumer to the next. The car example comes to mind once again. Some people make their decision based on purely technical criteria, such as fuel consumption – in other words, based on the central product. Some may choose one brand over another because of the manufacturer's warranty or the dealer's post-purchase maintenance service plan – that is, according to services associated with the product. Still others may base their decision on the social standing linked to product use. Sometimes this symbolic value becomes the main reason for buying a product.

2.1.3 The Cultural Product and Its Specific Characteristics

Cultural products are also characterized by these different components, although with a few nuances.

Components of the Cultural Product

While the artist remains at the centre of the cultural product, it should be kept in mind that all cultural products are characterized by four components: the artistic product itself, spin-off products, related services, and the consumer's experience of the product (including the value he or she attaches to the product). The artistic product is the central product; it is the work itself as produced by an individual creator or a team of creators. An organization markets this work by inviting customers to come into contact with the fruit of the artist's labour. Three aspects revolve around this central component: spin-off products, related services, and the consumer's experience (including the value attached to the product). In some organizations, the artistic director considers these three other components integral to the work and therefore makes the decisions concerning them (pure product orientation); in other organizations, these components are left to the discretion of the marketing director.

For example, some people attend the Montreal International Jazz Festival to see a specific show (artistic or central product), while others attend for the atmosphere (the experience). Customers who have to choose between two theatres, each presenting a show they wish to see, may make the decision based on the fact that one theatre offers parking and the other does not; or they may choose a venue that has a bar, so they can have a drink before or after the performance (related service).

Example 2.1
The Oregon Bach Festival: Developing a Product Portfolio

The Oregon Bach Festival strives to keep its centuries-old music tradition fresh by integrating artistic program decisions with audience development initiatives. While specializing in choral orchestral masterworks, the festival appeals to a variety of musical interests through chamber music, small ensembles, solo performances, and innovative interpretive works. It leverages landmark events associated with premières of new and innovative works in an integrated approach designed to introduce new audiences, strengthen ties with established ones, and provide deeper sponsorship value.

This approach resulted in a national William Dawson Award for the Arvo Pärt *Litany* project in 1994 and a Grammy Award for 1998's *Credo* by Krzysztof Penderecki. In 2005, for the regional première of *La Pasion Segun San Marcos* by Osvaldo Golijov, it assembled a diverse 10-person committee that included representatives from the Latino community and a large synagogue as well as a rock-music scholar. Recommendations by the committee included a DVD sampler, a study guide, free talks, and sponsor exclusives. George Evano, the Festival's director of communications, explains: "These varying 'points of entry' introduced more than 7,000 people to the work in some way. The two performances of *La Pasion* were the highest attended concerts in the Festival 17-day schedule, and 40% of those audiences were first-time attenders. Its success paved the way for a multi-year, extensive audience research grant from the project funder."

Source: Patricia Dewey, Assistant Professor, Arts and Administration Program, University of Oregon, USA.

In each case, the consumer's decision is based on the benefit he or she hopes to gain, whether that benefit is related to the artistic (or central) product, related services, the experience, or symbolic value.

The Cultural Product: A Complex Product

The complexity of a product may vary greatly according to the specific features of the product, the consumer's characteristics, or the consumer's perception of the product. Some products are considered more complex because their technical specifications require substantial personal effort on the part of the consumer just to be familiar with product features. For example, the first-time inexperienced buyer of a personal computer confronts technical complexity; this shopper may find the emotional burden associated with buying a computer rather unsettling. Before buying a new car, a consumer may seek advice from several friends, since their opinions are important in combatting emotional complexity. This consumer will buy other products automatically, however, as is the case for many common convenience goods, which could be called "simple products."

Most cultural products may be defined as complex, especially when the works produced require specific knowledge or rely on abstract notions that require the consumer's ability to appreciate such concepts. Complexity becomes even greater when the consumer is unfamiliar with a particular type of product (lack of references).

The cultural or artistic sector does, nonetheless, include' less complex products, such as work drawing on stereotypes known to most people or using very concrete concepts. These products are often labelled popular. "Pop" music and summer-stock theatre may be considered simple products in comparison with a classical repertoire or an avant-garde production.

The Artistic Product: Multidimensional

Another way of approaching the notion of a product, which applies in the case of a cultural product, is to define the artistic work using three dimensions (see Table 2.1): referential, technical, and circumstantial.

The referential dimension enables consumers to situate a product according to various points of reference (discipline, genre, history, etc.). These reference points increase or decrease according to the individual consumer's experience or knowledge of the product. This dimension defines the product through comparison with both whatever else exists and what once existed. A contemporary-dance work, for example, could be situated as a product in comparison with other pieces in the same show, with the artist's other works, or with other styles of dance (modern, jazz, etc.). This product could also be situated in relation to dramatic works, which also compete for audiences, or

Table 2.1
The Three Dimensions of an Artistic Work

Referential dimension	Technical dimension	Circumstantial dimension
Discipline	of the product consumed	Ephemeral components
Genre	of the production process	The consumer
History		The artist
Competitors' products		
Substitute products		

to other leisure activities. When the product is evaluated, it is also situated within a certain context of distribution or diffusion and within a particular market where other products exist or existed. This inherent complexity explains why the critic's task is exceedingly difficult, since he or she must be aware of these several reference points.

This complexity also explains why some artistic products are more popular than others. For example, the average consumer is surrounded by popular music from childhood on, thus acquiring, over the years, references that shape his or her choices and preferences; on the other hand, the language of dance is not nearly as pervasive in everyday life, making this art form less penetrable to the average consumer.

The technical dimension includes the technical and material components of the product as received by the consumer. It could be the product itself (a sculpture), the vehicle (a CD or book), or a component of the performance of the work (a show). The consumer buying a compact disc is acquiring the technical dimension of an artistic work. As a spectator, however, the same consumer may see the technical dimension integrated into the work but be unable to possess it. In any event, the technical dimension influences the quality of the work produced.

The circumstantial dimension is related to the ephemeral circumstances surrounding product perception. An artistic work cannot be seen twice in exactly the same way – even by the same person! Consumer perceptions are a basic, indispensable component in the appreciation of a product. The same may be said of the perception of the context in which the product is presented. For example, a sculpture will look different with a sunset as a backdrop rather than a cloudy sky. Moreover, the individual perceiving the product has different moods, physical states, comfort levels, and so on. All of these fleeting factors play a role in the overall perception of a product and influence the consumer's opinion. Indeed, as soon as human perception becomes part of the equation, it becomes a key variable. It is this aspect that raises the quality of the consumer's experience.

Although the consumer's perception is an influential factor for all products, it must be noted that perception plays a special role in the performing arts, where an artist's mood, physical condition, and perception of the audience's reaction are also circumstantial factors influencing product quality and proving once again that a product cannot be the same twice.

The Cultural Product: A Specialized Purchase

In marketing literature, there are several ways of classifying products. Here, we describe the best-known method, which involves classifying products, according to the amount of effort expended by the consumer, into convenience goods, shopping goods, and specialty goods.

Convenience goods are those that the consumer buys often, though with very little brand loyalty. The normal brand of milk, bread, or butter, for example, is easily replaced by whichever brand the corner store sells when a consumer does not want to travel all the way to the supermarket.

If a purchase is well thought out, however, the consumer will buy only after comparison shopping among substitute products. When clothes shopping, for example, most consumers compare the style, colour, and fabric of several similar garments before finding the one that meets their current criteria best.

A specialized purchase involves a product, often a particular brand, for which the consumer is prepared to make a significant effort. The consumer will refuse all other brands if the product desired is unavailable, and will even make a special trip to wherever that product is sold.

Cultural products usually fall under the category of specialty goods. The consumer wants to see a particular show or film and/or to buy a specific recording by a favourite performer. This consumer will not compromise and will put considerable effort into buying tickets in advance, lining up for hours or even travelling great distances to the venue where the event is being held.

In some situations, a cultural product can be categorized as a thought-out purchase (shopping goods). For example, in buying a book, a consumer might browse through a bookshop for something that suits his or her mood. This consumer may opt for a novel and then leaf through the best-sellers or read jacket blurbs before choosing one title out of a group of interesting novels.

The Cultural Product: Characteristics of a Service

Many cultural products share the four characteristics that define service enterprises, namely intangibility, perishability, simultaneity, and the circumstantial dimension.[1] For example, in the case of the performing arts, movie theatres, and museum exhibitions (found in quadrants 1 and 4 of Figure 1.2, Marketing and Cultural Enterprises), the consumer does not purchase a tangible product; since the consumer does not take the work home, the purchase can be said to be intangible. Cultural products are also perishable, since one cannot stock a performance or relive the experience of a visit to a museum. The consumption of the work can be said to be simultaneous with its purchase in that one cannot acquire the work and consume it at a later time (as one can in the case of a piece of clothing), although it is possible to purchase a ticket in advance. Finally, the quality of a performance will vary according to the prevailing conditions at the time (circumstantial dimension). These characteristics give added weight to the role played by the employees who come into contact with customers, since they can influence the consumer's satisfaction. Telephone personnel, box office staff, ushers, security guards, guides, and all the other people who play a role in the delivery of a service can have an impact on the quality of the cultural product and the consumer's experience. This aspect will be examined in greater detail in Chapter 4, "Consumer Behaviours."

2.1.4 Brand

For most businesses, the use of a brand is an important component of their marketing strategy. Customers in the various markets differentiate among products based on their recognition of a product's attributes as conveyed by the brand. The brand can be either a name or a symbol (design). For example, Mickey Mouse's ears are recognized worldwide as the Disney logo.

All cultural enterprises have a brand or trademark, even if it is only the name of the company. The name of a well-known company conjures up images in the mind of the client (whether this be a consumer or a donor), who associates it with a particular product. Even people who have never set foot in Milan's La Scala or New York's Museum of Modern Art (MoMA) have some idea of what these institutions represent.

A strong brand not only attracts consumers but makes possible the creation of franchises. The Guggenheim Museum, for example, has capitalized on the strength of its brand name to expand its market and establish franchises throughout the world: there are now the Peggy Guggenheim Collection in Venice, the Deutsche Guggenheim Berlin, and the Guggenheim Museum Bilbao.[2]

Thus, the role of the brand is to differentiate the products of one firm from those of other firms, or to set the firm itself apart from the competition. The brand serves to summarize the benefits offered by a company. It can also represent a response to consumers' expectations. For example, fans of the pop star Céline Dion know exactly what to expect when they buy one of her compact discs. The brand can also serve as a convenience: readers of Harlequin romances, for instance, do not have to search through all the titles in the market, but can fall back on the Harlequin brand and thus save themselves time and effort and avoid the risk of making a bad choice. The brand can even become, whether consciously or not, a symbol of membership in a group, as is the case for certain brands of clothing.

The Characteristics of a Brand

Brands are usually defined in terms of the following five characteristics:

1) perceived quality: the different markets and market segments can get a sense of the quality of a brand even if they have never used or consumed that brand

2) name awareness: the larger the percentage of the population that is able to name a brand (with or without assistance), the stronger the brand

3) customer loyalty or satisfaction: loyalty can be measured using the number of repeat purchases and the rate of subscription renewal

4) association with relevant elements: the markets may, for example, identify the brand with the quality of a museum's collections

---

Example 2.2
Harlequin Enterprise: Publishing and Branding

Harlequin Enterprise Limited is a Canadian publisher founded in the early 1950s. It publishes around 110 titles per month, in 27 languages in 95 international markets on 6 continents. Harlequin novels are written by 1,300 authors. In 2004, the company sold 130 million books.

Harlequin considers itself an expert in branding strategy within the publishing industry. The company develops brands that correspond globally to the tastes of its readers. It offers its readers an array of romantic storylines (traditional, suspense, inspiring, etc.) in a wide selection of brands linked to each theme. The brands include Harlequin Books, MIRA Books, Red Dress Ink, LUNA Books, HQN Books, Steeple Hill Books, and Steeple Hill Café. In 2003, 12 of the company's titles made it to the *New York Times* bestseller list.

http://www.eharlequin.com

Source: Johanne Brunet, Guest Professor, HEC Montréal, Montreal, Canada.

---

5) tangible and intangible assets associated with the brand: the architecture of the Sydney Opera House is a key element in the market's perception of the brand; this performing arts centre is recognized worldwide for its unique shape – the building is even used as an emblem by the Australian tourism department.[3]

The higher a brand scores on each of these characteristics, the more it will be considered a strong brand and the higher its market value will be. In the cultural field, a strong brand is particularly important since a cultural product constitutes a specialized purchase.

2.1.5 Customer Service

The satisfaction that the customer derives from consuming a work of art is different from the satisfaction (or lack thereof) that is derived from the relationship established with the company offering the work. Poor customer service can ruin the quality of the artistic experience, lower the customer's satisfaction, and, ultimately, harm the brand image. The role of customer service is to provide the best possible experience for customers in their dealings with the organization and to manage their expectations through this experience.[4] Good customer service is a way of setting oneself apart from the competition and building customer loyalty; indeed, it is ultimately more expensive to attract a new customer than to keep an existing one.

It is essential for an organization to analyze and understand the expectations of its clientele. The chief expectation is reliability. The others are responsiveness, accessibility, rapidity, employee competence, courtesy and respect, consideration, advice, empathy, customer recognition (in the case of a regular customer), discretion and confidentiality, flexibility and adaptation, convenience, and equity.

An effective organization that truly cares about its customers will study the "moments of truth" between itself and its customers – that is, any time the customer comes into contact with the organization, whether by telephone, over the Internet, at the box office, in the bookstore, or at the cash register, or any time a customer makes a complaint. The organization analyzes each of these points of contact – or "moments of truth" – and looks for ways to increase the customer's satisfaction at each one. Through this process, it puts itself "in the customer's shoes" in order to understand his or her expectations. Walt Disney was known to line up to purchase a ticket to Disneyland and to then test each attraction in order to evaluate first-hand the quality of the consumer experience. This is a simple way for a company to assess its customer service. It should be kept in mind that, very often, the client's only contact with the organization is through its front-line employees – receptionists, counter attendants, ticket agents, or ushers – and that this contact can determine

Example 2.3
The Alabama Shakespeare Festival:
Adjusting Customer Service

Focus groups and surveys conducted by the Alabama Shakespeare Festival revealed that customer service was an important criterion for the consumer. When lapsed subscribers were asked why they had not renewed, many were able to recall instances when the theatre seemed to forget that the customer is always right. When pressed for examples, they remembered encountering what they perceived to be cumbersome ticket-exchange policies, inflexible date-selection rules, annoying latecomer seating policies, or generally impersonal service by a box office or front-of-house staff member. It should be noted that the norms and culture in the American South have some distinctive idiosyncrasies, sometimes considered part of the "Southern charm." Many Southerners will tell you that when a customer service representative of any kind says "no" to a request, he or she is seen as downright rude! With this "no" equals "rude" paradox in mind, it was time for the Alabama Shakespeare Festival to make substantive changes to its customer service.

All ticketing and front-of-house policies were carefully reviewed and staff discussed the rationale behind each. Managers were surprised by how many archived policies (rules that could result in a "no" to the customer) could easily be made more flexible or even eliminated. Managers and staff were empowered to bend or even break the rules when necessary. No front-of-house chaos ensued. Customer service was made a marketing priority and became a function of all training and orientation procedures. Training was reinforced through the use of helpful human resource videos. Every patron was greeted by a friendly employee who strived to meet any request. Subscribers were given an exclusive hotline number for their "personal concierge" (an assistant box office manager). Management even placed an inviting and plainly visible desk in the lobby, clearly marked "Concierge" and tended by a friendly and well-informed assistant front-of-house manager. Follow-up surveys revealed that the elimination of "no" yielded positive results.

Source: Steven Morrison, Assistant Professor and Associate Director, Arts Administration Graduate Program, University of Cincinnati College-Conservatory of Music, USA.

whether or not the client will accept the organization's offering and purchase its product. This focus on customer satisfaction is just as important for the consumer market as it is for the other markets of the cultural enterprise.

2.2 THE PRODUCT LIFE CYCLE

2.2.1 The Concept of a Life Cycle

The concept of a life cycle for a product stems from the notion that everything, from people to products, is born, grows, and dies. Some products know moments of glory, only to later fall into disuse or oblivion. This is the case for papyrus, the quill and inkwell, and the gramophone and record player. All of these products were replaced by easier-to-use, more efficient products that fulfilled certain needs better than their predecessors did.

In short, the idea of a product life cycle exists because consumer needs and preferences change as technology continues to evolve. Taste and technology are two interdependent phenomena that influence each other and often speed up a product's life cycle.

The following four stages make up the life cycle of a product: introduction, growth, maturity, and decline. Although it is difficult to pinpoint the exact stage a product may be in at any given moment, each phase does have specific characteristics. Figure 2.1 shows the theoretical curve of the life cycle.

This curve is actually the demand curve for a product over a period of time. Unfortunately, the elegant line shown in Figure 2.1 is rarely reproduced in reality, where each phase may not be equal in length. Demand for a prod-

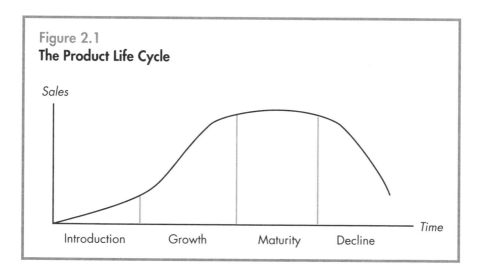

Figure 2.1
The Product Life Cycle

Sales

Introduction   Growth   Maturity   Decline   Time

uct may be a mere flash in the pan or may blossom slowly to reach maturity only years after the introduction stage. The number of possibilities is infinite: some performing artists fade into obscurity after a single CD, while others, including groups such as the Rolling Stones, seem to be able to remain in the maturity stage indefinitely.

The expression "product life cycle" should be considered in its broadest sense. The concept may apply to a group of products offered on the market (market life cycle) or to a specific brand or product. Generally, the life cycle of a market is composed of a series of superimposed product life cycles, which, in turn, are made up of superimposed brand life cycles. Organizations also have a life cycle. In the cultural sector, for example, a company that is closely linked to its founder or in which the founder and the organization are synonymous may come to an abrupt end if that person dies, retires, or resigns.

The notion of a life cycle in the arts can be illustrated in the example of summer-stock theatre and summer theatre festivals in the province of Quebec, Canada. Figure 2.2 follows the life cycle of summer-stock theatre in Quebec from its inception to the year 2000.

The product was introduced gradually. As a result, the number of summer-stock theatres rose slowly from 1957 to 1974, a period corresponding to the introduction phase. The year 1974 marked the start of tremendous

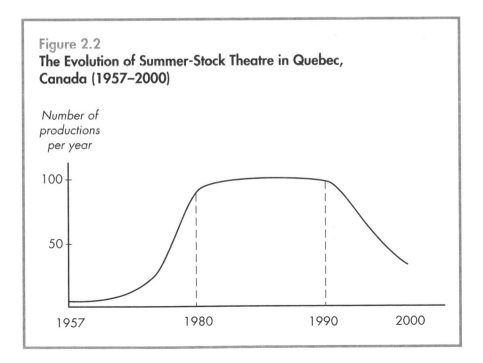

Figure 2.2
The Evolution of Summer-Stock Theatre in Quebec, Canada (1957–2000)

Number of productions per year

100

50

1957   1980   1990   2000

growth, which stopped in the early 1980s, when the market hit the ceiling (100 productions), corresponding to the start of the maturity phase. The number of troupes and products remained stable until 1990. After this period, the proliferation of festivals and other popular events caused the number of productions to fall to approximately 30.

The museum product, as a whole, has long been considered elitist. During the 1970s, the client base was broadened and the number of visits rose. Some people have called this the democratization of museum-going. Marketing specialists, however, might consider it an example of a market life cycle that has experienced a new growth stage after years spent at one level. This market, however, has not developed evenly. Art museums, for example, were slow to draw a large clientele. Indeed, only in the past decade have they managed to increase in popularity. On the other hand, museums of civilization, a newer product, were an instant success and remain quite popular. Science museums also attract ever-increasing numbers of visitors.

2.2.2 The Product-Adoption Process

Although some consumers are hesitant to stop using a product, others are constantly looking for novelty and are always ready to try something new. As we have seen, the demand for a product corresponds to the number of units purchased by consumers. The greater the number of units, the stronger the demand. However, not all potential consumers will become customers at the same time. Some take more risks and agree to consume a product just introduced; others are more conservative and wait until the product has passed the test of public approval. Rogers[5] created a model that describes how innovations are diffused. He based his research on how quickly American farmers adopted new products. Figure 2.3 illustrates the results of Rogers's study.

So-called innovators are prepared to consume a new product as soon as it goes on the market. After a certain period, the initial consumers, a group characterized by strong personal leadership, play a key role in spreading the innovation. These initial consumers gather in their wake the early and late majorities. The laggards are the last to both start and stop using the product.

When the cycle occurs as illustrated in Figure 2.3, consumer purchases create, over time, a curve representing the demand. This curve can be seen as the life cycle of the product. In fact, when only the so-called innovators buy a new product, the life cycle of that product does not go beyond the introduction stage. If, however, adoption of the product progresses quickly, the maturity stage will soon be reached (within just a few years, 80% of the North American population acquired a DVD player). Of course, if the adoption process is swift because of the characteristics of consumers within the target market, other factors may play a major role. One factor is certainly the lower selling price of

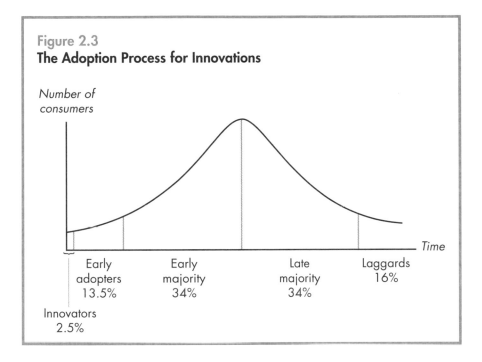

Figure 2.3
The Adoption Process for Innovations

Number of consumers

Time

| Innovators 2.5% | Early adopters 13.5% | Early majority 34% | Late majority 34% | Laggards 16% |

the product, if it is a durable good. The videocassette recorder/player provides an excellent example of this factor. The VCR spread like wildfire throughout the industrialized countries: the percentage of households owning a video-cassette player hovered at 0% in 1980 and shot up to 70% within one decade; today, ownership rates surpass 90% in many countries. Although this piece of equipment initially cost several thousand dollars, it can now be purchased for less than a hundred dollars. The onslaught of the VCR led to a boom in the number of video clubs, creating a whole new industry. In turn, this phenomenon helped develop the market potential for the VCR itself. A similar boom is now taking place in the DVD and cell phone markets; the cell phone market is particularly important because it is now possible to download movies, music, photographs, and so forth onto cell phones.

In short, the curve representing the diffusion of an innovation is the graphic image of the number of consumers purchasing a product. The curve representing the product life cycle illustrates the demand for that product.

2.2.3 The Four Stages of a Life Cycle

Development

Before they can launch a product (before the life cycle can begin), cultural enterprises must engage in a crucial period of development. In the cultural industries, the development phase often entails the investment of substantial human and financial resources. In the case of many film and drama series, the development phase can last months or even years.

Introduction

In a life cycle, the introduction of a new product after the development phase is characterized by slow sales, financial losses, and the absence of competitors. This phase can last a long time, depending on consumer response. The sooner the bulk of consumers change their habits and adopt an innovation, the sooner the growth stage is reached. Market penetration may be slowed by a variety of factors, such as the consumer's resistance to change, a distribution network that limits accessibility to the new product, a robust offensive by companies selling substitute products, an overly high price, and so on.

Normally the selling price is highest during the introduction stage, when the manufacturer has enormous expenses to cover. Not only are manufacturing costs per unit high, but promotion costs have to be included in the selling price to ensure that the innovation is accepted. The manufacturer must also include a certain percentage to amortize the design and development of the product.

Table 2.2 shows four product-introduction strategies based on a combination of two hypotheses of price and promotion: low or high price and light or heavy promotion.

The "top-of-the-line" strategy involves launching a product at a high price through a powerful promotional campaign. This strategy is applicable

Table 2.2
Product-Introduction Strategies

		Promotion	
		Heavy	**Light**
Price	**High**	Top-of-the-line strategy	Selective penetration strategy
	Low	Massive penetration strategy	Bottom-of-the-line strategy

when the potential market does not yet know the product – for example, a real novelty item – but a sufficient number of consumers are likely to buy it even at a high price. The company, in this case, foresees competition in the near future and seeks to forge a strong brand image.

The massive penetration strategy consists of launching a product at a relatively low price with a very strong promotional campaign. The company is then likely to obtain a high level of market penetration and capture a large share of the market. This second strategy is useful if the product is little known but likely to interest a vast market of price-conscious consumers. The number of units produced must allow for economies of scale[6] in order to ensure profitability.

The third strategy, called the "bottom-of-the-line" strategy, enables a company to increase profits by economizing on promotional costs. In this case, the market must be extremely large, the average consumer must be price-conscious, and the type of product must already be known, even if the brand is new.

Last is the selective penetration strategy, which involves launching a new product at a high price with little promotional input. This approach may be used if competition is weak, if the generic product is known, and if the consumer is prepared to pay the price. Marketing this product allows for a high profit margin with little money spent on promotion.

Growth

As more consumers join the innovators, the product enters the growth stage. The ranks of the "early adopters" are swelled by the "early majority." At this point, the demand becomes strong enough to allow a drop in price, to encourage other groups of consumers to buy the product.

This stage is characterized by a rapid jump in sales figures and a noticeable increase in competition, since the market can now absorb new competitors. The arrival of additional consumers enables new manufacturers to earn enough without jeopardizing the sales of existing companies. In the consumer-goods sector, this is a period when both the number of consumers and the rate of consumption per person rise.

During this period, companies face a major dilemma: should they take immediate advantage of the short-term profits generated, or invest those profits in the hope of developing a better competitive stance during the next stage of the product life cycle? In taking the second option, an executive could choose to allot a percentage of corporate profits to improving the product, expanding distribution routes, seeking new categories of consumers, intensifying promotional campaigns, and so on. In all of these cases, immediate profits are sacrificed for the betterment of the company's future position.

Maturity

Sooner or later, once all potential customers have been reached and the rate of consumption per person has stabilized, overall demand will plateau. This is the maturity stage, which generally lasts longer than the previous stages.

The maturity stage may be subdivided into three periods. The first is increasing maturity, at which point the rate of sales growth starts to slow down. Although laggards start adopting the product and join the group of current buyers, they are relatively few in number. Product sales then reach a plateau. This is the saturation period, during which the demand comes essentially from replacement sales. The third period is that of declining maturity, characterized by a drop in sales volume, since some consumers are already looking at substitute or new products.

When demand levels off, there are serious consequences in terms of competition. Although the market is saturated, new companies or product brands are constantly springing up and trying to find a niche. The increasingly intense competition forces the most vulnerable companies to close their doors.

Strategically, a company may now choose among three different approaches: modify the market, modify the product, or modify other variables in the marketing mix.

The market may be modified by seeking out new, as yet untapped segments. The company must then either persuade consumers to buy more of the product or reposition the brand by modifying the average consumer's perceptions of the product.

Product modification consists of reviving sales by improving quality, changing style, or developing features specific to that product. This tactic is effective as long as the consumer perceives these changes as both real and relevant.

Lastly, a company may choose to adjust other variables in the marketing mix. It may lower prices, attack the market through a powerful promotional campaign, hold a contest, offer coupons, or turn to higher-volume distribution channels, such as discount stores.

It is not always easy to recognize where a product is in its life cycle. Although the introduction and growth stages are usually the easiest to pinpoint, the other stages may prove difficult to analyze in detail. For example, how can a temporary plateau in sales be distinguished from the saturation phase? A diagnostic approach would likely include the following three elements: the product's rate of penetration, the possibility of finding new market segments, and the amount of consumption per person. If a company cannot increase the number of consumers in a given segment or hunt down other segments likely to buy the product, and it is impossible to increase consumption per person, the market saturation point has been reached.

A company can restart a product's life cycle by adopting a new artistic orientation that repositions the brand. Since the arts sector is an extremely dynamic sector, many companies are required to undertake such a reorientation at one time or another. This was the strategy adopted by Montreal's Les Grands Ballets Canadiens (considered here as a brand) when it shifted away from its image as a classical ballet company by adding more modern ballet works to its repertoire, in addition to taking on the role of distributor by including foreign troupes in its programs. Interesting examples elsewhere include the Australian Ballet and the Steppenwolf Theatre in Chicago.[7] Such strategies are also common in the cultural industries, such as in the pop music sector; Céline Dion's career, to cite one example, has been repositioned several times over the years as the pop star evolved from a child to a woman and mother.

Decline

The decline stage is undoubtedly the most difficult for any company to handle. In fact, the company may not even be able to tell whether its product has really started to decline or its sales have simply slumped temporarily. Only a detailed analysis of the situation can provide any answers to this question, and even then no one can be sure. The problem of distinguishing between a temporary decrease and a definitive drop in sales should not be underestimated. This kind of uncertainty leads to difficult decisions, especially if the product was marketed over a very lengthy period. The human factors involved in this type of decision should not be underestimated either. A sentimental attachment or a resistance to the idea of defeat may make a promoter insist on pursuing a project.

A company may prefer to pull its product off the shelves, maintain the status quo, or adopt the concentration strategy. This strategy involves concentrating efforts on the most profitable market segments and distribution channels. A company may also decide to use a pressure strategy, which lowers promotion costs and allows the product to "float" while generating short-term profits.

The main indicator used in diagnosing the decline stage is the presence of superior substitute products. This stage is usually reached as soon as superior substitute products that cannot be outdone hit the market. The compact disc, which almost eliminated the vinyl record, is an excellent example of this indicator, as are the DVD, which now competes with the CD, and music downloaded from the Internet, which is affecting CD sales. Yet even with this indicator nothing is certain. Some thought that television would sound the death knell for radio, but this was not the case. TV and radio seemed like the same product, using two different technical supports, destined for one and the same market. Some products were transferred – for example, radio soap operas to TV "daytime dramas"; however, each mode of communication developed its own specialties, so as to co-exist with the other yet still serve the same clientele for different needs and in different circumstances.

2.2.4 The Limitations of the Life-Cycle Concept

Some authors have seriously questioned the value of the concept of a product life cycle.[8] Their main argument is that the concept is modelled after the human life cycle, which has strict time definitions (childhood, adolescence, adulthood, and old age). Products, on the other hand, may experience a revival, extend their growth stage, or even become eternal! Products that follow the elegant curve shown in Figure 2.1 are actually rare. Jagged, less symmetrical curves are the norm.

Unfortunately, the model is not very useful during the course of business. In fact, a product's current stage is never known for sure, especially with respect to the decline and maturity stages. Although some indicators do help marketing professionals to determine approximately where the product is in its life cycle, much remains uncertain. As a result, a drop in sales may not necessarily mean that the product is in decline, and hasty corporate decisions made at that point may later be regretted.

For some cultural products, especially those whose technical dimension cannot be bought, the model is not very useful at all. In fact, the life cycle of a product is often predestined at its launching. Many cultural products, particularly in the arts sector, are created to be performed or exhibited for a limited time only. They have a set number of performances or a pre-scheduled exhibition length, then they disappear. Even if the production is a success, it closes by a certain date. This style of product management is imposed by the restrictions inherent in the cultural sector. For example, a theatre company may offer a seasonal subscription and therefore be obliged to set dates and reserve seats. Meanwhile, performers accept or decline contract offers according to the date of their last performance. In most cases, the company cannot "hold over" the life cycle indefinitely, since contracts have been signed with the theatre and cast. Few theatres want to remount a play for either artistic or financial reasons (more rehearsals, another promotional campaign, different performers and hence a different product). A tour offers an interesting way of extending the life cycle of a product, but it may not always correspond to the company's mission.

The typical life cycle of the cultural product described above therefore follows a curve similar to that shown in Figure 2.4. As for productions that, once mounted, are allowed to run as long as there is still demand for them: these generally follow the standard product life cycle curve. This is the case for many of the commercial productions that play on New York (Broadway) and London stages, but also for repertory theatres that perform productions once or twice a week in rotation with the other productions in the company's repertory, until demand for them has run out. This type of concept is found at La Comédie-Française in Paris and in several Eastern European countries.[9] These companies typically have a permanent troupe of actors who appear in some capacity in nearly all of its productions. Often, actors will rehearse a new production in the morning and dedicate the afternoon to rehearsing the production they are to perform that very evening.

2.3 DESIGNING NEW PRODUCTS AND THE RISKS THAT THIS INCURS

2.3.1 Developing New Products

Large manufacturing firms have a special department working on new products. The research and development (R&D) department has the exclusive task of developing product ideas in order to fill a market need. All expenses are financed through the profits generated by products sold by the firm. Large firms accept the fact that they must invest sizeable sums of money in R & D to ensure the future success of both new products and the organization itself.

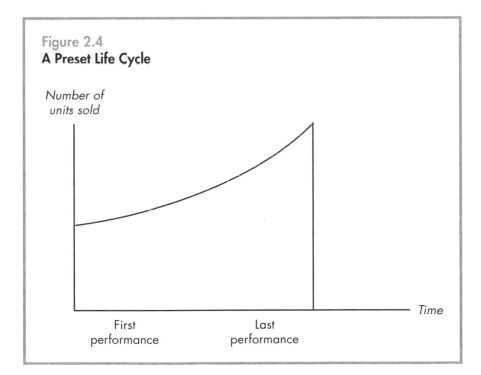

Figure 2.4
A Preset Life Cycle

Number of units sold

First performance

Last performance

Time

The idea of special units devoted to research and development is foreign to the arts milieu. In fact, the R & D role is often undertaken by specialized companies, which must obtain a significant percentage of their revenue through government grants that require artistic as opposed to commercial success. These groups are not mandated to both conduct research and market successful products; they bear names beginning with adjectives like "contemporary," "alternative," or "parallel."

However, in the cultural industries there is usually a division, department, or person in charge of developing new products (such as movies) or new artists, and marketing and financial resources are sometimes involved during the development phase. In fact, the development phase is extremely important for the cultural industries as a whole, since it is in this phase that the organization has an opportunity to ensure its longevity. While teams are at work producing a feature film or documentary, for example, the company is already looking ahead to its next project, not only so that it can move on to a new venture when production wraps up, but (ideally) so that it can produce more than one project at a time.

The development phase can last several months, or even years, and often requires substantial investments and the allocation of significant resources. It involves elements such as the development of ideas, synopses, and scripts; in the pop music industry, it may involve the circulation of a demo by the artist, with the aim of attracting the interest of record companies.

Example 2.4
Pilots in the TV Industry

In the American television industry, the cost of developing pilot programs reached US$364 million in 2005. Every year, hundreds of projects are submitted to the major TV networks (or to production companies). Of these, the 30 or so that appear to have the most potential are chosen, and only half of those will eventually go into production as a pilot. The approximate cost of a pilot for a one-hour drama is $4 million, for a 30-minute situation comedy $2 million. If the pilot does not get chosen by a network, the producer will have to assume the cost of development. Because of financial constraints, few broadcasters outside of the United States use pilots as part of their development.

Source: Johanne Brunet, Guest Professor, HEC Montréal, Montreal, Canada.

In the manufacturing sector, as in the cultural sector, new products designed by the R & D department are evaluated by a series of specialists in engineering, marketing, or finance. Their expert opinions are given throughout the product-development process using product prototypes that are not yet marketed or ready to be field-tested by a sampling of the population. In the cultural sector, a product usually undergoes this critical process after it has been marketed, unveiled, or premiered. The specialists, in this instance, are the critics or members of the artistic community and the "connoisseurs" among the general public.

The development and marketing of new products is an extremely risky undertaking for any organization, regardless of its sector. In the manufacturing sector, the product mortality rate is very high. In fact, the marketing literature shows that, out of 60 product ideas, only one will actually be developed, produced, and launched on the market. Furthermore, many of the products that do find their way to market ultimately fail (80% in the case of frozen food products). Thus, success does not come as easily to commercial products as one might expect.[10] This is why producers tend to exercise extreme caution when deciding whether or not to tackle a new project.

Administrators seek to minimize the inherent risk by using a very rigorous development process.[11] This process (see Figure 2.5) involves a series of precise steps, each one requiring a decision before continuing to the next step, in which the manager must once again decide whether or not to continue developing the product. Since the high cost of product development actually increases with each step, this process helps companies pinpoint losing projects early, and thus saves them a considerable amount of money.

The creative act characteristic of the development of an artistic product does not fit well with the approach taken in the business sector, although an artistic work can be tested in certain circumstances. In the performing arts sector, for example, only on opening night can a company know how the product will be received by the audience. Even experts can be mistaken in their predictions of the commercial success of a script. There is, of course, an enormous difference between the text and the finished product. Casting, group dynamics at rehearsal, and direction are all intangible factors with a tremendous influence on this product.

In the performing arts, the concept of a "work in progress" provides a noteworthy exception. Several creative artists present the fruit of their labours to a limited audience prior to the final shaping of their work, after a certain stage has been reached in rehearsal but without all the production elements (sets, props, costumes, and lighting) in order to test certain ideas or effects on a select clientele.

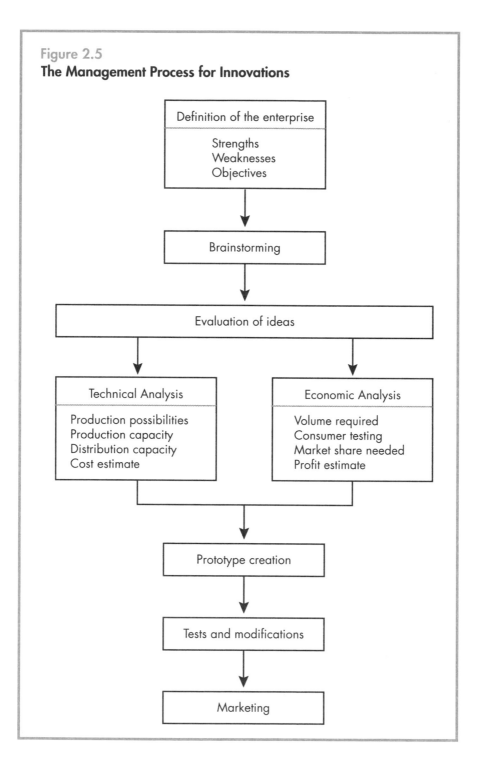

Figure 2.5
The Management Process for Innovations

Definition of the enterprise

Strengths
Weaknesses
Objectives

Brainstorming

Evaluation of ideas

Technical Analysis

Production possibilities
Production capacity
Distribution capacity
Cost estimate

Economic Analysis

Volume required
Consumer testing
Market share needed
Profit estimate

Prototype creation

Tests and modifications

Marketing

In Hollywood, films are frequently screened in front of a test audience before they are finished, during the editing process, the aim being to gauge the audience's reaction and/or to discuss the movie's ending with the audience. After gathering the audience's feedback, the director goes back to the editing room and makes the changes he deems appropriate.

Obviously, certain elements surrounding the "manufacture" of an artistic product may be tested – for instance, elements in an advertising campaign. The product may also be adapted according to cultural differences when exported – for instance, a new ending to a film. These adjustments, however, are minor.

Example 2.5
The Barbarian Invasions, an Oscar-Winning Film

The France/Canada co-production *The Barbarian Invasions* won the Oscar for Best Foreign Film in 2004. The Canadian producer, Cinémaginaire, its co-producer, Pyramide Productions, and the film's director, Denys Arcand, decided to adapt the movie for the international market. The film was re-edited and 11 minutes were cut, since some of the content was considered too "local": scenes about the Canadian health-care system, cable system, and media convergence. Both versions are available in Canada.

Source: Johanne Brunet, Guest Professor, HEC Montréal, Montreal, Canada.

2.3.2 The Risks Incurred

It goes without saying that products with a high degree of novelty, such as those in contemporary or parallel art, carry a high degree of risk for the producer, both financially and in terms of acceptance. With classical, popular, or familiar products, risk is always present but to a lesser degree.

While it is true that the cultural producer faces certain risks, there is also pressure on consumers, who, in making their choices, are limited to what other people have said about a product, with no opportunity to sample it themselves.[12] Producers, distributors, and performing arts organizations attempt to attenuate this pressure by offering potential customers a subscription for several new productions. The idea is to reduce consumers' perceived risk by selling them a "proven" product, which is in fact the organization itself, as opposed to each production being purchased separately; the organization becomes the "brand." Thus, the spectator is really buying the Comédie-Française, the Opéra de Montréal, or the New York Philharmonic, rather than Molière's *Le malade imaginaire*, *Madame Butterfly*, or Beethoven's Symphony No. 2 in D major. In the cultural industries, companies take advantage of the halo effect created by their reputation to influence the perception of their customers. For example, the Canadian children's publishing company Les Éditions de la courte échelle benefits from its brand's established reputation when launching a new book for young readers; the hope is that consumers will continue to place their trust in the company, based on their positive experiences with its products.

The combined effect of all these elements is that cultural enterprises are highly risky endeavours without equivalent in other sectors of the economy. At the same time, one of the defining characteristics of a cultural enterprise is the perpetual launching of new products. Indeed, managers of artistic products are required to invest heavily in the creation of products without being able to pre-test them – all the while knowing that, even if the product is successful, they will have to deliberately put an end to that success and start the whole process all over again with another product that also cannot be stored for future use.

SUMMARY

There are several recognized ways of defining products. One way is to classify them according to the effort that consumers expend to purchase them. This is how popular consumer products are categorized. The notion of a product is, however, much broader than a simple physical entity. We can therefore distinguish among the central product, related services, and the symbolic dimension. In the arts and cultural sector, the notion of product can be broken down into four components: the artistic product, spin-off products, customer service, and the consumption experience. The consumer may, in fact, want to buy one or more of these components.

A cultural product may also be defined according to three dimensions: referential, technical, and circumstantial.

Cultural products are often perceived as complex, because the notion of aesthetics, a subjective, non-quantifiable element related to taste and upbringing, is involved. The degree of complexity of a cultural product may vary according to corporate mission. For the marketer, the product may be defined as the set of benefits the customer perceives.

The life cycle of a product is a key concept in marketing. It is usually defined in terms of four stages: introduction, growth, maturity, and decline. The life cycle is represented by a curve that represents the demand. The time line for the life-cycle curve varies according to the consumption level of the target market. The notion of a life cycle is useful but far from definitive. For cultural enterprises whose products have predetermined life spans, its practical application is extremely limited.

The launching of a new product represents a major risk for any firm. Production in the arts and cultural sectors must be considered a particularly high-risk venture, since each product is actually a new one. The normal risk is exacerbated by three characteristics of cultural products. First, in the performing arts, for example, the product cannot be tested before its opening night; hence, production and promotion costs must be assumed ahead of time. Second, these products often have a predetermined life span regardless of their commercial success. Third, this type of product cannot be stored by either the producer or the consumer. As a result, the level of risk rises and the nature of the competition is affected.

QUESTIONS

1. Can you give an example of a consumer's definition of a product in the cultural sector?

2. Why is the main or central product not always the most important aspect for the consumer making a purchase?

3. Why does the circumstantial dimension of an artistic product have a double impact in the performing arts?

4. Can you give some examples of the importance of customer service in the cultural sector?

5. How is the notion of a product life cycle useful?

6. Can you describe how innovations spread?

7. What do "top-of-the-line" and "massive penetration" entail as strategies?

8. What are the characteristics of the growth phase in a product life cycle?

9. What strategies are available to a company in the maturity stage?

10. What are the three elements that help us decide that a product is in the decline stage?

11. What risks are normally associated with the launching of a new product?

12. How is risk different for cultural products?

Notes

1. Evrard, Y., and F. Colbert. 2000. "Arts Management: A New Discipline Entering the Millennium." *International Journal of Arts Management*, Vol. 2, n° 2 (Winter), p. 4–14.

2. Caldwell, N.G. 2000. "The Emergence of Museum Brands." *International Journal of Arts Management*, Vol. 2, n° 3 (Spring), p. 28–34.

3. Colbert, F. 2003. "The Sydney Opera House: An Australian Icon." *International Journal of Arts Management*, Vol. 5, n° 2 (Winter), p. 56–69.

4. Caru, A., and B. Cova. 2005. "The Impact of Service Elements on the Artistic Experience: The Case of Classical Music Concerts." *International Journal of Arts Management*, Vol. 7, n° 2 (Winter), p. 39–55.

5. Rogers, E. 1962. *The Diffusion of Innovations*. New York: Free Press.

6. "Economies of scale" refers to how a company can reduce unit costs by manufacturing in large quantities.

7. Radbourne, J. 2000. "The Australian Ballet – A Spirit of Its Own." *International Journal of Arts Management*, Vol. 2, n° 3 (Spring), p. 62–69; Ravanas, P. 2006. "Born to Be Wise: How Steppenwolf Theatre Mixes Freedom with Management Savvy." *International Journal of Arts Management*, Vol. 8, n° 3 (Spring), p. 64–74.

8. Dhalla, N.K., and S. Yuspeh. 1976. "Forget the Product Life Cycle Concept." *Harvard Business Review*, January–February, p. 102–112.

9. Levshina, E., and Y. Orlov. 2000. "General and Specific Issues in Russian Theatre." *International Journal of Arts Management*, Vol. 2, n° 2 (Winter), p. 74–83.

10. Power, C., et al. 1994. "Flops." *Business Week*, 16 August, p. 77.

11. Cooper, R.G. 1976. *Winning the New Product Game*. Montreal: McGill University Publication Services.

12. Crealy, M. 2003. "Applying New Product Development Models to the Performing Arts: Strategies for Managing Risk." *International Journal of Arts Management*, Vol. 5, n° 3 (Spring), p. 24–34.

For Further Reference

Bennett, R. 2001. "Lead User Influence on New Product Development Decisions of UK Theatre Companies: An Empirical Study." *International Journal of Arts Management*, Vol. 3, n° 2 (Winter), p. 28–40.

Leemans, H. 1997. "A PMC-Model for Cultural Organisations: The Case of a Public Library." In *Proceedings of the 4th International Conference on Arts and Culture Management*. San Francisco: Golden Gate University, p. 381–394.

Rentschler, R., and A. Gilmore. 2002. "Museums: Discovering Services Marketing." *International Journal of Arts Management*, Vol. 5, n° 1 (Fall), p. 62–72.

Scott, C. 2000. "Branding: Positioning Museums in the 21st Century." *International Journal of Arts Management*, Vol. 2, n° 3 (Spring), p. 35–39.

PLAN

Chapter **3**

The Market

OBJECTIVES

- Understand the specificity of the four markets open to cultural enterprises
- Give a profile of the culture consumer
- Point out the different levels of demand experienced by a company
- Understand the specificity of demand for enterprises in the arts sector and in the cultural industries
- Describe the pressures exerted on the market by macro-environmental variables
- Understand the effect of the synergy between markets and the dangers of a narrow view of the competition

INTRODUCTION

In order to adopt the perspective of the consumer, an organization must identify the characteristics of its target market. Consequently, one of the roles of the marketing manager is to study the firm's markets and to measure real and potential demand, not only for the company but for its markets overall. The evolution of demand in the entertainment sector is an interesting topic that merits special attention.

The marketing manager who wants to understand the forces influencing the market must adopt a broader view of the competition while taking into account globalization of the competition. Competition and globalization, combined with industry fragmentation in some cultural sectors, oblige companies to rely on a competitive advantage to ensure their own survival.

Lastly, in this chapter we examine how environmental forces exert tremendous pressure on every market, the company, and even the competition.

3.1 THE MARKET

As a rule, one organization targets several markets. A cultural enterprise may serve four different markets: the end consumer (or the consumer market), partners, governments, and the private sector. Each of these markets is driven by different motivations and expects different benefits. Therefore, organizations must pay special attention to the decision-makers in each one by developing marketing strategies designed specifically for that market.

3.1.1 The Consumer Market

The consumer market is composed of individuals who buy a specific good or service.

Rarely does one product interest the entire population. This statement applies even to staples, such as sugar, flour, and salt. A small percentage of households do not eat these products, so even if a company did target the entire population, not everyone would be a potential consumer.

The same statistical truth applies to cultural products. However, because of the extremely fragmented nature of the cultural sector, some distinctions are in order. For example, looking at this sector as a whole, it can be said that nearly 100% of the population consumes one type of cultural product or another. Indeed, in its broadest sense, the cultural sector encompasses everything from the performing arts (high and popular), to heritage, compact discs, movies, book and magazines, and radio and television, with each of these disciplines appropriating a share of global demand.

In Canada, for example, statistics[1] show that 37.0% of families attend an arts event at least once a year: movies 62.2%, museums and art galleries 32.9%. In the United States the figures for cultural consumption are: classical music 15.6%, opera 4.7%, musicals 24.5%, plays 15.8%, ballet 5.8%, art museums 34.5%, and historical parks 46.9%.[2] In Australia[3] the figures are: musical theatre 19.3%, classical music 7.7%, festivals 21.9%, concerts 23%, and museums 27.8%. Of course, within each of these sectors, consumers cluster according to specific poles of interest. This leads to sharper market segmentation. The consumer makes a discriminating choice among various cultural products to acquire or consume the type of product desired.

The distribution of consumers according to various market segments differs in both time and space. Markets undergo and reflect the influence of opinion leaders, trends, tastes, and societal characteristics. Markets also vary from country to country according to different social structures.

Over the past 40 years, various surveys focusing on the sociodemographic profile of consumers of cultural products have been carried out in nearly every European country (both East and West), as well as in Canada, the United States, Australia, and Japan.[4] It is fascinating to note that, regardless of whether the surveys were conducted in the 1970s, 1980s, or 1990s, they all obtained the same attendance rates and the same sociodemographic profiles. Differences in the measuring tools used can sometimes make it difficult to compare countries (different nomenclature for sectors, questions formulated differently, etc.); nonetheless, these studies have consistently and systematically revealed strong polarization of audiences between high art and popular culture across all countries over the past four decades. They show, for example, that cultural products catering to high art attract educated consumers, whereas those catering to popular culture draw on all segments of the population, in accordance with the relative weight of each. The proportion of university graduates making up Canadian audiences, for example, ranges between 50% and 70% for high art (symphony orchestras, arts festivals, fine arts museums, etc.), compared with 10% to 25% for popular culture (pop music, historical parks, etc.). By way of comparison, the overall percentage of university graduates in Canada is 25%. Similar results have been found in other countries, most notably in France[5] but also in Russia, where university graduates make up 50% of performing arts audiences but only 7% of the general population.[6]

Other sociodemographic variables are also linked to attendance, including average income (higher among consumers of high art than consumers of popular culture) and type of occupation (white-collar workers account for a larger proportion of high art consumers while blue-collar workers are drawn to popular culture in greater numbers). It should be pointed out once again that this profile is based on averages. Less-educated individuals with lower income may be great consumers of culture, as is the case for students and those specialized or working in the cultural milieu. Indeed, it is well known that, as a rule, many people active in the arts are highly educated yet so poorly paid that they struggle to stay above the poverty line. On the other hand, there are people with both very high salaries and very high educational levels who are not interested in the arts and gladly keep their distance. Four factors are known to influence an individual's penchant for complex cultural products:

Capsule 3.1
The Development of Tastes among Arts Consumers

Several studies have attempted to identify the factors that motivate people to consume high art, while few studies have focused on popular culture. Researchers have identified four main factors that influence the preference of consumers for high art products: family values that encourage the consumption of high art, the educational milieu and the value it places on high art, childhood attendance at performances or visits to museums, and the practice of amateur art.

Values transmitted by the family constitute the main factor influencing the development of a taste for the arts. The sociologist Bourdieu[7] calls this phenomenon "cultural capital." When asked what has most influenced them, arts consumers typically say that their parents encouraged them or had a positive attitude toward art. In cases where this factor is not present, the values transmitted in school are often cited as an influence; for example, a music lover might identify a teacher's enthusiasm as the source of his or her own passion for music.

Several studies also identify childhood attendance at performances or visits to museums as an important factor in fostering a taste for the arts; a person who had this type of opportunity as a child or teenager will tend to develop a greater interest in high art than a person who did not.

Finally, there is a link between the pursuit of amateur art and being a consumer of high art; many consumers of high art are people who took up the practice of amateur art at school or as a leisure activity.

family values that encourage or discourage high art, the educational milieu and the value it places on high art, the fact of having attended performances or visited museums as a child, and amateur art practice.

A more detailed analysis of the typical cultural consumer's traits reveals other nuances based on the different disciplines (see Capsule 3.1 for a discussion of the development of tastes among arts consumers). For example, dance audiences are relatively younger and even more female in composition than those of the other performing arts; similarly, more women than men read novels, although a larger proportion of men read daily newspapers. In the film sector, there are two very different segments of avid cinema-goers; one of these segments is dominated by a young clientele (15–25 years), while the other is made up of educated people. The majority of consumers in the film sector belong to one or the other of these two segments.

Thus, arts enterprises and certain organizations belonging to the cultural industries (those offering products labelled "art house" or "contemporary") whose audiences include a high proportion of university graduates are targeting a rather limited market, even if these people are big consumers of cultural products. Popular art caters to a much larger market segment.

Figure 3.1 illustrates the relationship between the popular and high arts, the number of units consumed, and the complexity of the product.

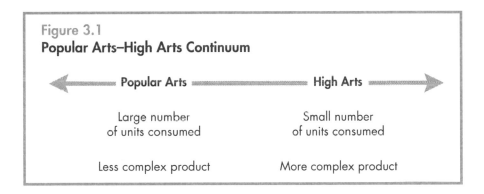

Figure 3.1
Popular Arts–High Arts Continuum

Popular Arts — High Arts

Large number of units consumed   Small number of units consumed

Less complex product   More complex product

3.1.2 The Partner Market

Although some companies sell their product directly to the end consumer, many others use the services of a partner. This may be the result of a strategic decision or it may be a necessity, dictated by limited resources, by the way in which the product is consumed, or by the structure of the sector or geographical territory.

A partner is an organization with which a firm associates on an ad hoc basis while sharing, to varying degrees, the risks and successes arising from an operation ultimately intended for the consumer market. Cultural enterprises have four main types of partner: distribution intermediaries, co-producers, distribution partners, and the media. Each can be considered a market in itself or a segment of the partner market.

Distribution Intermediaries

In the performing arts sector, for example, the local promoter or presenter is a distribution intermediary. A touring company will turn to the local promoter to help it reach consumers living in a specific city or region. In this case, the marketing of a cultural product can be said to be a two-step process: the first step consists of the touring company convincing the local promoter to include its show on the season's program and to thereby share the risk; the second step consists of the local promoter reaching potential consumers in the region. As a rule, the producer must develop a specific strategy aimed at local promoters, as well as designing promotional tools to support the local promoter's efforts to sell the product to the end consumer.

Sometimes producers present an artist or show that is so popular the producers can pick and choose which local promoter they want to deal with and dictate their own terms and conditions. The Quebec (Canada) reality TV show *Star Académie* is one example of this phenomenon. To cite an example from the film industry, during the last instalment of the *Star Wars* series, the producers not only chose the theatres where they wanted the movie to be screened, but also imposed a different fee structure. In such cases, the role of the distribution intermediary is closer to that of a supplier than a market.

Co-production

Many cultural productions would never see the light of day if the producer was unable to find a co-producer to support the project financially. It is very common for films to be co-produced by foreign partners. This approach not only ensures adequate financing for the project, but also increases the film's likelihood of succeeding as a result of the partner's greater familiarity with the local market. (The different modes of co-production are described in Appendix 3.1.)

Distribution Partners

A company may decide to join forces with another producer, or, alternatively, it may seek to form a partnership with a distributor. The National Arts Centre in Ottawa (Canada) occasionally takes on this role by investing in a production mounted by a producer partner; by integrating this partner's production into its programming, the NAC becomes co-producer and distributor. Distributors at both the local and the international level often play a similar role; some dance companies, for example, find foreign distribution partners when they accept a residency with a partner.

Media

Finally, most cultural enterprises strive to secure the cooperation of the media in promoting their product. This is especially true of small companies that cannot afford ambitious advertising campaigns. In such cases, the media represent a key partner that the company must try to win over. However, this is no easy task given that media representatives are in high demand and the number of productions to be covered often exceeds the time they have available to attend them. A conscientious marketing manager will devise a strategy that respects the benefits perceived by this sub-market.

3.1.3 The State as a Market

"State" is used here to denote the different levels of government – federal, provincial (regional), and municipal (local) – that support cultural enterprises in various ways. The state plays a dominant role in the cultural sector in most Western countries. Sometimes it acts as a consumer, or it may intervene to varying degrees, from simple partner to patron controlling the entire cultural sector of a nation.

The notion of the state as grant giver and as market implies that a cultural enterprise must define its own strategy to convince decision-makers to become partners in its activities. This type of cultural enterprise faces competition from others in the same field, and the efforts of each company to obtain more state support are essentially efforts to capture a larger share of a specific market. Since the arts budget is not sufficient to meet the needs of the entire cultural sector, the arrival of a new company or the success of an existing one may mean that the money allotted to one company will be reallocated to the benefit or detriment of another company.

There are several government agencies prepared to assist cultural organizations and companies through various forms of financial support. Some programs allow for the funding of infrastructures; others allow for the completion of specific projects; and still others contribute to the operational budget of the company itself.

Capsule 3.2
Public Investment in Culture and the Arts

The level of public investment in culture and the arts varies according to a country's traditions. Countries in Continental Europe have a long history of state participation in this sector; major theatres and museums can expect to receive as much as 80 to 100% of their budget in the form of government funding. In the United States, public investment in the arts is much less pronounced and the private sector and individual donors play a major role in the life of cultural enterprises; for example, on average, only 3.2% of opera company[8] budgets and less than 10% of theatre company [9] budgets come from public sources. The approach adopted by Canada and Australia is modelled after that of the United Kingdom, where the state has a hand in the cultural sector but to a lesser degree than in Continental Europe.

With regard to the structures created to distribute these public funds, again the models vary from one country to the next. Some countries, such as France, have a centralized model in which a culture minister fixes the priorities and objectives that define cultural policy. On the other hand, the United States has adopted a highly decentralized model based on the creation of nearly 3,000 Local Arts Councils that play a major role in the cultural life of communities; even the National Endowment for the Arts, whose budget is very low considering the country's size (about US$130 million in 2005), is obliged to distribute a portion of its budget to the State Arts Councils and Local Arts Councils. In Canada, Australia, and the United Kingdom (whose model the first two countries have borrowed), a national arts council plays a major role in awarding funding for the arts; however, this strong presence does not preclude other ministries and regional authorities from establishing their own financial aid programs.

An interesting feature of the funding situation in Canada is that arts enterprises can seek support from three levels of government – federal, provincial, and municipal. Of the approximately $7 billion in cultural expenditures at these three levels, 46% is contributed by the federal government, 32% by the provinces, and 22% by municipalities.[10] This degree of involvement by different levels of government is not found in all countries. In Europe, the political approach to cultural funding reflects a historical tradition rooted in the customs of

Capsule 3.2 (continued)

princes and the nobility. These traditions continue to have a profound influence on state intervention in culture in Europe today. France, for example, does not have a provincial level of government; the central state plays a predominant role that reflects the monarchic system from which it originates, while cities play a supporting role. In Germany, the post-World War II constitution prohibits the federal government from intervening in cultural affairs, which fall under the jurisdiction of the Länder (provinces) and cities, which have upheld the traditions of the former principalities to which they trace their origins. In Sweden, the provinces account for a mere 7% of the country's cultural budget. In Italy, in contrast, cultural enterprises can seek funding from four levels of government – federal, provincial, regional, and municipal – some of which contribute very little in the way of cultural subsidies.

3.1.4 The Private-Sector Market

For our purposes here, the private sector encompasses individual and corporate donors, foundations, and corporate sponsors.

In the early 1980s, the different levels of government in Canada began to encourage cultural enterprises to turn to private donations and sponsorships in order to increase their revenues. This shift coincided with the discovery by private corporations that the arts clientele represented an attractive market for their business, which led to an increase in the participation of the private sector in arts funding. In the province of Quebec , private support for the arts lags behind that of the other provinces and is substantially lower than that in the United States. In Quebec, the contribution of the private sector to the performing arts overall accounted for 8.4% of total revenues in 1981,[11]10% in 1995, and 14.8% in 2003; for the same years, the Canadian averages were 13%, 17.7%, and 21.1%.[12]

Of all the causes that attract the generosity of the public or of private enterprise, the arts are at the back of the pack. This phenomenon is not specific to Canada but can be observed in all countries, including the United States. Religious groups consistently rank first in terms of private sector funding. Figure 3.2 presents the data for Australia.

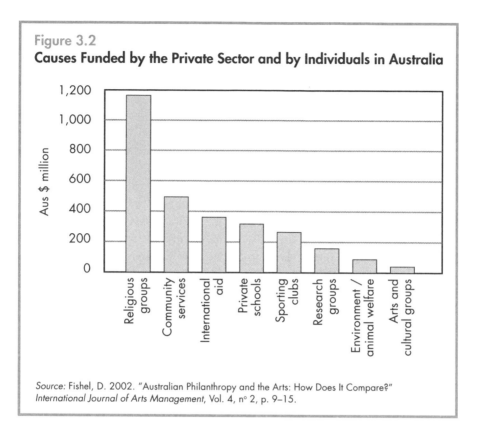

Figure 3.2

Causes Funded by the Private Sector and by Individuals in Australia

Aus $ million

Religious groups | Community services | International aid | Private schools | Sporting clubs | Research groups | Environment / animal welfare | Arts and cultural groups

Source: Fishel, D. 2002. "Australian Philanthropy and the Arts: How Does It Compare?" *International Journal of Arts Management*, Vol. 4, n° 2, p. 9–15.

3.2 MARKET DEMAND

3.2.1 Defining Demand

Market demand for a particular product is the expression, in volume or dollars, of purchases made. The demand may be expressed either quantitatively in units (volume) or monetarily, according to need and availability of data. It is possible to calculate demand for each of the cultural enterprise's markets; this section uses demand in the consumer market as an example, but the same logic can be applied to the other markets of the cultural enterprise (governments, private sector, partners).

Demand expressed in terms of volume often gives a more realistic picture of the market, since the results are not inflated through price increases. It is therefore easier to compare data from one year to the next since the basis of comparison is similar. Sometimes, an increase in demand in dollars is merely the result of higher prices, while the real market level remains the same. If the demand is given in dollars with no adjustment for price, the measurement is considered to be in current dollars. If a marketing analyst eliminates the inflation factor by using the same year of reference, the measurement is said to be in constant dollars. If data on volume are unavailable, demand must be calculated in constant dollars, to neutralize variations in price and provide a true picture of the situation.

Although expressing demand in terms of volume may be useful, especially to see how demand evolves, it may at times be difficult to do. The data, as such, may not exist, or the product may comprise a range of diverse elements. In the leisure market, for instance, the demand cannot be evaluated in terms of volume because the category of products combines proverbial apples and oranges that do not add up – for instance, theatre seats, trips, and book purchases.

Market demand (MD) and corporate demand (CD) are normally considered separately. Corporate demand is the expression in volume or in dollars of purchases made of one product manufactured by a specific company. Market demand embraces all the corporate demands.

CD = Number of units sold by a company

$MD = \sum CD_i$

Since the market demand (MD) for a product consists of all the individual corporate demands (CD), the overall demand may reveal one trend while the CD indicates the opposite. For example, the overall demand for theatre tickets may have risen one year, while the demand for tickets for a particular theatre company may have plummeted during the same period. The same possibility exists in the overall demand for a specific industry, such as leisure activities, with regard to the demand for its parts, such as shows or sporting events.

It is possible to measure demand at different points along the chain, from creation to production to distribution to consumption. In this case, demand for a specific link is equal to the volume in units or dollars of purchases made by all those active in the link.

Sometimes, several firms or "players" join forces to stimulate overall market demand. These firms presume that an increase in overall demand is possible and is beneficial for each firm in proportion to its importance in the marketplace. In Canada, for example, Montreal Museums Day is an open house organized annually by the Board of Montreal Museum Directors as part of the festival "Musées en fête" presented by the Société des musées québécois. Both of these events are inspired by International Museum Day (www.museesmontreal/site/idmmhtm.org), launched by UNESCO. On Montreal Museums Day the public can discover the treasures of the city's museums admission free.

Similar initiatives may take place at the local or regional level. In the United States, for example, some museums have formed associations with a view to joint promotional campaigns designed to increase the overall demand within a particular region.

3.2.2 Market Share

The market, as defined here, comprises all the individuals or companies consuming a product. Each firm encourages its part of the market segment to consume its product in order to acquire a percentage of the demand. In current marketing terms, this is called the "market share," and it describes not the consumers buying the products, but the proportion of the demand belonging to one company. It would be more accurate to speak of "demand share" rather than market share, but the accepted expression is market share. The term also means share of the demand and is used in that sense here.

The market share of a company is calculated as follows:

$$\text{Market share} = \frac{\text{CD}}{\text{MD}}$$

A company with sales of $400,000 in a very specific $1 million market that it shares with other companies is said to have a market share of 40% ($400,000 ÷ $1,000,000). This information is extremely useful, since it enables a firm to compare itself to other firms and thus determine its position relative to the competition. It is possible to calculate a company's market share in each of its markets.

3.2.3 The State of the Demand

Demand for a product may be considered from two vantage points: real and potential. For each aspect, there are three periods: past demand, current demand, and forecast demand.

Real Demand

The real demand of a company corresponds to its sales volume at a specific time. The same applies to the market demand, which is a measure of the demand at a specific moment, be it now or in the past. It is possible to obtain the historical background chronicling the dynamics of a sector, industry, or company by measuring the evolution of demand from past years. At the same time, the future level of demand can be forecast for a company or market in general terms.

Potential Demand

The potential demand is the maximum level that may be reached by a product in a given context. Not all consumers buy all the products offered on the market, although for commonly bought consumer goods consumption is often believed to be generalized. The entire consumer population is almost never reached. People who do not consume a particular product but may do so are called potential consumers. Manufacturers work to persuade these potential purchasers to try their products in order to increase sales. If the percentage of sales per capita can be increased, manufacturers will try to convince their clientele to consume more.

There is, however, a threshold for any demand. This depends on the consumers' means, tastes, and preferences, as well as on their receptivity to a marketing strategy and their environment. The marketing manager's task is to estimate the maximum level of market demand at any given time – in other words, the potential market demand. Similarly, the manager can estimate the potential demand for the company.

Just as in the case of real demand, potential demand may be calculated at a point in the past or the present, or forecast for the future.

Market Demand in Different Situations

Real demand is often lower than potential demand. In this case, a company may hope to increase its sales or its market share. If real and potential demand are equal, then the market is said to have reached the saturation point, after which the product enters the maturity stage of its life cycle.

Any sales projections must therefore take into account the foreseeable actions of the competition and the predicted evolution of the potential demand. The marketing manager may expect an increase in potential demand and an increase in company sales figures. On the other hand, when potential demand in a market dips, companies must expect to have greater difficulty in maintaining their current level of demand and market share (see Figure 3.3).

These concepts apply not only to the demand but also to the market. A market may also be considered real or potential and be measured in the past, present, or future.

Here is a concrete example of these concepts. A touring theatre troupe offers its show to a presenter in a specific region. The current potential market for the troupe in that area corresponds to the total number of venues or presenters likely to buy the show. The real market is known, since the troupe knows which halls or theatres it has already played that year. The predicted market is composed of the number of buyers forecast for the following year. This forecast may be made by considering two different areas: the number of presenters in the market (potential market) and the number of presenters that will buy the show (real forecast market).

3.2.4 The Evolution of Demand in the Leisure Market

The world leisure market experienced tremendous growth between the 1960s and the 1980s. In fact, the increase in demand has benefitted almost

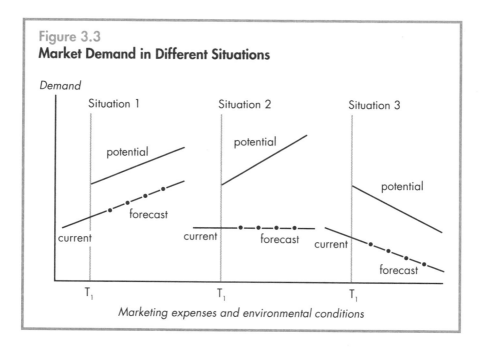

Figure 3.3
Market Demand in Different Situations

Demand

Situation 1

potential

forecast

current

Situation 2

potential

current

forecast

Situation 3

potential

current

forecast

T_1 T_1 T_1

Marketing expenses and environmental conditions

all cultural sectors. It is worth noting that, in a country such as Canada, stage productions have surpassed sports events in terms of consumer popularity. Table 3.1 shows that in terms of the percentage of families responding, the percentage of dollars spent on these two leisure products reversed in 1974, with stage productions surpassing sports events by far in popularity.

This trend can be attributed not only to an increase in artistic and cultural offerings, but also to significant changes at the level of demand.

Underlying Trends and Current Challenges

Five factors explain the steep rise in demand in the leisure market, including the arts, that occurred in industrialized countries between 1960 and 1980: 1) population growth, 2) increase in leisure time, 3) increase in disposable personal income in constant dollars, 4) increase in level of education, and 5) increasing participation of women in the workforce.

These five powerful factors combined to drive the rapid rise in demand in the leisure market. However, their beneficial effect on demand has worn off somewhat. For example, despite a slight increase in the overall level of education, the population is growing at a snail's pace, the amount of leisure time available has reached a plateau (or even declined in some job categories), disposable personal income in constant dollars has either levelled off or

Table 3.1
Evolution of Average Family Expenditures on Cultural Outings

	Sports events		Stage performances		Museums		Cinema	
	%	$ con-stant	%	$ con-stant	%	$ con-stant	%	$ con-stant
1964	35.5	10.6	26.0	5.1	n/a	n/a	61.0	16.1
1974	31.6	15.2	32.2	8.7	n/a	n/a	62.5	20.0
1984	28.4	8.3	43.1	11.8	39.5	5.4	59.9	13.4
1992	25.7	7.0	35.1	9.9	32.9	4.3	48.9	9.3
2003	19.3	7.2	37.0	13.3	32.9	5.6	62.2	17.2

Source: Statistics Canada, 2000. *Family Expenditure in Canada.* Catalogue 62.555

increased only slightly, and new generations of women have long been integrated into the workforce.

Among the factors that have contributed to the increased demand for cultural products, two in particular warrant attention by marketing managers: the presence of women, and population growth. The spectacular growth in participation in cultural leisure activities can be attributed in part to a predominantly female clientele. The women's liberation movement of the 1960s and the arrival of women on the labour market created a new group of consumers – educated, financially secure women with leisure time on their hands and with tastes that differed from those of male consumers. Free to make their own decisions, independently of their husbands, and eager for leisure activities outside the home, women turned in large numbers to arts and culture. At the time, they represented a new segment of consumers. In 2006, one is likely to hear the media discuss the phenomenon of the "superwoman," exhausted from the demands of fulfilling her multiple roles of mother, professional, wife, and homemaker and having to balance work and family. Considering that the majority of consumers in many fields are women, marketing managers would do well to keep this phenomenon in mind.

The increase in demand that was seen between 1960 and 1980 is also largely attributable to the coming of age of the baby boomers starting around 1960. This consumer group has dominated and set the tone for cultural behaviour for the past few decades. Moreover, it is a generation that chose to have children later in life and to have fewer of them. This caused a gradual decline in the number of children per woman of child-bearing age, which was followed, starting in 1980, by an increase in the birth rate. This rise in the birth rate translates into an increase in the segment of the population that is presently under the age of 18. This new generation, often referred to as the echo generation, is larger than the generations preceding it but smaller than the baby boomer cohort, and it is expected to comprise an important segment of the market within the next 10 to 15 years.

In fact, by around 2015 the two largest segments of the market for cultural enterprises will be situated at opposite extremes of the age pyramid: the baby boomers, who will be over 50, and their offspring, who will be between the ages of 15 and 35. Each of these two segments will be larger than the third segment, made up of the 35–50 age group. The main question raised by this phenomenon is whether these two consumer groups will have similar preferences or will be attracted to different cultural products. In the latter case, firms will be faced with a dilemma: they will have to either choose between these two segments or adjust their products in order to reach both of these potentially incompatible segments at the same time. For companies that offer only one product, the dilemma will be absolute, while for those offering a program consisting of several performances or exhibitions, there will be greater room for adjustment, although this will not necessarily be easy to achieve.

Indeed, studies based on age cohorts in Canada, the United States, and Europe suggest that the behaviour adopted by younger generations differs from that of their elders,[13] all the more so when it comes to music. For example, the cohort born between 1966 and 1976 (thus ranging in age from 17 to 26 at the time of the American study) displayed a clear preference for jazz and a marked lack of interest in classical music and opera. If this trend is carried over to the following generation (that born after 1976), barring a reversal, the audience for symphony orchestras and opera companies could go into a free fall within the next few years, especially in light of the drop in patronage observed among the very elderly.

This problem is compounded by the fact that senior citizens have very specific needs, described by Motta and Schewe[14] as both physical and psychological. Their physical needs involve diminished hearing, vision, physical endurance, and mobility due to age, while their psychological needs have to do with a diminished capacity for abstraction and memory. For example, many elderly people are unable to perceive certain sounds, or they may like to sit down more frequently. Generally speaking, this age group prefers events which offer the opportunity to socialize with other people, as opposed to events involving more solitary contemplation.

Thus, beyond the preferences for particular works or a specific repertoire, it is the whole context of consumption that is affected by these trends.

3.3 MARKET AND COMPETITION

3.3.1 A Broad View of Competition

In any discussion of competition within culture and the arts, the cultural product must be situated in a much broader context – the leisure market. Even if people do not consider cultural products simply as pastimes, they can consume them only during non-working and non-sleeping hours. The cultural product is therefore in competition not only with other cultural products, but also with various other products designed to occupy the consumer's free time (such as sports and other physical activities, restaurant dining, travel, and continuing education), regardless of whether they are consumed within the home (television, the Internet) or externally and regardless of whether the competition is local, national, or international.

There are essentially four types of competition. First, there is competition within one category of products; this is the case in a regional market – for instance, for an exhibition offered by different museums. Second, there is competition between different genres of cultural product – for example, between a classical music concert and a dance performance. Third, there is competition between cultural products and other leisure products – for example, between movies and skiing. Lastly, there is competition between local cultural products and international cultural products that have become available as a result of technological advances: radio, magazines, and daily newspapers, as well as educational materials prepared by museums, are now all accessible via the Internet.

Competition is quite strong for leisure organizations trying to capture their share of the precious moments and dollars consumers allot to free time. Competition is fiercer in large cities, where the number of cultural products and leisure activities reaches dizzying heights. One look at the newspapers in a major city like New York, Sydney, Rome, or Toronto reveals tremendous variety in the supply.

The competition is all the keener since the life span of certain products is short and ephemeral; this is particularly the case for cultural organizations and products in quadrants 1 and 4 of Figure 1.2, Marketing and Cultural Enterprises (see Chapter 1). Exhibitions are offered for a limited time only, so these products cannot be stored for future presentation and the consumer cannot postpone consumption beyond a certain date. The consumer must therefore make his or her choice immediately. This time pressure intensifies the competition among products.

3.3.2 The Interdependence of Markets and the Ripple Effect

Companies that earn revenue in several markets – which is the case for the majority of companies – face stiff competition within each market. This competition is simultaneous but involves different actors in each market. Two firms that approach a sponsor may not be applying to the same government funding program or to the same distribution partner. It is therefore essential that managers study the competition from all angles. Moreover, managers must take into account the synergy and ripple effects between the markets, instead of considering them individually and developing a separate strategy for each. By analyzing existing interrelations, a company can use one market to generate a leverage effect over its other market(s), thus triggering a growth spiral. For example, a company has to know its consumers well not only in order to communicate effectively with this market, but also in order to be able to offer more information to sponsors, partners, and even (in some cases) governments.

The opposite is also true. A company that begins to weaken in a given market can enter a negative growth spiral, leading to its demise. A decline in clientele can cause a drop in the number of sponsors and the erosion of funding, with the result that the company begins to look less attractive to potential partners. In such a case, the company must analyze the situation based on all four markets and take vigorous action in order to reverse the direction of the spiral. This is not always an easy task, however.

3.3.3 The Effect of Globalization on Competition

Globalization of competition has opened up new vistas to consumers and has made possible the export of certain cultural products. In exchange, other products can be imported from foreign countries. These imports mean additional competition for local products. Moreover, while international markets may appear to be very attractive, the marketing manager of an arts enterprise must keep in mind that competition in the respective markets is very strong in all industrialized countries; while in many cases the population will be greater, in these countries supply may also exceed demand.

In the cultural industries, companies are clustered or concentrated, so that a small number of multinationals control the creation of a large number of cultural products. These multinationals diversify their activities so that each one controls businesses in each cultural sector: artist management, record production, live performance, performance venues, ticket offices, entertainment equipment (CD players, VCRs, etc.), film production and distribution, publishing, radio and TV networks, stage productions, and so on. The cultural enterprises in a country with a small population must work together, using synergy to combat foreign competition. This united front, so to speak, must include not only products, but also the many other partners or links that form the production channel, including suppliers and the distribution network. This idea of the industrial cluster is part of Porter's[15] strategy for a country seeking to position itself advantageously at the international level. Porter also points that, just like corporations, countries are competing among themselves.

3.3.4 Industry Fragmentation

Another trend that can intensify competition is fragmentation of the industry. Porter gives five sources of pressure that might cause an industry to fragment (see Figure 3.4). These are (1) intra-industry rivals; (2) new entrants – for example, companies just starting in the industry; (3) suppliers; (4) purchasers; (5) and substitute products.

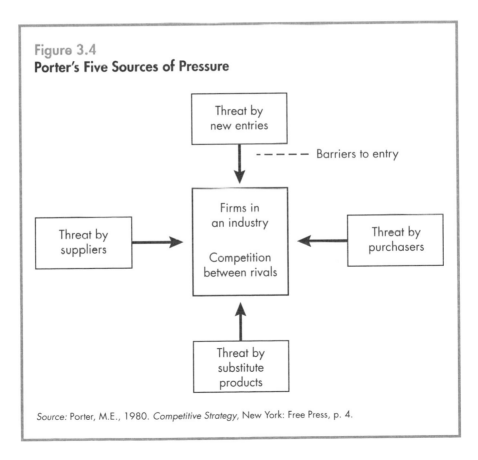

Figure 3.4
Porter's Five Sources of Pressure

Threat by
new entries

- - - - - Barriers to entry

Firms in
an industry

Competition
between rivals

Threat by
suppliers

Threat by
purchasers

Threat by
substitute
products

Source: Porter, M.E., 1980. *Competitive Strategy*, New York: Free Press, p. 4.

An industry is said to be fragmented if competitors are small yet numerous, if barriers blocking their entry into the industry are weak, and if buyers or suppliers have control over companies within the industry. This last point is particularly important when there are few suppliers or buyers and they are both large and powerful enough to lay down the law within that industry, and keep competitors small so as to enjoy their position of power. If, on top of that, the sector grows slowly and there is little possibility of differentiation among firms, competition becomes cut-throat among small firms that are unable to expand. The usual result is a perpetual price war. The competing firms may jeopardize their own profitability and end up bankrupt.

An industry may change from an extremely fragmented to a less fragmented one if it becomes highly concentrated. By concentrating, an industry can have a balanced number of large and small companies. The former regulate the market. Some industries, however, will never experience this type of concentration. Porter lists 16 traits that may prevent concentration (see Table 3.2), any one of which is enough to sustain the fragmentation.

The high arts sector is a fragmented industry, with many small companies. The industry does not, however, offer any possibility for concentration, since it possesses at least four of the 16 traits likely to block concentration. First, fragmentation in the arts may be explained by the lack of barriers to entry. It is, in fact, easy to find a string quartet or a theatre troupe since little initial outlay is required, in comparison with the financing needed to open a traditional commercial enterprise like an auto manufacturing plant. Second, economies of scale are not possible due to the very nature of the product. A symphony orchestra, for example, always needs the same number of musicians and the same amount of rehearsal or performance time. Third, artistic content is very important for the cultural enterprise. In fact, this is the main distinguishing feature of companies active in the arts. Lastly, the "exit barrier" helps to explain why many artists prefer to toil away rather than renounce their art. Their devotion enables their employer (cultural enterprises) to survive.

A similar situation can be found in certain cultural industries. The rise of the digital age has served to break down the entry barriers to the recording and film industries, for example. Now, all one needs is a computer and a little talent. To cite just one example, Lhasa de Sela is said to have recorded her debut album in a Montreal (Canada) kitchen before it went on to sell hundreds of thousands of copies.

A company in a fragmented industry must find its positioning in order to stand out from the crowd – in other words, the competition. The principle of a competitive advantage is, therefore, vitally important.

Table 3.2
The Sixteen Causes of Industry Fragmentation

1. Low overall entry barriers
2. Absence of economies of scale
3. High transport costs
4. High inventory costs or erratic sales fluctuations
5. No advantages of size in dealing with buyers or suppliers
6. Diseconomies of scale in some important aspect
7. Low overhead crucial to success of operation
8. Made-to-measure products for diverse market needs
9. Heavy creative content in product
10. Close local control and supervision of operations required
11. Abundant personalized service
12. Local contacts required simply to do business
13. Exit barriers
14. Local regulation
15. Government prohibition of concentration
16. Newness of industry

Source: Porter, M.E. 1980. *Competitive Strategy.* New York: Free Press, p. 196.

3.3.5 The Principle of a Competitive Advantage

Pressure from the competition in its broadest sense, including global competition, obliges any cultural enterprise to define and use its competitive advantage to appear unique in the consumer's eyes; the nature of this uniqueness can vary from one market to another, since needs are different in each market.

Any company must try to adopt a strong position that enables it to stand out. This position of strength is achieved only by highlighting some distinctive aspect or competitive advantage of the company or product. Naturally, this aspect must be positively perceived by consumers. The advantage may be a product feature, a promotional tool, a different way of using the distribution networks, or an interesting pricing policy. It is up to the company to find its own unique niche that will enable it to outdistance the competition.

The marketing manager must consider the question: Why did the consumer (or sponsor) prefer the product offered by my firm over that of the competition? This question is an important one, because in a saturated market such as the arts, the consumer is faced with a virtually unlimited number of choices; in many cases, consumers must choose between several possibilities, each as interesting as the next. In the consumer market, decisions may be based on related factors (proximity of parking, atmosphere, ease of ticket purchase, politeness of staff, presence or absence of a bar, etc.), the effort required, or the quality of a previous experience.

Faced with the enormous pressure exerted by the competition at both the national level and the international level, a cultural enterprise has no choice but to develop a competitive advantage in its target market, whether it is the consumer, government, private sector, or partner market.

Example 3.1
Cines Albatros Y Babel: A Competitive Advantage

The Albatros and Babel cinemas are the only two multiplexes in Valencia (Spain) that show only films in the original version. They represent approximately 7% of screens in the city. The main reason for this distinction, originally, was interest on the part of the funders. Other reasons were the difficulty of obtaining dubbed films, due to ownership concentration, and complex relationships with distributors. The two cinemas finally targeted a market niche in order to gain a competitive advantage and establish a more fluent relationship with suppliers.

European films account for 70% of the films screened, followed by independent American films and South American and Asian films. The audience consists mainly of women between the ages of 30 and 40 and academics. Within this audience, three groups can be distinguished: university students, language students, and high school teachers/university professors. Focusing on these segments, the cinemas' managers have broadened their timetables and instituted such features as premières, conferences, telephone and Internet ticket sales, film brochures, and special discounts and promotions. They have developed a group of highly satisfied and loyal consumers.

Source: Manuel Cuadrado, Associate Professor, Universitat de València, Spain.

3.4   THE MARKET AND MACRO-ENVIRONMENTAL VARIABLES

Macro-environmental variables, also known as uncontrollable variables, exert an ongoing influence on both the market and the life of an organization. Firms must sometimes adapt to radical changes over which they have no power to act. There are five main variables in the macro-environment: demographic environment, cultural environment, economic environment, political-legal environment, and technological environment. These variables must be taken into account by the company not only in relation to the domestic or national market, but also when entering the global market.

3.4.1 The Demographic Environment

Demographics play a key role in the market, since a shift in the population may mean a rise or fall in the demand. How the population is spread out within an area, which age groups dominate, and which ethnic groups live there are only a few of the important dimensions of the environment that influence marketing. For example, teenagers 15–17 years old buy the most pop-music recordings. Naturally, a variation in the number of teens aged 15–17 will have a definite impact on the music sector. This is also the case for products designed for children, a product category that depends on the number of children in each age group.

3.4.2 The Cultural Environment

The values of a society, also called the cultural environment, play a leading role in the marketing of a product. As values change, so do consumer habits. Thus, what was unthinkable in the 1940s now seems normal. The traditional role of women, for example, was once that of homemaker, and a large family was the ideal. This is no longer the case; most women over 18 are now in the job market. At the same time, modern couples are having fewer children and having them later in life – in their thirties rather than in their twenties. This helps to explain why today's young couples have more leisure time in which to consume cultural goods. Naturally, these changes influence cultural organizations.

3.4.3 The Economic Environment

Firms, like individuals, must deal with their economic environment. Inflation, unemployment, and recession are all now household words. During a recession, for instance, there are fewer potential consumers and fewer dollars available per consumer. This situation affects not just cultural enterprises, but sponsors too: the corporate budget for sponsorships or donations shrinks immediately. Any corporation trying to cut costs will slash peripheral activities, and donations and sponsorships are the first to go. Entire towns may disappear when the international economic situation triggers a drop in the price of certain raw materials. At that point, shock waves travel throughout the cultural sector, since the cultural demand often absorbs the consumer's discretionary income.

3.4.4 The Political-Legal Environment

Laws and regulations are another key variable, since government action can radically change the face of an industry. A direct tax on the price of cultural products may lower demand. The effect of government intervention or action may also be positive – for instance, tax measures designed to stimulate the film-making industry.

3.4.5 The Technological Environment

Every company is subject to influences from the technological environment. Science has made tremendous advances and discoveries that have left few areas untouched. Technology has also had an impact on the arts. In some areas, such as audiovisual equipment, there is ongoing competition spurred on by innovations that constantly flood the market and can radically change the way a work is produced or distributed. Other areas may be less affected by technological developments in terms of production and preservation yet be greatly affected in terms of distribution. For example, traditional artisans such as glassmakers, whose craft often consists in using ancient methods, would produce an entirely different product if they used modern technology. However, these artisans cannot afford to ignore the Internet as a distribution channel and promotional tool; they need the Internet in order to reach their markets. On the other hand, the development of holography and computer graphics has changed or enhanced traditional painting techniques. Artists can now create more durable and more soluble synthetic pigments. Recent chemical discoveries have led to new binding substances and varnishes that provide more malleable, reliable tools for the conservation of art works.

Cinema provides a very dramatic example of technological impact on a market. Movies were originally meant to be consumed collectively, in a theatre equipped with a large screen. The emergence of television, cable TV, pay TV, video, satellite TV, DVDs, Internet broadcasts, and, recently, downloading of images on cell phones and iPods, has presented the consumer with an ever increasing range of choices.

3.4.6 The International Market

In addition to these variables of the macro-economic environment, a company must take into account two other variables when entering the global market or exporting products: the geography of a territory, and its infrastructures. The accessibility, climate, and road network of a territory are just some of the constraints that can influence the manner in which a product is exported and also its timing. If, for example, the country's electrical system functions at 220 volts, this must be taken into account when bringing into the country any electrical equipment designed to run on 110 volts. In addition, television sets in some territories use the PAL system whereas in others they use the NTSC system. In the case of a touring show, the availability of a road network is another key consideration.

When the time comes to distribute the exported product, the company must be familiar with the distribution structures in place, including their effectiveness and reliability. For instance, in order for audiences to view a feature film in movie theatres, there must be an intermediary in the target territory who can manage or coordinate the distribution of the film to those theatres.

Example 3.2 – Museum Card in the Italian Context: Stimulating Demand within a Market

In Italy over the last few years an assortment of museum cards have been developed to promote the country's rich stock of museums and to make them as accessible as possible. The most interesting examples are those cards offered in the cities of Turin, Naples, Venice, and Rome. The cards vary in terms of benefits and target markets, but they all provide access to virtually every museum in the respective city, at a reasonable price. In Naples, Venice, and Rome the card is mainly targeted at tourists, while in Turin it is targeted at local residents in a bid to win their loyalty.

The technology used in these cards permits sophisticated analysis of their usage, for the purpose of marketing by particular institutions or for comparison among institutions.

L'Abbonamento Musei Torino Piemonte: Targeting the Local Community

In use since 1995, the Abbonamento Musei Torino Piemonte (Turin Piedmont Museum Subscription) includes free admission to an unlimited number of permanent collections, temporary exhibitions, and the other offers of participating museums. It also entitles the bearer to discounts at cinemas, theatres, shops, and other exhibitions.

The card is valid for one year. The number of participating institutions has grown progressively, and the steady increase in the number of cards sold testifies to their value (38,700 cards sold in 2005, for a total of 130,278 visits, compared to 17,000 cards in 2002 and 7,000 in 2000). Visitors can pick and choose and are free to experiment.

Sales of cards and number of visits

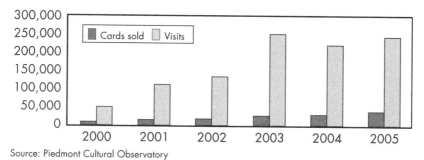

Source: Piedmont Cultural Observatory

Data analysis reveals that in the first year, patrons use the card to explore the various possibilities offered by the museum system, while in the succeeding years they use it to access their favourite exhibitions. Data analysis also shows that the card raises the visibility of lesser-known institutions while at the same time reinforcing the positioning of the museum network.

The Campania Artecard: Targeting Tourists

The Campania Artecard was introduced at the end of 2002. After a three-month experimental phase in central Naples, it was extended, over a period of five months, to Campi Flegrei on the outskirts of the city and then to the entire region of Campania.

The Campania Artecard entitles the bearer, over a one-week period, to free or half-price admission at 30 museums and sites, free urban transport, and discounts on other cultural services in the region. The success of this initiative led, in 2006, to a 365-day card, mainly targeting Campania residents.

The Artecard is sold as part of a kit that includes a city map, a guide to participating museums and sites, and, where provided, a transit ticket.

The card uses digital technology (a chip and bar code), which not only validates the card (free or half-price admission) but also includes personalized information by each participating institution.

Between 2003 and 2005 the number of Artecard visitors increased by 28.6%, while the number of other visitors increased by only 4.8%.

	2003	2004	2005	Var. % 2003–05
Regular visitors	5,114,789	5,289,333	5,359,702	4.8
Artecard visitors	88,875	117,696	114,328	28.6

The card entitles local residents to free or reduced admission and one free transit ticket. It provides tourists with an additional benefit: instant information on how to reach the museum or site, where to buy a transit ticket, where to find out about opening hours, and so on. Moreover, the card guarantees the bearer direct admission, so one can avoid queues at the entrance to museums and sites.

The participating institutions benefit in terms of increased revenues and shared promotion. Moreover, smaller museums have the advantage of being able to piggyback onto the fame of the better-known institutions.

Source: Alessandro Bollo, Research Coordinator, Fitzcarraldo Foundation, Turin, Italy, and Ludovico Solima, Università degli Studi di Napoli, Federico II, Naples, Italy.

SUMMARY

The cultural market can be subdivided into four main groups: the consumer market, the partner market, the government market, and the private sector market. Each of these markets responds to different motivations and covers specific aspects of the product. It is therefore worth developing different marketing strategies for each.

According to research carried out in several industrialized countries, high-arts consumers have higher than average levels of income and education while fans of the popular arts draw on all segments of the population.

State subsidies represent a substantial chunk of the budget for cultural enterprises in most countries, but not in the United States. However, the absence of government from the arts in the United States is offset by the fact that private enterprise and individual donors invest heavily in the arts.

Demand is the expression in volume or dollars of purchases made by members of the market. The notion of demand is useful in accurately judging a company's competitive position in a given market in the past, the present, or the future.

Demand in the leisure market rose substantially from 1960 to 1980. The main factors were an increase in the population, an increase in leisure time available to consumers, and a rise in the levels of both income and education. The fact that the arts garnered a larger share of the leisure market than sports can be attributed to the emergence en masse of a female clientele in the 1960s. During the same period, the supply side also experienced significant growth.

Competition in the leisure and cultural-products markets may take many different forms, yet it remains fierce. In order to survive, a company must acquire a competitive advantage enabling it to resist competitive pressures, which are intensified by technological progress and the globalization of the marketplace. Moreover, the arts sector is fragmented, with many small companies, and is destined to remain that way.

QUESTIONS

1. Why does stating that the consumer of cultural products is educated and well off not give a full picture of the situation?

2. Why is the percentage of revenue from government sources different in Canada, the United States, and Europe?

3. How important is the private sector in the budgets of cultural companies?

4. What is the difference between the notion of demand and the notion of market?

5. What differences do you see in comparing real and potential demand?

6. Can you describe how demand has changed since the 1960s in the leisure market?

7. Why does the problem of fragmentation in the arts sector seem impossible to resolve?

8. What does the expression "gain a competitive advantage" mean?

9. What has been the impact of technological developments on cultural enterprises?

Notes

1. Statistics Canada. 2005. *Family Expenditure in Canada.* Ottawa: Author. Catalogue n° 62-555.

2. National Endowment for the Arts. 1997. *Survey of Public Participation in the Arts: Summary Report.* Washington: Author, p. 17.

3. Australian Bureau of Statistics. *Australia Now – A Statistical Profile.* http://www.abs.gov.au/

4. See, for example, Conseil de l'Europe. 1993. "Participation à la vie culturelle en Europe : Tendances, stratégies et défis." Table ronde de Moscou – 1991. Paris: La Documentation française, 229 p.; Donat, O. 1996. *Les amateurs: Enquête sur les activités artistiques des Français.* Paris: Département des études et de la prospective, ministère de la Culture, 229 p.; Fernandez-Blanco, V., and J. Prieto-Rodriguez. 1997. "Individual Choice and Cultural Consumption in Spain." In *Proceedings of the 4th International Conference on Arts and Cultural Management,* A.W. Smith, ed. San Francisco: Golden Gate University, p. 193–205; Ford Foundation. 1974. *The Finances of the Performing Arts,* vol. 2. New York: Author; Japan Council of Performers' Organisations. 1995. "Professional Orchestras in Japan." *Geidankyo News,* Vol. 1 (Spring), p. 6–7; McCaughey, C. 1984. *A Survey of Arts Audience Studies: A Canadian Perspective 1967–1984.* Ottawa: Canada Council for the Arts; Myerscough, J. 1986. *Facts about the Arts 2: 1986 Edition.* London. PSI Policy Studies Institute; Rubinstein, A. 1995. "Marketing Research into Theatre Audiences in Russia." In *Proceedings of the 3rd International Conference on Arts and Cultural Management,* Michael Quine, ed. London: City University, p. 51–67; Throsby, C.D., and G.A. Withers. 1979. *The Economics of the Performing Arts.* New York: St. Martin's Press.

5. Donnat, O. 2002. *La démocratisation de la culture en France à l'épreuve des chiffres de fréquentation. Circular* n° 14, Ministère de la Culture et de la Communication de la France, Département de la recherche et de la prospective, p. 2–3

6. Rubinstein, A. 1995. "Marketing Research into Theatre Audience in Russia." In Proceedings of the 3rd International Conference on Arts and Cultural Management, M. Quine, ed. London: City University, p. 51–67; Levshinal, E., and Y. Orlov. 2000. "General and Specific Issues in Russian Theatre." *International Journal of Arts Management*, Vol. 2, no 2 (Winter), p. 74–83.

7. Bourdieu, P. 1984. *Distinction: A Social Critique of the Judgment of Taste*. Boston: Harvard University Press.

8. Opera America. 2005. "The 2003 Annual Field Report." *Newsline*, Vol. 14, no 5, p. 19–32.

9. Theatre Communication Group. http://www.tcg.org/

10. Statistics Canada. 2005. *Government Expenditures on Culture*. Ottawa: Author. Catalogue no 11-001-XIE.

11. Groupe de recherche et de formation en gestion des arts, HEC Montréal. 1986. *La levée de fonds : panacée ou utopie*. Montreal: Author.

12. Statistics Canada. 2000. *Canadian Culture in Perspective: A Statistical Overview*. Ottawa: Author, Catalogue no 87-211-XIB.

13. Colbert, F. 1997. "Changes in Marketing Environment and Their Impact on Cultural Policy." *Journal of Arts Management, Law and Society*, Vol. 27, no 3 (Fall), p. 177–187; Colbert, F., ed. 1998. "Changes in Demand and the Future Marketing Challenges Facing Cultural Organisations." In *Cultural Organisations of the Future*. Montreal: Chaire de gestion des arts, HEC Montréal, p. 69–87; Conseil de l'Europe. 1993. *Participation à la vie culturelle en Europe : Tendances, stratégies et défis, Table ronde de Moscou – 1991*. Paris: La documentation française; Pronovost, G. 1998. "Shifting Cultural Practices: An Intergenerational Perspective." In *Cultural Organisations of the Future*, F. Colbert, ed. Montreal: Chaire de gestion des arts, HEC Montréal, p. 89–110.

14. Schewe, C.D., and P.C. Motta. 1993. "Targeting Mature Adult Patrons: Some Marketing Directives." In *Proceedings of the 2nd International Conference on Arts and Cultural Management*, Y. Évrard, ed. Jouy-en-Josas, France: Groupe HEC School of Management.

15. Porter, M.E. 1990. *The Competitive Advantage of Nations*. New York: Free Press.

For Further Reference

Colbert, F. 2003. "Entrepreneurship and Leadership in Marketing the Arts." *International Journal of Arts Management*, Vol. 6, no 1 (Fall), p. 30–40.

Cuadrado, M., and A. Molla. 2000. "Grouping Performing Arts Consumers According to Attendance Goals." *International Journal of Arts Management*, Vol. 2, no 3 (Spring), p. 54–60.

Donat, O. 1994. *Les Français face à la culture. De l'exclusion à l'éclectisme*. Paris: La Découverte.

Fishel, D. 2002. "Australian Philanthropy and the Arts: How Does It Compare?" *International Journal of Arts Management*, Vol. 4, no 2 (Winter), p. 9–15.

Gainer, B. 1993. "The Importance of Gender to Arts Marketing." *Journal of Arts Management, Law and Society*, Vol. 23, no 3, p. 253–260.

Gainer, B. 1997. "Marketing Arts Education: Parental Attitudes towards Arts Education for Children." *Journal of Arts Management, Law and Society*, Vol. 26, no 4, p. 253–268.

Octobre, S. 2005. "La fabrique sexuée des goûts culturels : construire son identité de fille ou de garçon à travers les activités culturelles." *Développement culturel*. Paris: Département des études et de la prospective, ministère de la Culture, no 150.

Porter, M.E. 1980. *Competitive Strategy*. New York: Free Press.

Statistics Canada. 1997–2002. *Spending Patterns in Canada*. Ottawa: Author. Catalogue no 62-202.

Appendix 3.1
Co-productions

More and more, cultural industries are using co-production as a means of internationalization. This type of collaboration allows partners from different countries to become involved in a project creatively as well as financially.

In television and film production, many countries are now negotiating bilateral agreements. These arrangements, which follow certain rules, allow a co-production to qualify as national content for each respective country, even if the participation of the country is not a majority one.

Why co-produce?
There are many reasons why producers choose co-production:
- Access to new markets: international co-production provides access to a new market that might otherwise be unavailable
- Government protectionism: certain governments may impose particular restrictions, in which case only international collaboration will permit access to the said market or the resources
- Sharing of financial risks: co-productions allow for the sharing of the risk on major projects
- Economy of scale: on major projects, collaboration may allow for certain economies of scale with regard to various aspects of production, and therefore allow the partners to better compete within the industry
- Transfer of know-how: co-production allows each partner to benefit from the know-how of the other

Co-production: minority or majority
A co-production may be a minority or a majority arrangement between the different partners. Co-productions are now used in most cultural industries. The Oscar-winning film *The Barbarian Invasions* was a co-production between Canada and France, with Canada having the majority stake. Many documentaries are produced by the United Kingdom in partnership with Canada or the United States. In the publishing industry, co-publishing allows for lower unit production costs. Museums are now co-producing exhibitions, which then travel from one museum to the other.

The disadvantages of co-production
The disadvantages of co-producing are as follows:
- Coordination costs will usually be higher, since the project will be more complex
- There may be some loss of control over the content of the project and also a loss of cultural specificity
- The foreign partner may wish to take advantage of the situation, and could thus become a competitor instead of a partner

Appendix 3.2
Key success factors in co-productions

Partnerships are not easy to manage. The objectives of one partner might not be in agreement with those of the other partner. However, experience has shown that certain elements can contribute to the success of a partnership.

The choice of partner

The choice of partner is the first and most important element to consider. It is essential that there be coherence between the choice of partner and the objectives of the project. It would be dangerous for an enterprise to team up with the first potential partner that comes along.

The relationship between the partners will greatly influence the atmosphere of the project and, ultimately, its success or failure. The partners should have complementary assets and possible synergies. If they are different in size, at least their objectives and interests should be compatible. They should have the same corporate culture. The relationship should be flexible, committed, and trusting.

The choice of project leader

The project leader (manager) should be both experienced and sensitive to different cultures. He or she must be able to work in a turbulent environment, in a matrix type structure. He or she must be a strong communicator and an excellent diplomat, so that the team and the partners function in a climate of trust. The project manager must be able to meet the objectives of all the partners involved.

The choice of team

The members of the team must be able to work in a semi-structured environment. They have to be autonomous yet able to collaborate in a complex environment. Their tasks are non-repetitive. They must be able to work in teams, at the same pace as their colleagues, and to focus on the process and the structure. They should possess intuition, tolerance for ambiguity, and plenty of self-confidence.

The contract

From the start of the project, there should be a very clear, precise, detailed contract in order to avoid any disagreements. The contract may help to clear up any confusion that arises during the project. It should specify roles and responsibilities. The contract should also contain clauses dealing with conflict resolution.

PLAN

Chapter **4**

Consumer Behaviours

by Jacques Nantel

OBJECTIVES

- Describe in detail the various decision-making processes that form the basis of consumer behaviours
- Present the main variables that influence the structure and nature of decision-making processes
- Highlight the connection between decision-making processes, the information that consumers use, and corporate marketing strategies
- Link the information used by consumers to various corporate marketing strategies
- Discuss these concepts within the context of arts management

INTRODUCTION

Why is it important to look at consumer studies and behaviour? Why is describing the consumers within a market in sociodemographic terms alone not enough? The answer to these questions is found in the very essence of marketing. One of the basic functions of marketing is meeting consumer needs. A marketing manager must accurately identify and fully understand these needs in order to create a product that fulfils a specific need, to position a product in terms of a specific segment of the population, and, in the case of product-oriented companies, to attract the target clientele. This is, however, easier said than done. The manager who wants to position a product properly must have a good description of the consumers targeted by the company and must also know why these consumers will or will not buy a cultural product.

This chapter first explores the basic triad (individual–product–situation), that determines the consumer's motivation in purchasing a product. We then look more closely at the notion of motivation and the individual variables in the main decision-making processes. The variables related to the purchasing situation will follow, and, lastly, we will see how a consumer processes information before making a choice, which then translates to a purchasing behaviour.

4.1 THE CONSUMPTION OF CULTURAL AND LEISURE PRODUCTS

The consumption of leisure products – including cultural products – cannot be approached in the same way as the consumption of other products. There are three reasons for this. First, in addition to the financial investment, the consumption of leisure products requires that the consumer be willing and able to spend time pursuing consumption. Second, the consumption of leisure goods is first and foremost "experiential,"[1] meaning that the product can be assessed only at the moment of consumption. Finally, leisure goods are targeted at the hedonistic and affective aspects of consumption, as opposed to its utilitarian dimension.[2]

Since the "consumption" of cultural goods as leisure products requires time, and since the amount of leisure time available varies according to the life cycle of individuals and households, the tendency to consume certain cultural products varies with the person's age, income, and level of physical fitness. Figure 4.1, taken from the Statistics Canada annual survey *Spending Patterns in Canada,* shows that demand for the performing arts peaks when consumers over the age of 50 no longer have young children, are still healthy, and are still able to go out. Figure 4.1 reveals a different trend in video rentals; being younger and having young children increases annual spending in this product category. Studies published regularly by the Canada Council for the Arts and Statistics Canada describe the main sociodemographic variables that affect the propensity to "consume" different types of cultural products.

In addition to the budgeting of time, the consumption of leisure products and cultural goods can be characterized as "experiential." Unlike products such as cars, which can be evaluated prior to purchase, most cultural products, including films, operas, concerts, and exhibitions, cannot be judged until the moment of consumption. The experiential nature of cultural products creates an additional element of risk for consumers. A corollary of this is that cultural products appeal not only to consumers' minds but also to their emotions.

For all of these reasons, when developing a marketing strategy for a cultural product the marketing manager must consider more than just the

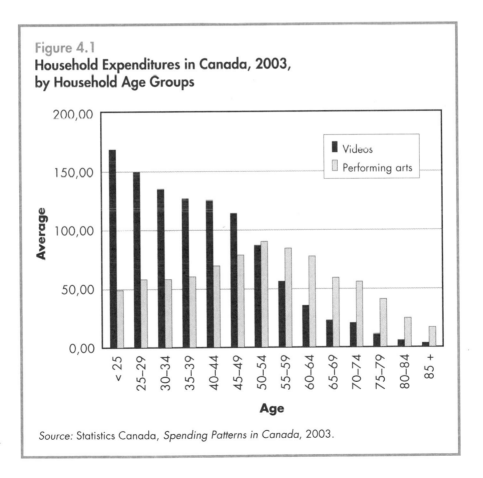

Figure 4.1
Household Expenditures in Canada, 2003, by Household Age Groups

Source: Statistics Canada, *Spending Patterns in Canada*, 2003.

sociodemographic profiles of the product's target consumers; he or she must undertake a refined psychological analysis of consumer behaviours.

4.2 INDIVIDUAL–PRODUCT–SITUATION: THE BASIC TRIAD

Analysis of consumer behaviours rests on the assumption that consumers always make their decisions based on a certain amount of information. This information can be divided into two categories: internal (past experience) and external (type of product, word of mouth, etc.). For example, consumers targeted for a season subscription to the opera would base their decision on both their personal knowledge of operatic music (past experience) and the information provided (choice of works, featured artists, price, reviews, friends' comments, etc.). In order to develop an effective marketing strategy, therefore, the marketing manager must be knowledgeable about both the type of information that consumers use to make purchasing decisions and how that information is perceived and utilized – in other words, the decision-making process.

Consumers' decision-making process is influenced by three key elements: information related to consumers themselves, information related to the purchasing situation, and information related to the products being considered. These three elements form the "basic triad" of consumer behaviours.

Figure 4.2 illustrates the main elements used in analyzing consumer behaviours.

This triad is one of the principles of the study of consumer behaviours. It stipulates that the dynamics of a market, or even of a market segment, can be understood only if the consumer, the product purchased, and the purchasing situation are all taken into account – only then can the tremendous wealth and complexity of consumer behaviours be appreciated. Let us take the example of two consumers who are both loyal fans of baroque music. It would be tempting for a marketing manager to assume that the two consumers are similar and that their future behaviour will also be similar since they share the same tastes. But what if the first consumer developed a taste for baroque music as a child, whereas the second is a recent convert who was influenced mainly by the popularity of artists such as Daniel Taylor or Karina Gauvin? For the first consumer the decision-making process is tied to deep-rooted attitudes, while for the second it is linked to social influences and trends.

This example shows how the consumer-product relationship can differ from one consumer to the next. Given the differences, any corporate strategy drawing on customer loyalty would have to be adapted for each case. In the example, can it be said that the first consumer is less susceptible to social

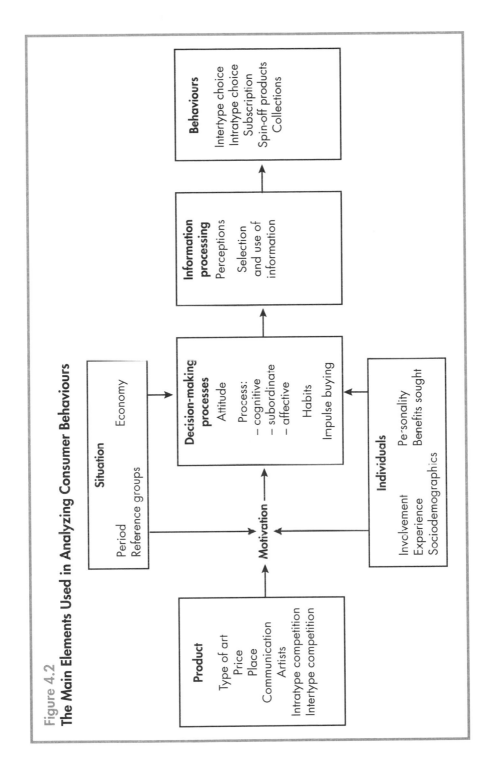

Figure 4.2
The Main Elements Used in Analyzing Consumer Behaviours

Situation

Period
Reference groups   Economy

Product

Type of art
Price
Place
Communication
Artists
Intratype competition
Intertype competition

Motivation

Individuals

Involvement
Experience
Sociodemographics   Personality
Benefits sought

Decision-making processes

Attitude

Process:
– cognitive
– subordinate
– affective

Habits

Impulse buying

Information processing

Perceptions

Selection
and use of
information

Behaviours

Intertype choice
Intratype choice
Subscription
Spin-off products
Collections

influences than the second? Such a conclusion would be rather hasty, if not dangerous. It may well be that the first consumer, while perhaps not easily swayed by external influences when it comes to music, is more sensitive to such influences when making decisions about the theatre. Moreover, a consumer's behaviour may vary according to the situation. For instance, a consumer may adopt one kind of behaviour on vacation and another at home, so that plays that are well received in the summertime may not have the same appeal if programmed during the regular season.

4.3 MOTIVATION

It should be remembered when studying consumer behaviours that consumers will not consider buying a product unless they are strongly motivated to do so. Although this may seem like common sense, when forgotten it causes grief and frustration among managers and artists alike. Motivation lies at the very heart of consumer behaviours; it has its roots in an imbalance between the consumer's current and desired states. The wider the gap between the two states, the stronger the consumer's motivation will be. This imbalance may stem from the consumer (e.g., an older consumer may want to read poetry or spend more time on leisure activities) or arise in a particular situation (e.g., at Christmastime, listening to holiday music in the mall encourages shoppers to buy). It may also be the result of promotion (e.g., advertising for *Phantom of the Opera* encourages the consumer to buy a ticket). More often than not, the consumer will not be influenced by any stimulus, regardless of the pressures applied. Consumer motivation to buy a product is largely related to previous experience and level of product involvement. These two variables have a tremendous influence on the nature of the decision-making process used by consumers.

Whether the product is a cultural product, a consumer good, or a service, the complexity of the decision-making process varies according to the individual–product–situation triad. It should be emphasized that in most cases there is a close link between how complex the decision-making process is and how extensively the information is processed. In other words, the more complex the decision-making process, the more diversified the consumer's information. For marketing managers, this statement is crucial, since it suggests that their marketing mix is analyzed more closely when the consumer is involved and the decision-making process is complex. In some situations, however, the marketing manager is better off if the consumer does not want too much information. This would be the case for a company that has a clientele with well-entrenched habits. On the other hand, a company might want consumers to have as much information as possible in order to understand why the product offered is superior to the competition's. In this case, customer involvement, if present, becomes a real advantage.

4.4 INDIVIDUAL VARIABLES

This section focuses on an analysis of five individual variables: consumer involvement in the product offered, consumer experience, consumer sociodemographic profile, consumer personality, and product features considered desirable by consumers.

4.4.1 Involvement

Of all the consumer variables, product involvement is by far the most important.[3] In the arts sector, research has confirmed that childhood experience is one of the most important variables explaining the propensity to attend museums and the theatre as well as consumers' level of involvement with these artistic products.[4] Although researchers in this area have defined involvement in different ways over the years, according to research trends popular at the time, the consensus is that the term can be understood as the feeling of importance or personal interest associated with the product in a given situation.

Involvement can be defined as the importance, for an individual, of a given product in a given situation. Involvement can be structural or "conjunctural" – that is, linked to the situation. For example, one consumer may perceive theatre as a product with a consistently high level of involvement while another may feel that level of involvement only in a specific situation, such as when choosing the only play he or she will see all year.

Whether involvement is related to an individual's interest in one product or an entire category of products, involvement is largely a function of the risk that consumers associate with the purchase or use of a product or service. The riskier the purchase or use of the product, the greater the consumer's involvement. There are several types of consumer risks.[5] They are not mutually exclusive, although they may well exist independently. The main risks influencing the purchase of a product are functional, economical, psychological, and social.

Functional Risk

In terms of cultural products, functional risk has the most impact on consumer behaviour. This type of risk may be defined as the possibility that the product will not meet the consumer's expectations. It is common in the service and cultural sectors since products in these sectors have a strong "experiential" dimension that makes a priori evaluation difficult. A consumer can, however, reduce functional risk dramatically by seeking as much information as possible on the play to be seen or the book to be bought. Critics' reviews, advertising (which often repeats positive reviews), or the opinions of friends may also reduce functional risk.

A recent study found that consumers who read movie reviews can be divided into four segments[6] (each characterized by distinctive behaviour), based on how the consumer processes the information he or she reads. The impact of a review, whether positive or negative, on each of these segments appears to be determined by four elements: the regularity with which the consumer reads reviews, the consumer's degree of self-esteem, the consumer's sensitivity to social pressure, and the consumer's knowledgeability about film. In each case, the promotional strategy adopted should either capitalize on the effects of a positive review or lessen the impact of a negative one.

Another way for the consumer to reduce the functional risk is to opt for a "safe bet." Cultural products such as the latest Spielberg film, *The Nutcracker* ballet, or an indoor concert at the Montreal International Jazz Festival do not require a complex decision-making process: they are considered safe bets and as such are not perceived as representing a high functional risk. These examples show how the presence of a functional risk can influence the consumer's decision-making process. In the first case, the consumer reduces the risk by seeking more information about the product. In the second case, the consumer is faced with a "safe bet": he or she does not perceive a high functional risk and therefore does not feel the need to seek more information. In short, the greater the perceived risk, the greater the degree of involvement and the greater the likelihood that the consumer will engage in a decision-making process that reduces that risk.

Economic Risk

Economic risk is the easiest to understand: the more expensive the product, the more complicated the decision-making process. This relationship may be greatly attenuated by the consumer's income level. The latest studies on this topic[7] reveal that an increase in income generates long-term demand for cultural products, while a significant increase in the price of cultural products leads to a short-term drop in demand.

Economic risk is affected not only by the cost of purchasing the product itself, but also by the total expense incurred in consuming the product. The consumption of cultural products often involves related expenses such as parking, babysitting, and dining out either before or after the show. All of these costs are taken into account by the consumer when evaluating economic risk.

Psychological Risk

Psychological risk is frequently experienced in the consumption of cultural products. It may be defined as the risk associated with the purchase or consumption of a product that does not correspond to the consumer's desired self-image. One consumer may be reluctant to confront his or her latent inner feelings and elect to avoid movies containing violence. Another may be tempted to try certain art forms in order to increase his or her self-esteem. A marketer of a cultural product may try to take advantage of the psychological aspect of risk by sending consumers the message that its product is essential to their personal culture. This approach has the effect of increasing the consumer's involvement.

Social Risk

Whereas psychological risk is related to the individual consumer's self-image, social risk is related to the image others have of the individual. Some people may subscribe to the opera to be part of a particular reference group rather than to enjoy the music. Conversely, some consumers may forgo the pleasure of a cultural event simply to avoid their friends' or colleagues' disapproval. Naturally, this risk is not present for all consumers. In fact, social risk is present only in cases in which the form of consumption is visible or the consumers are sensitive to their environment.

4.4.2 Experience

Experience, like involvement, has a significant impact on the complexity of the consumer's decision-making processes. The broader the experience, the shorter the decision-making process. The experience accumulated by the consumer – whether in poetry, jazz, or Russian theatre – influences the type of decision-making process he or she will use. In all cases, past experience facilitates decision-making by telling the consumer what criteria to consider and how to analyze these criteria.

Experience affects the complexity of the decision-making processes that consumers use, because consumers categorize their previous experiences into subsets of possibilities that are known, unknown, retained, or rejected.

If, however, a product requires a high degree of involvement and the consumer's experience is both substantial and satisfactory, the consumer develops a strong affective predisposition that acts upon his or her perceptions. The product will have more merit than can be attributed to it objectively. This predisposition explains the phenomenon of groupies and die-hard fans.

4.4.3 Personality

Personality is the most intriguing yet least conclusive variable of all in terms of consumer behaviours. Marketing experts would like to believe that a single

Example 4.1
Customer Satisfaction, Functional Service or Prosocial Values? A Study of Two U.S. Theatres

"A recent study conducted with audience members at two U.S. theatres examined which image perceptions lead to satisfaction for men and women. Results suggest that satisfaction is higher for men when they perceive an elevated level of functional service quality (i.e., they were treated well by the theatre's staff) and for women when they perceive that the theatre possesses prosocial values (i.e., its top priority is expanding community access to and appreciation for art). Both women and men are more satisfied when they perceive that the theatre holds either market or artistic values (i.e., the theatre either prioritizes a commitment to customer satisfaction or an intrinsic drive for artistic creativity, innovation, and independence). Surprisingly, no direct link surfaced between perceived quality of the work on stage and customer satisfaction. It appears, instead, that performance/production quality is important to both men and women, driving their engagement in further elaboration of image attributes, but it is not important enough to directly stimulate satisfaction when other factors of the consumption experience are taken into account. Men and women at both theatres sat in the same audience, watched the same production, and came away with a diversity of images of the experience.

"Apparently, it is patrons' *image* of the theatre's values that drives satisfaction, regardless of what values that theatre holds as core to its mission and what messages it communicates about these values through words and actions."

Source: Voss, Zannie G., and Véronique Cova. 2006. "How Sex Differences in Perceptions Influence Customer Satisfaction: A Study of Theatre Audiences." *Marketing Theory*, Vol. 6, n° 2, p. 201–221.

consumer, given his or her personality, will prefer rock to opera, or that some consumers like safe bets while others prefer innovation and novelty. However, these hypotheses are rarely backed by empirical research.

Even though personality traits do not provide an exhaustive explanation of consumer behaviours, they can be of some interest. Some consumers tend to imitate peer behaviour, while others tend to behave according to their own predispositions. This trait, called "self-monitoring," has a significant effect on the perceived social risk and, as a result, influences the type of decision-making processes the consumer will use.

4.4.4 Benefits Sought

A consumer may wish to purchase a book or visit a museum for various reasons, such as exoticism, relaxation, cultural enrichment, or escapism. He or she may also consider this purchase on the basis of price or other tangible attributes (the author, genre, or format in the case of a book; the dates, type, or location of an exhibition in the case of a museum).

For many products, the nature of the decision-making process is largely a function of the benefits sought. The consumer deciding among four films and one play could simply compare the five possibilities by looking at the various attributes of each one as well as the benefits of going out. The benefits gained through the use of a product may vary from one consumer to the next. In this sense, they are closely linked to the functional risk.

The concept of benefits sought enables managers to understand the structure of the decision-making process that consumers use and thus how to select the elements of their marketing mix. Nevertheless, an analysis of consumer benefits is valid only if consumers actually consider such benefits. Yet, unlike other types of goods and services, cultural products, because they are by definition "experiential," rarely give rise to decision-making dominated by consideration of tangible attributes. The decision-making process is usually influenced by highly emotional factors.

4.5 THE MAIN DECISION-MAKING PROCESSES

The different elements examined so far provide the framework for an intelligent discussion of the types of decision-making processes that might explain a consumer's decision to purchase or consume a cultural product. Figure 4.3 details the main decision-making processes used and some of the variables that characterize them.

4.5.1 Attitude

A decision-making process based on attitude requires both experience and involvement in the particular cultural product or the particular category of cultural product. Of course, this type of process becomes apparent only if the product implies a high level of involvement, if the attitude is based on either very good or very bad experiences, and if the consumer's social context and personality allow this attitude to affect the decision-making process.

Example 4.2
La Triennale di Milano: Offering Services to Enrich the Cultural Experience

La Triennale di Milano is a foundation dedicated to research and documentation as well as single-sector and interdisciplinary exhibitions on architecture, town planning, decorative arts, design, industrial production, fashion, and audiovisual communication (www.triennale.it).

Since 1929, the Triennale has hosted an international exhibition every three years. Its Palazzo dell'Arte houses a permanent collection of Italian design objects and mounts various temporary exhibitions each year.

Today, the Triennale is a focus of scientific debate and research on innovation, while also attracting a broad and loyal public. Its specialized services, which generate substantial revenues, constitute a unique environment for the Triennale's events. The Art Book specializes in books on design and architecture and also offers selected design items, while the Coffee Design café exhibits cult design objects, offers themed lunches as well as serving drinks and other meals, and hosts various special events. In collaboration with Fiat, Italy's leading automobile manufacturer and a major design influence, the Triennale recently launched the elegant Fiat Café La Triennale, which is located in the park surrounding the Palazzo dell'Arte.

In the words of the architect and designer responsible for La Triennale's new layout, these facilities are meant to create an attractive atmosphere where we can "enjoy the time we manage to extract from our daily routine to dedicate to art and culture."*

* Del Drago, E. 2004. *La Triennale di Milano*. Rome: Arti grafiche la Moderna, p. 13.

Source: Antonella Carù, Associate Professor, Bocconi Business School SA, Milan, Italy.

Attitude is a particularly effective mechanism: it allows the consumer to reach a decision easily, quickly, and effectively on the basis of past experience and personal judgement. In the arts sector, this is the type of mechanism that gives rise to fan clubs and explains the phenomenon of "groupies." For the cultural organization, author, or rock group concerned, a consumer's positive attitude is a precious asset, particularly since attitude is extremely resistant to change. In other words, since it is difficult to change an attitude that is based

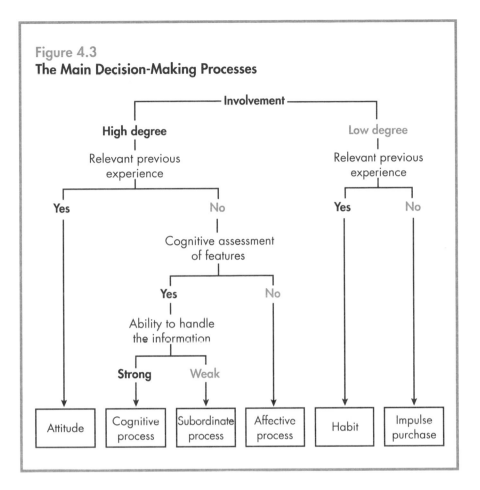

Figure 4.3
The Main Decision-Making Processes

on past experience, this mechanism works in favour of the organization or artist while at the same time blocking the competition. The enduring influence of attitude as a mechanism can be attributed in large part to the fact that it creates a bias in the mind of the individual.

It should be noted that consumers' attitudes can relate to either products as a whole or the components of a product (a musical genre, a type of theatre, a particular culture).

In order to fully grasp how attitudes affect consumers' decision-making processes, one must first understand how attitudes are formed.[8] Most attitudes are based on past experiences, which may originate in a subordinate process, a cognitive process, or an affective process. These processes are rarely of a single type; usually, they represent a combination of types. Often, however, an attitude is related to a learned mechanism of unknown origin that gets caught up in a combination of socialization, learning, and acculturation mechanisms. For example, why does a particular shopper dislike the colour yellow? Or why does a particular opera buff have a preference for baritone? One of the mechanisms involved here is known as "classic conditioning": a neutral stimulus becomes associated with an emotionally charged one whereby the emotional charge is transferred to the neutral stimulus. A taste for culture and the arts is a mechanism that is acquired at a young age, and the manner in which this socialization is produced (association of a cultural event with either a pleasant outing or a chore) is a determining factor.

4.5.2 Cognitive Processes

In the case of products that require a high degree of involvement, the inexperienced consumer tends to use cognitive decision-making processes. Both longer and more complex, these processes require some judging of the various attributes of the product offered. The following example illustrates the factors involved in cognitive processes. A consumer wishing to acquire a portable sound system must choose among four brands: Sony, Sharp, Koss, and General Electric. To make her choice, she considers the various benefits that she deems important for this type of purchase: price, length of warranty, quality of sound, and ability to program several CDs. By weighing the importance of each attribute and judging each choice according to these attributes, the consumer can make an optimal choice objectively and rationally. This approach, which is largely based on the work of the psychologist Martin Fishbein, is known in marketing as the "linear compensatory model of decision-making." It requires an exhaustive and very specific decision-making technique that is highly cerebral.

The conjunctive model, like the linear compensatory model, is a simple one designed to describe the structure of decision-making processes used by consumers. In this model, the consumer sets a minimally acceptable threshold for each criterion considered. If one of the options remains under par, it is automatically rejected. For example, if a consumer will attend the theatre only if the lead role is played by a well-known actor, then any play featuring a cast of young actors will be automatically rejected. In practice, if a large portion of the target clientele makes its decisions based on either conjunctive or linear compensatory cognitive mechanisms, the marketing manager would do well to approach the cultural product to be marketed as he or she would a recipe for a cake, where flour is an essential ingredient but the decision to use milk or water depends on the clients and the benefits they seek.

The identification and understanding of these processes constitute an important advantage for managers seeking to reach a specific clientele. A marketing manager who knows what attributes consumers are looking for, and the relative importance of those attributes, will be able to adjust the elements of the marketing mix accordingly.

Naturally, understanding sophisticated cognitive processes is useful only if consumers actually use the same processes. Interestingly, this is not always the case in cultural products or the arts. Given the unique, innovative quality of some cultural products, the trouble many consumers have in judging cultural products cognitively, and the very emotional component characteristic of the decision-making process, marketing managers should consider additional decision-making mechanisms in order to understand consumer behaviours. These additional mechanisms are called subordinate processes and affective processes.

4.5.3 Affective Processes and Hedonistic Consumption

The principal decision-making processes presented thus far depict consumers as cognitive beings who analyze the various characteristics of a product in order to optimize their consumption of it. While this concept, which is based on a utilitarian view of consumers' decision-making processes, dominates marketing theory, other approaches – notably, those involving affective processes – must also be taken into account. Some products are not bought solely on the basis of objective attributes or specific features; rather, their purchase constitutes a total experience aimed at gaining a sense of hedonistic gratification. This is the experiential perspective. As a decision-making process, the total experience relies more on affective elements (love, hate, joy, boredom, fatigue, etc.) than on cognitive elements such as the evaluation of a product. This type of decision-making process is particularly common among consumers of cultural products. It is important that marketers be aware of this affective dimension of decision-making, since most decision-making processes are neither entirely cognitive nor entirely affective but a blend of the two.

The acquisition of preferences is a process based on a series of conscious experiences from which the consumer derives a sense of pleasure. The task of identifying the parameters of this process is a difficult one for marketers, since consumers typically have trouble explaining their preferences. For managers targeting a group of pleasure-seeking consumers, "trial and error" may be the only available marketing strategy. This is where marketing strategy is more art than science. This is particularly true for cultural products in that the marketing strategy depends on the ability of a work to appeal to consumers without the benefit of a proven recipe.

Two cultural sectors – film and music – have proved particularly adept at using the Internet to develop marketing strategies that capitalize on the affective aspect of purchasing decisions. In the film industry, promotional campaigns that once relied on movie posters to elicit an emotional response from consumers now use trailers and other promotional material on Web sites. According to a study by eMarketer,[9] Internet advertising for videos and films jumped from $30 million in 2000 to $385 million in 2006 and could reach $1 billion by 2008. The same study found that this form of advertising, which relies on affective processes, is not only popular among teenagers and young adults but also reaches 45% of those between the ages of 35 and 50. Moreover, 30% of movie tickets are now sold over the Internet, in most cases following the viewing of an Internet-based trailer.[10]

Marketing strategies in the music industry have been turned upside-down by the online sampling of music. For years, Amazon (see Figure 4.4), the global leader in e-commerce, has been allowing Internet surfers to sample songs for free before purchasing them. While a number of other retailers were already offering this service, Amazon made it available for millions of titles, thus radically changing the way that music is marketed. The online music store iTunes, meanwhile, allows consumers to download entire CDs. This method of selling music has contributed to the revolution. In both of these cases, the opportunity to test the product before purchase reduces the functional risk for consumers.

4.5.4 The Experiential Facet of Consumer Behaviours
(*by Yannik St-James*)

During the last 20 years, researchers have been giving more attention to the experiential facet of consumer behaviours. This perspective complements the more traditional study of consumers' decision-making processes, by exploring other dimensions of consumption. It favours the affective aspects of consumption over its utilitarian functions, the symbolic dimensions of products over their tangible attributes, and consumers' imagination over their understanding of an objective reality.

The experiential facet of consumption thus refers to the affective, symbolic, creative aspects that define the consumption experience.[11] The domain of culture and the arts is a unique sphere of experiential consumption because it offers multisensory experiences that fire the imagination and elicit a high level of affective involvement. Furthermore, cultural or aesthetic experiences are rich in symbolic meaning, as they constitute a stage where social affiliations and distinctions are expressed and reinforced. This section introduces the hedonic and symbolic dimensions of consumption experiences and discusses some implications for the marketing of cultural products.

Hedonic Dimension of Consumption Experiences

Aesthetic products engage multiple senses simultaneously through images, sounds, scents, tastes, and tactile cues. Consumers interpret these multi-

Figure 4.4
Example of Audible Musical Samples

sensory stimuli subjectively as they generate images in their mind and as their emotions are aroused.

Consumers do not simply encode multisensory stimuli; they also use these stimuli to generate images within themselves. They use the symbols offered by cultural products to construct imaginary narratives relating to their personal history and fantasies. Consumers therefore interpret cultural products in multiple ways by imbuing them with subjective meaning beyond their tangible attributes. Consequently, the meaning of a cultural product does not reside in the object itself but is created in the mind of the consumer. This is why Colin Campbell refers to the consumer as an "artist of the imagination."[12]

Cultural products also arouse emotions. Consumers often seek them out for the pleasure they give, from the simple joy of watching an entertaining movie to the complex emotions of delight and transcendence triggered by the beauty of a work of art. But consumers are attracted not only by pleasurable experiences. Sometimes they choose aesthetic products that will induce negative emotions. For instance, a work of art that depicts violence may elicit painful emotions such as fear or sadness. Such affective experiences can help consumers to cope with difficult life situations. For example, visits to museums and historic sites are often associated with nostalgia, a bittersweet longing for a time past. Nostalgia may be experienced differently, depending on the consumer's life circumstances. The findings of one study[13] suggest that elderly museum visitors who belong to tight social groups and who are comfortable and empowered in their life situation experience nostalgia as a temporary, amusing emotion, whereas those who feel alienated and lack control over their life situation seek refuge in nostalgia, using it as a temporary escape in order to manage their negative emotions.

In sum, the hedonic dimension of consumption reveals the playful, pleasurable nature of aesthetic experiences and underscores the meaningful role that these experiences can play in consumers' lives. Cultural products are not only a source of entertainment; they provide emotional and fantasy outlets that help consumers cope with emotional conflict.

Symbolic Dimension of Consumption Experiences

In addition to their hedonic component, cultural experiences provide a stage for social interaction by giving the consumer an opportunity to strengthen interpersonal bonds and share impressions with others. For instance, a painting may serve to stimulate conversation and storytelling among a group of museum visitors.[14] Similarly, a consumer may enjoy attending the ballet because it makes him or her feel part of a like-minded group of balletomanes.

Moreover, consumers select cultural products for their symbolic value, since these products allow them to define and express their identity to themselves and to others. For example, it has been suggested that for many museum visitors, "having been" to a museum is a greater motivation than actually being at a museum.[15] The consumption of cultural products constitutes a powerful status symbol. This relationship has been described in terms of three patterns: distinction effects, effacement effects, and omnivore effects.[16]

The distinction effect means that the consumption of cultural products serves to preserve and accentuate class differences. From this perspective, which draws heavily on the work of the sociologist Pierre Bourdieu, cultural capital predisposes people to prefer certain types of cultural product.[17] Cultural capital consists of the distinctive tastes, skills, knowledge, and practices one acquires from one's family, friends, education, and training. It is a socially rare resource and is distributed unevenly across the social hierarchy: members of the higher classes can be expected to prefer highbrow products such as classical music and theatre, while members of the lower classes can be expected to prefer lowbrow products like popular music and movies. Class-related factors thus influence consumption patterns, which, in turn, symbolize status and reinforce the social hierarchy.

The effacement effect, in contrast, means that differences between highbrow and lowbrow cultural products are disappearing, giving way to increasingly similar preferences among consumers from different social classes. This blurring of boundaries is associated with the growing popularity of lowbrow over highbrow cultural products due to the commercialization of culture.[18] John Seabrook illustrates the effacement effect persuasively in his book *Nobrow*, arguing that "the culture of marketing" now pervades "the marketing of culture" so that class distinctions are replaced with a "hierarchy of hotness."[19]

Finally, the omnivore effect suggests that members of the higher classes are characterized by their appreciation for a broad range of cultural products, both highbrow and lowbrow, whereas members of the lower classes consume mostly popular cultural products. Although consumption of cultural products still reflects social distinctions, these distinctions are no longer expressed strictly along a highbrow-lowbrow continuum. Now, they are expressed in terms of the diversity of cultural products consumed, reflecting multiple dimensions of consumer tastes and practices. For instance, consumers from the higher classes tend to have more cosmopolitan tastes and to interpret art works more critically than consumers from the lower classes, who tend to have local tastes and to interpret art works in a self-referential manner.[20] In sum, our social environment shapes our preferences for certain types of cultural product (highbrow versus lowbrow) as well as our consumption motives (e.g., appreciation versus entertainment).

Distinction, effacement, and omnivore effects are not mutually exclusive; they may provide complementary explanations of consumer behaviours.[21] For instance, one study has found that the Spanish performing arts market is made up of people who consume few cultural products, people who consume mainly lowbrow or highbrow cultural products, and people who consume a wide variety of cultural products.[22]

Implications for Marketing of Cultural Products

Adopting an experiential view of consumer behaviours affects our perception of the role played by the consumer and by the cultural enterprise in the aesthetic experience. It adds to our understanding of consumers' motivation to choose certain cultural products and provides strategies for identifying different consumer segments.

The hedonic and symbolic dimensions of consumer behaviours stress the active nature of consumption. Consumers of cultural products are not merely passive observers; they are co-creators of the experience. Their participation may be manifested physically – applauding during a performance, sharing impressions with others – but it also entails reactions that may not be observable. In this perspective, the cultural organization does not provide a rigid, uniform experience for all consumers; rather, it provides them with the symbols and tools to create their own meaning, fires their imagination, and guides their subjective experience.

Because aesthetic experiences involve interpreting, evaluating, and responding affectively, consumers must expend considerable emotional resources in the process. This process is often described as absorbing[23] or flow[24] experiences in which consumers exert psychic energy to produce a feeling of well-being. Such experiences are "autotelic" – they are pursued as an end in themselves and not for utilitarian purposes – and require engagement and involvement. As with other resources, such as time or money, the allocation of emotional resources is likely to influence consumption decisions.[25] A contemporary dance performance is a more challenging cultural product than a rock concert, and an experimental theatre production is a more intellectually and emotionally demanding cultural product than a light romantic movie. Therefore, consumers' willingness to deploy the emotional resources necessary to interpret, evaluate, and respond affectively to an aesthetic experience at a given time may determine whether they will consume a cultural product and what type of cultural product they will choose.

Finally, the experiential aspects of consumption suggest several useful variables for segmenting the cultural products market. For instance, one study has found that consumers from different social backgrounds have different experience-based motivations for attending performing arts events: those with low levels of cultural capital tend to seek diversion and togetherness, prefer familiar and popular products, and evaluate performances naïvely, whereas those with high levels of cultural capital are attracted by strong affective and cognitive stimulation, favour innovative and authentic products, and use sophisticated appreciation criteria.[26] Similarly, an analysis of visitors to contemporary art centres has identified three groups of visitors on the basis of type of experience sought[27]: *hedonists* possess little expertise, prefer interactive exhibits, and evaluate their experience self-referentially and on the basis of entertainment value; *activist* consumers expect an exhibit to exemplify the cultural field and to express and decry social conflict; finally, *intellectuals* seek to understand and interpret the exhibit by adopting a cognitive focus in order to evaluate the beauty of the art work. These studies illustrate how groups of consumers are motivated to consume aesthetic products for various hedonic and symbolic purposes. By understanding these preferences, a cultural enterprise can better identify those consumers who will be most receptive to its aesthetic product and which elements of the experience should be communicated to entice various consumer types.

In sum, the experiential dimension of consumption enriches our understanding of consumers' motivation for seeking cultural products as well as their consumption experience. It enables us to see the central role played by creative, affective, and symbolic processes in consumer behaviours.

4.5.5 Subordinate Processes

A consumer with a high degree of involvement in a cultural product but with little experience may engage in a cognitive decision-making process. However, if such a consumer lacks the time or ability (either in perception or in reality) to absorb product information, he or she will likely opt for a subordinate process whereby the decision is based on imitation, recommendation, or compliance. In all of these cases, the decision-making process is subordinated, in whole or in part, to a third party. For such a mechanism to work, the third party must be credible from the consumer's point of view. Often, the source of imitation or compliance is a friend or relative – hence the determining influence of the reference group on consumer behaviours with regard to products whose consumption is visible (music, TV shows, etc.). In other cases, the influential party is a perceived expert – a spokesperson, critic, or specialized organization such as the Academy of Motion Pictures, which awards the Oscars. Organizations influence consumer decisions by making their recommendations public. In such cases, due to the complex nature of the information to be processed and the consumer's unwillingness or inability to evaluate the information, the consumer's decision-making process may be subordinated to that of the organization. A similar phenomenon occurs when a shopper relies solely on the advice of a salesperson. The role of the critic can be seen in this context: reviews are simultaneously based on and favour a subordinate decision-making process, while reducing the functional risk perceived by certain consumers.[28]

4.5.6 Habit

Habit is another decision-making mechanism used by consumers. Like attitude, habit allows a consumer to decide on a product quickly. Unlike attitude, habit is characterized by a low level of involvement. The following example highlights this distinction. Mrs. Smith has a strong positive attitude toward Minute Maid® frozen orange juice; she buys it automatically every week.

Mrs. Jones does the same, although with a lesser degree of involvement. One day, the grocery store where both women shop stops carrying Minute Maid® orange juice. Given Mrs. Smith's high level of involvement, she might decide to shop elsewhere, not to buy orange juice, or to pick another brand after analyzing the features of similar products. On the other hand, Mrs. Jones is likely to substitute another brand of orange juice much more mechanically.

In short, habit provides consumers with an easy, routine way of selecting a product or category of products whose purchase or consumption represents very little risk. However, since most cultural products represent a high level of involvement, habit is a less frequent decision-making mechanism.

4.5.7 Impulse Purchasing

The decision-making process used by the consumer purchasing on impulse is characterized by a low degree of involvement and experience. These purchases are generally unplanned and of little consequence. Sometimes, product placement or the colours on the packaging are enough to prompt the consumer to buy. Some video-club members use this process. For these consumers, renting a DVD requires little involvement; hence, their decision-making process may entail simply taking the most familiar title they find among the recent releases.

4.6   SITUATIONAL VARIABLES

Decision-making processes, along with the related information-processing strategies, are influenced by certain situational variables. The main situational variables are the period (month, day, season) when the purchase is made, the time available to the consumer to shop for the purchase, the presence or absence of reference groups, the economic climate, and the place where the decision is made.

The period during which a purchase is made influences the decision-making process. A snowfall in early December, for instance, encourages consumers to do Christmas shopping. Tchaikovsky's *The Nutcracker* may be a holiday season favourite, but would it be sold out or held over in July?

The amount of time a consumer has to make a decision also influences the decision-making process adopted. If there is little time, the consumer will rely more on subordinate processes and processes based on past experience.

The presence or absence of reference groups also influences the decision-making process. If a consumer is aware of signals in his or her environment and must make a decision, the presence of a reference group or person of influence will increase the tendency to use a subordinate process.

The economic climate also plays an important role. If the consumer is living through a recession or is keenly aware of the economic situation, he or she will tend to use a cognitive decision-making process in which price becomes more significant.

The physical environment is another element influencing the consumer's choice of decision-making process. This factor is especially important, since the presence or absence of affective or cognitive stimuli would determine the process used.

4.7 CONCLUSION

All decision-making processes are based on a minimum amount of information. Consequently, a key function of marketing is to provide consumers with information that can be adapted to both the type and the structure of the decision-making process selected. The greater the consumer's experience with a particular product or product category, the less inclined he or she will be to seek information from outside sources and the less sensitive he or she will be to solicitation.

The development of an effective marketing strategy depends to a great extent on a clear understanding of consumers' decision-making processes. Unless the marketing manager has a firm grasp of these processes, any marketing initiative is doomed to failure.

SUMMARY

Consumers, as human beings, base their behaviours on a certain amount of information, which has already been processed according to particular decision-making processes. These processes are, in turn, based on the basic triad of individual–product–situation. Notable among the variables influencing both the type and the structure of the decision-making processes are the consumer's previous experience and level of involvement with the product.

Marketing managers must have an excellent grasp of the information-processing system that a consumer uses when buying their company's product. A good understanding of the factors that make up these processes will enable managers to optimize their company's marketing strategy. This understanding will, in turn, enable the company to do the following:

1) better segment its markets

2) better position the company's products vis-à-vis the competition and the segments targeted

3) select more suitable distribution modes and networks

4) set up a price structure based not only on costs or competitors' prices, but also on the target consumer's perception

5) develop a communications strategy that provides consumers with the information they want in the most suitable form.

QUESTIONS

1. You are the new marketing director of a decorative-arts museum. Over the past two years, the number of museum visitors has dropped considerably. Given the degree of product involvement implied, what marketing action will you take to improve the museum's position in the market?

2. Compare the linear compensatory process and the conjunctive process.

3. Why is it important for a manager to be well acquainted with the decision-making process that targeted consumers are using?

4. What is the difference between a decision to buy with low product involvement and a decision to buy with high product involvement? Support your answer with examples of cultural products.

5. What are the advantages and disadvantages of using sociodemographic variables as determining factors in consumer behaviours?

6. Which elements explain the influence of reference groups on consumers?

7. What role does attitude play in the decision-making process? Use an example to back up your answer.

8. How do situational variables influence the decision-making process and the processing of information?

9. What are the consequences of selective perception for a marketing manager designing an ad campaign for a new play?

10. What do we mean by "the experiential facet of consumption"?

Notes

1. For an in-depth discussion of products that can be evaluated only upon consumption, see Sénécal, S., and J. Nantel. 2004. "The Influence of Online Product Recommendations on Consumers' Online Choices." *Journal of Retailing*, Vol. 80, n° 3, p.1–12.

2. As we shall see in the chapter on segmentation, the utilitarian aspect is more concerned with the attributes of products and services as well as their tangible benefits. On the other hand, the affective and hedonistic aspects concern the sensory and emotional pleasure derived from a product or service. For a discussion of these notions, see Nantel, J., and Y. Grégoire. 1998. "Une segmentation de la clientèle des centres commerciaux." *Gestion*, Vol. 23, n° 2 (Summer), p. 45–54.

3. For details, see Park, C.W., and B. Mittal. 1985. "A Theory of Involvement in Consumer Behavior: Problems and Issues." In *Research in Consumer Behavior*, J. Sheth, ed. Greenwich, CT: JAI Press, Vol. 1, p. 201–232.

4. Gainer, B. 1993. "An Empirical Investigation of the Role of Involvement with a Gendered Product." *Psychology and Marketing*, Vol. 10, n° 4 (July/August), p. 261–283.

5. See Ingnene C., and M.A. Hughes. 1985. "Risk Management by Consumers." In *Research in Consumer Behavior*, J. Sheth, ed. Greenwich, CT: JAI Press, Vol. 1, p. 103–158.

6. d'Astous, A., and F. Colbert. 2002. "Moviegoers' Consultation of Critical Reviews: Psychological Antecedents and Consequences." *International Journal of Arts Management,* Vol. 5, n° 1 (Fall), p. 24–35.

7. Brito, P., and C. Barros. 2005. "Learning-by-Consuming and the Dynamics of the Demand and Prices of Cultural Goods." *Journal of Cultural Economics*, Vol. 29, n° 2, p. 83–106.

8. To gain a better understanding of attitude, see Holbrook, M., and R.M. Schindler. 1989. "Some Exploratory Findings on the Development of Musical Tastes." *Journal of Consumer Research,* Vol. 16 (June), p. 119–124; Fazio, R.H. 1986. "How Do Attitudes Guide Behavior?" In *The Handbook of Motivation and Cognition: Foundations of Social Behavior*, S. Richard and H. Tory, eds. New York: Guilford; and Snyder, M. 1982. "When Believing Means Doing: Creating Links between Attitudes and Behavior." In *Consistency in Social Behavior: The Ontario Symposium,* M. Zanna, E. Higgins and C. Herman, eds. Hillsdale, NJ: Lawrence Erlbaum, Vol. 2, p. 105–130.

9. eMarketer. 2005. *Online Video Is Not Just for Kids.* December. http://www.emarketer.com/eStat-Database/ArticlePreview.aspx?1003716

10. ComScore Media Metrix. 2006. *Ticket Buyers Get Online Instead of In Line.* January.

11. For a discussion of the tenets of the experiential view of consumption, see Hirschman, E.C., and M. Holbrook. 1982. "Hedonic Consumption: Emerging Concepts, Methods, and Propositions." *Journal of Marketing*, Vol. 46 (Summer), p. 92–101.

12. Campbell, C. 1994. "Consuming Goods and the Good of Consuming." *Critical Review*, Vol. 8, n° 4, p. 503–520.

13. Goulding, C. 1999. "Heritage, Nostalgia, and the 'Grey' Consumer." *Journal of Marketing Practice*, Vol. 5, n° 6/7/8, p. 177–199.

14. Goulding, C. 2000. "The Museum Environment and the Visitor Experience." *European Journal of Marketing*, Vol. 34, n° 3/4, p. 261–278.

15. Kelly, R.F. 1985. "Museums as Status Symbols II: Obtaining a State of Having Been There." In *Advances in Non-Profit Marketing*, R. Belk, ed. Greenwich, CT: JAI Press, Vol. 2, p. 1–38.

16. Holbrook, M.B., M.J. Weiss and J. Habich. 2002. "Disentangling Effacement, Omnivore, and Distinction Effects on the Consumption of Cultural Activities: An Illustration." *Marketing Letters*, Vol. 13, n° 4, p. 345–357.

17. Bourdieu, P. 1984. *Distinction: A Social Critique of the Judgment of Taste.* Cambridge, MA: Harvard University Press.

18. For a review, see Holbrook, M.B. 1999. "Popular Appeal versus Expert Judgments of Motion Pictures." *Journal of Consumer Research*, Vol. 26, n° 2, p. 144–155.

19. Seabrook, J. 2000. *Nobrow: The Culture of Marketing + The Marketing of Culture.* New York: Knopf.

20. Holt, D.B. 1998. "Does Cultural Capital Structure American Consumption?" *Journal of Consumer Research*, Vol. 25 (June), p. 1–25.

21. Holbrook, M.B., M.J. Weiss and J. Habich. 2002. "Disentangling Effacement, Omnivore, and Distinction Effects on the Consumption of Cultural Activities: An Illustration." *Marketing Letters*, Vol. 13, n° 4, p. 345–357.

22. Sintas, J.L., and E.G. Álvarez. 2005. "Four Characters on the Stage Playing Three Games: Performing Arts Consumption in Spain." *Journal of Business Research*, Vol. 58, p. 1446–1455.

23. Swanson, G.E. 1978. "Travels through Inner Space: Family Structure and Openness to Absorbing Experiences." *American Journal of Sociology,* Vol. 83 (January), p. 890–919.

24. Csikszentmihalyi, M. 1990. *Flow: The Psychology of Optimal Experience.* New York: Harper & Row.

25. Hirschman, E.C., and M. Holbrook. 1982. "Hedonic Consumption: Emerging Concepts, Methods, and Propositions." *Journal of Marketing*, Vol. 46 (Summer), p. 92–101.

26. Caldwell, M., and A.G. Woodside. 2003. "The Role of Cultural Capital in Performing Arts Patronage." *International Journal of Arts Management,* Vol. 5, n° 3 (Spring), p. 34–50.

27. Aurier, P., and J. Passebois. 2002. "Comprendre les expériences de consommation pour mieux gérer la relation client." *Décisions Marketing*, Vol. 28 (October/December), p. 43–52.

28. Colbert, F., and A. d'Astous. 2003. "La consultation de critiques de films et son impact sur la consommation." *Gestion*, Vol. 28, n° 1, p. 12–17.

For Further Reference

Amazon. http://www.amazon.com/

Statistics Canada. 2003. *Spending Patterns in Canada.* Ottawa: Author.

PLAN

Chapter 5

The Private Sector Market

by J. Dennis Rich

OBJECTIVES

- Understand the various components of the private sector market
- Learn about the history of philanthropic activity in the United States
- Explore the possibility of sponsorship as a promotional tool
- Review the steps involved in making a successful sponsorship application

INTRODUCTION

Artistic enterprises are increasingly dependent on the participation of the private sector to make ends meet. Following the example of the United States, many industrialized nations have taken steps over the past 20 years to facilitate the participation of individuals, foundations, and corporations in culture and the arts through various tax incentives. Faced with increasingly scarce public funds, governments have encouraged cultural organizations to seek other sources of revenue. Private sector contributions can take the form of donations or sponsorships.

The first part of this chapter provides an introduction to the donor and sponsorship markets and makes essential distinctions between the two. In addition, it provides a brief history of private sector participation in the community, revealing the key role played by the private sector in civic life in the United States, particularly in the artistic and cultural milieu.

The second part of the chapter looks at the different aspects of sponsorship. Sponsorship can be described as an essentially commercial operation in which a corporation uses an artistic or cultural enterprise as an advertising vehicle or as a tool to enhance its image.

5.1 THE DONOR MARKET

In recent years, the competition for donated money has brought concepts traditionally associated with marketing into the cultural fundraising arena. Few arts organizations seek support solely on the basis of quality programs or even on the basis of the services they provide to the community. It is common for cultural institutions today to refer to economic impact, the creation of jobs, or the role they play in attracting tourists. In essence, they are seeking to effect an exchange of value.

The sponsorship and fundraising market comprises individuals, foundations, and private companies likely to provide support to cultural institutions. This is a special market in that cultural enterprises often must compete with each other to capture the market share representing high potential earnings. Sponsors and donors, on the other hand, make support decisions using criteria that are different from those of the state and the consumer. Each sponsor has its own criteria for selecting an enterprise to support.

Support may take two forms: contributions, and sponsored events or products. Contributions may be made by individuals, foundations, or companies. Sponsorships come mainly from companies. A contribution is normally a philanthropic act, whereas sponsorship is a promotional initiative in exchange for publicity or advertising. Sponsorships are awarded based on promotional benefits that are calculated in advance. The corporate sponsor then evaluates the performance of its investment in terms of visibility, top-of-the-mind awareness, and the vehicle's reach – that is, the number of consumers receiving the message.

Companies that sponsor artistic and cultural events are looking for prestige advertising vehicles. Their hope is that the popularity of the group sponsored and the public's affection for that group will be transferred to the sponsor. Usually, funds are drawn from the company's advertising or public relations budget. The public targeted by cultural organizations is an extremely lucrative market for commercial enterprises seeking a market segment with strong purchasing power. In fact, many organizations in the cultural industries serve a broad-based market and are therefore perceived by the private sector as excellent advertising vehicles. Faced with media fragmentation, companies are looking for new ways to get their message across in a cost-effective and competitive manner. Sponsorship can meet this need.

The gamut of companies seeking a sponsorship role proves this point. Today, organizations such as the Toronto International Film Festival, the Chicago Symphony Orchestra, and the Salzburg Festival are so successful that large private corporations do not hesitate to become associated with them. These events not only attract large audiences but also enjoy tremendous public approval and appeal.

Individual donors, on the other hand, provide assistance based on personal taste and commitment. In the case of a foundation, its mission and goals determine the choice of a cause. Donors usually are rewarded with some form of recognition, but this does not generally result in a philanthropic gesture.

In Canada, the private sector provides 21% of the revenue of performing arts companies[1]; in the United States, the figure can exceed 40%.[2] In Canada, support for all the performing arts, from the different levels of government, comes to as much as 40%; in the United States, government support for the performing arts averages 5.5% or less.[3]

Certain fields receive more private sector support than others. Orchestras, opera companies, and musical societies enjoy more success in this regard than dance or theatre companies. The size of the artistic enterprise or event also influences the choice of donors and sponsors, the latter tending to prefer larger venues and groups.

The United States is unique among the top industrialized nations in terms of private sector support for the arts. This may be partially explained by the lower rate of corporate taxation and the number of tax incentives available in the United States, where the state plays a lesser role in financing the arts. Indeed, the ratio of foundations supporting the arts in the United States in comparison with Canada is 35:1, whereas the population ratio is 10:1.[4] In Europe, the state historically has done little to encourage cultural enterprises to find partners in the private sector, though this situation is changing rapidly.

Cultural sponsorship in Western Europe began in the late 1970s. In the beginning, corporations in Germany, Spain, the Netherlands, and France limited their support to collections of art works. They gradually extended and broadened their role, supporting the visual arts (both collections and exhibitions), heritage (restoration of monuments and buildings), theatre, and classical music (sponsoring the touring activities of well-known companies). In Europe, corporate support and sponsorship of the arts and their implications are still low but are growing.

In the United States, donor support represents significant sums of money. Charitable giving in 2004 represented 2.1% of the GDP (gross domestic product), or $248.52 billion.[5] Of this total, individuals gave 83.6% (including bequests), corporations 4.8% (excluding sponsorship and cause-related marketing), and foundations 11.6%. Some $13.99 billion, or 5.6%, went to culture and the arts.[6]

In addition to providing financial support, 44% of all American adults volunteer their time to a charitable organization. And those Americans who volunteer also tend to make larger financial gifts. In households in which adults volunteered their time and services in 2001, total charitable giving came to 4.5% of personal income; among non-volunteering households in which adults made financial contributions, the average was 2.4% of personal income.[7]

5.2 HISTORY OF PHILANTHROPIC ACTIVITY IN THE UNITED STATES

Fundraising is not a new concept to managers in culture and the arts. From the beginning of recorded history, philanthropy has had a place in human society. It arrived in America with the Pilgrims. A basic tenet of Pilgrim society was that each member of the community had to willingly assume responsibility for the common good. An outcome of this historical circumstance is the association of volunteerism with philanthropy.

Communities preceded government in the New World. One result of this was that community needs were met through cooperative volunteer efforts. Leaders of such efforts were unpaid but achieved elevated social status, and, over the years, wealthy individuals founded institutions such as universities, schools, and libraries. In addition, they often bequeathed a part of their fortune to charitable organizations. As early as 1638, John Harvard bequeathed

> **Example 5.1**
> ## Festival Internacional de Benicassim (FIB): Retaining Private (and Public) Sponsors in Changing Times
>
> Every summer since 1995, the village of Benicassim (Spain), located on the Mediterranean coast, has hosted the indie rock music Festival Internacional de Benicassim, or FIB. The event was originally considered ill-suited to the traditional and family tourism of the area. Nowadays, however, nobody disputes its benefits. It was the first festival of its kind in Spain and is the most famous. In 2005, FIB attendees, or *fibers*, spent more than 10 million euros in just a few days.
>
> Fundraising has always been a difficult issue for the organizers. Currently, 40% of the total budget for the festival comes from sponsors and public bodies. Various firms sponsor the festival, seeking brand loyalty among young attendees. Local and regional authorities are also interested in funding the FIB, since it promotes tourism and is popular among young voters. The remainder of the funds come from the box office and peripheral services.
>
> All decisions concerning the festival take the interests of each stakeholder into account. In 2006, hotel managers in the area suggested that the festival be rescheduled for reasons of profitability. After consulting with the local authority, the organizers accepted this proposal and moved the FIB from August to July. This move, along with an appealing line-up and heavy international promotion, has resulted in higher attendance levels, greater benefits for the local area, and increased social impact.
>
> *Source:* Manuel Cuadrado, Associate Professor, and Juan D. Montoro, Associate Professor, Universitat de València, Spain.

a portion of his estate and his library to found Harvard College. In his will, Benjamin Franklin not only provided for his children but also included instructions regarding charitable donations.

As their circumstances improved, members of the American middle class followed suit and began to make charitable gifts.[8]

By the 19th century, fundraising activity was beginning to resemble modern philanthropy. Personal solicitation, letter solicitation, and fundraising events and campaigns came into being. In 1835, Alexis de Tocqueville (1805–59) commented on the unique nature of American philanthropy, characterized as it was by individual, private efforts and volunteerism. De Tocqueville was impressed by the willingness of people to give their own money to support social improvements. He observed that when local citizens saw the need for a school, hospital, church, or cultural service, they would form a committee to discuss the need, provide leadership, and seek out sources of support.

> The Americans make associations to give entertainments, to found seminaries, to build inns, to construct churches, to diffuse books, to send missionaries to the Antipodes; in this manner, they founded hospitals, prisons, and schools. If it is proposed to inculcate some truth or to foster some feeling by the encouragement of a great example, they form a society. Wherever at the head of some new undertaking you see the government in France, or a man of rank in England, in the United States you will be sure to find an association.[9]

By the early part of the next century, wealthy individuals such as John D. Rockefeller and Andrew Carnegie set the stage for large-scale support with the establishment of private foundations and the assertion that the wealthy had a moral obligation to distribute their fortunes for the good of society.

World War I was a cause for which American citizens contributed on a scale never before seen. Many communities established war chests. In 1917 the American Red Cross raised $115 million in a single month.[10]

During the Great Depression of the 1930s, the government began to help people meet their basic needs with such programs as the Works Progress Administration and the Civilian Conservation Core, while also encouraging corporate giving with passage of the 1935 Revenue Act, which legislated tax breaks for donor corporations.

Beginning in the 1950s, personal income in the United States rose dramatically, as did taxes. One result was an upsurge in charitable giving and the creation of family-sponsored and corporate foundations in an effort to gain a tax advantage. By the 1960s, during the "Great Society" era, Americans were supporting numerous causes, including culture and the arts. By 1965, when the National Endowment for the Arts and the National Endowment for the Humanities were established, Americans were giving to culture and the arts in record numbers.[11]

5.3 SPONSORSHIP

In the 1980s, corporate giving moved more and more toward "strategic philanthropy" based on the old concept of "doing well by doing good." Corporations began to form collaborations and partnerships with not-for-profit organizations, which increased recognition for both parties and enhanced the corporation's image.

Today, cultural and artistic enterprises turn to the private sector for financial support. Sponsorship represents a major source of revenue. It is actually a promotional tool for the sponsor, whose presence has an impact on the content of the advertising material for an organization or event.

5.3.1 Defining Sponsorship

The term "sponsorship" describes a relationship between a sponsor and an event, organization, or property in which the sponsor pays a cash or in-kind fee in return for access to the exploitable commercial potential associated with the event, organization, or property.[12] Sponsorship is part of a strategically planned promotional effort.

The related term "cause-related marketing" refers to a strategically planned *promotional* effort designed to increase a company's sales or improve its position in the marketplace through actions that also benefit a not-for-profit organization. Generally, this means that when consumers purchase the company's product or service, the company donates to the not-for-profit organization.[13]

Perhaps the first instance of cause-related marketing occurred during the 1983 restoration of the Statue of Liberty. American Express worked with the Ellis Island Foundation to promote both application for and frequent use of the American Express card, by donating to the Statue of Liberty restoration fund each time an application was approved and each time a cardholder used the card. The promotion raised $1.7 million for refurbishment of the statue and also resulted in a 45% increase in new cardholders and a 28% increase in card usage.

Money spent on sponsorship and cause-related marketing is a business expense, not a donation (as in the case of philanthropy), and is expected to contribute to the company's marketing effort and show a return on investment. Sponsorship involves interaction between two distinct parties: the sponsor, which provides funds, goods, or services, and the sponsored event or organization, which receives the funds, goods, or services in return for certain consideration. The business relationship assumes that each party is satisfied with what it receives in return for what it gives.

5.3.2 The Importance of the Sponsorship Market

Saturation in the mass media has forced companies to seek other means of reaching the consumer. Sponsorship and cause-related marketing is one of those means. Sponsorship is the fastest-growing medium in the market. When compared to advertising and sales promotion, sponsorship expenditures since 1983 have grown at a much faster rate.[14] Total North American sponsorship spending for 2004 was projected to reach $11.4 billion. Worldwide, sponsorship in 2003 came to $25.9 billion, and was projected to reach $28 billion in 2004.[15] Not surprisingly, most of the sponsorship money – 69% – goes to sports. However, corporations' demand for a new and better way of communicating with their target audiences has benefited every type of sponsorship, and 5% goes to the arts, 7% to festivals, fairs, and annual events, and 10% to entertainment, tours, and attractions.[16]

In the 1990s, a new concept of sponsorship and cause-related marketing began to emerge. Short-term sales-related promotional sponsorships began to be replaced by sponsorship and cause-related marketing integrated into the very identity of companies. The new form of strategic philanthropy seeks to affiliate not-for-profit events, organizations, or causes with a particular brand[17] as part of a comprehensive, integrated marketing strategy.

For example, when the Field Museum in Chicago purchased Sue, the largest Tyrannosaurus Rex ever unearthed, at an auction, it put together a groundbreaking deal with McDonald's and Walt Disney World Resorts.

In return for helping the Field Museum purchase Sue, both corporations gained access to Sue's image for use in their own promotions. The Field Museum name will be mentioned in conjunction with customer-savvy public relations and marketing efforts by two of the largest worldwide corporations. The three entities have a similar customer base: children under the age of 13 and their families. At the time of Sue's purchase, the agreement reached by the Field Museum, McDonald's, and Disney was heralded as innovative and was expected to be copied widely. The Field Museum's preparatory laboratory, where Sue's bones are being cleaned, has been named the McDonald's Preparatory Laboratory, and at Disney the public will be able to observe technicians and scientists as they work on Sue. One copy each of Sue's skeleton will be provided to McDonald's and Disney for their use. Because of these activities, the Field Museum will benefit from long-term relationships with each corporation.[18]

This sort of affiliation occurs regularly outside the realm of culture and the arts. Time will tell if this type of merger between commerce, education, and entertainment will be replicated.

5.3.3 The Decision-Makers

Sponsorship and cause-related marketing are not simple corporate contributions. Corporate contributions are donations not associated with a marketing program (see Table 5.1). People other than those who make decisions about sponsorship and cause-related marketing generally handle such contributions. Sponsorship and cause-related marketing involve the marketing,

Table 5.1
Sponsorship and Charitable Contribution Compared

	Sponsorship	**Charitable Contribution**
Publicity	Highly public	Usually little widespread fanfare
Source of funds	Typically, marketing, advertising, or communications budgets	Philanthropic or charitable contributions budgets
Accounting	Written off as a full business expense like promotional or media placement expenses	Write-off is limited by tax laws regulating charitable contributions; as a result, accounting/tax considerations are less likely to influence the way a corporation designates funding of a not-for-profit organization
Objectives	To sell more products or services: to increase positive awareness in markets and among distant stakeholders (customers, potential customers, geographic community)	To be a good corporate citizen, to enhance the corporate image with closest stakeholders (i.e., employees, shareholders, suppliers)
Partner/ recipient	Events, teams, or cultural organizations, projects, programs – a cause is sometimes associated with the undertaking	Larger donations are typically cause-related (education, health, disease, disasters, environmental) but can be cultural, artistic, or cause-related; at times, funding is specifically designated for a project or program; at times, it is provided for operating budgets

Source: *The Sponsorship Report.* http://www.sponsorship.ca/p-issues-callit.html

communications, promotion, or public relations functions of a company (see Table 5.2).

Both sponsorship and cause-related marketing are strategically planned *marketing* efforts designed to increase a company's sales or improve its position in the marketplace through actions that also benefit a not-for-profit organization. *Strategically planned marketing effort* is the key idea here. It means that sponsorship and cause-related marketing are based on a strategy and a

Table 5.2
The Corporate Sponsor's Decision-Making Process

Position/Department within the Organization	Participation in Cases (%)
Marketing director	46.4
President	45.7
Vice-president, marketing	45.7
General management	29.7
Sales department	29.7
PR department	26.1
Promotions department	23.9
Advertising department	21.0
Communications department	20.3

Source: Godbout, A., N. Turgeon and F. Colbert. 1991. *Pratique de la commandite commerciale au Québec : une étude empirique.* Montreal: Chair in Arts Management, HEC Montreal. Research Report n° GA91-02.

plan – they are not just coincidental activities. No such effort should take place without a carefully constructed plan, which should be drawn up jointly by the two partners – the sponsoring company and the not-for-profit organization.

In the collaboration between cultural organizations and companies, arts managers should be aware that the company is engaged in strategic philanthropy designed to improve its image or increase sales. Some arts and cultural organizations have a problem with this. Their leadership seems to believe that helping a company make money is inconsistent with their not-for-profit mission. However, as long as the activities of the sponsoring company are ethical and legitimate and the arts organization does not violate its tax-exempt status, there is nothing wrong with participating in a partnership that benefits both partners. The definition of sponsorship suggests collaboration, and it is clear that sponsorship and/or cause-related marketing must also benefit the not-for-profit organization. Whatever form it takes – unrestricted funds, financial support for a particular program, in-kind contributions, or increased public awareness – the chosen means of support should advance the mission of the arts organization.

A successful corporate sponsorship is a little like a successful marriage. Both parties have found the right partner – one with similar interests and goals. It takes hard work to ensure that a partnership will enjoy enduring, long-term success and that the needs of each party will be met.

5.3.4 Benefits Sought by Companies

In 1990, a study by Fisher and Brouillet found that companies seek the benefits shown in Table 5.3 when undertaking a sponsorship. Today, companies all over the world are seeking such benefits. In Ireland, for example, a study found that companies invest in sponsorship as a marketing tool for the reasons presented in Table 5.4. Interestingly, in the results of neither study does the idea that companies must stand for something appear as a response.[19]

5.3.5 Sponsorship and the Consumer

Consumers understand that a company is in business to make a profit, but today they expect the company to be involved. The *Cone/Roper Cause Related Trends Report*[20] reveals that public acceptability of sponsorship is overwhelmingly positive in the United States. It also reveals that sponsorship has the ability to influence what consumers buy and where they buy it.

Table 5.3
Benefits Sought in a Sponsorship Program

	(%)
Improved corporate image	37
Increased sales	22
Greater visibility	15
Social role	15
Support for a cause	5
Broader communications mix	4
Specific target group	2

Source: Fisher, V., and R. Brouillet. 1990. *Les commandites : la pub de demain.* Montreal: Éditions Saint-Martin, p. 15.

Table 5.4
Main Reasons for Undertaking Sponsorship

	(%)
Target marketing	54
Promotional tie-in	49
Entertainment opportunity	29
Sampling or couponing opportunity	26
Awareness	24
Image	22
Increased sales	18
Public relations	16
Employee incentive	9
Community relations	8

Source: http://www.onlinesports.com/sportstrust/sports11.html

The Cone/Roper report indicates that 74% of American consumers now find it acceptable for companies to engage in cause-related marketing, up from 66% in 1993. Sixty-one percent believe that cause-related marketing should be standard business practice. Eighty-three percent have a more positive image of a company they care about than one they do not care about. Approximately two thirds of American consumers (130 million people) are likely to switch to a brand or retailer associated with a good cause if price and quality are equal.

Leaders in the sponsorship field interpret these data to mean that sponsorship and cause-related marketing have become necessary for brands seeking a strong relationship with customers and communities.

The Cone/Roper report also shows that socially and politically active consumers – a key group for marketers – are especially receptive to companies that link with social issues. It reveals that 94% of Americans have a more positive image of such companies. This group is likely to switch brands or switch retailers to support a company associated with a good cause. Consumers also expect companies to support a cause in the long term and in a substantive way. Almost 80% of Americans consistently report that they favour companies that make a long-term commitment over those that focus on many different causes over short periods.

5.3.6 How Sponsorship Is Measured

Fisher and Brouillet found that, for companies, the value of a sponsorship arrangement for an event depends on the number of visitors or participants, the location of the company's logo on promotional material, visibility of the sponsor at the event, potential media coverage, image, social impact, and the commercial potential of the event.[21]

Sponsorship, then, can be measured with these criteria in mind. It can also be evaluated by measuring awareness of or attitude toward the sponsor's product or services, quantified in terms of sales results, and comparing the value of sponsorship-generated media coverage to the cost of equivalent advertising space or time.[22]

5.3.7 Selection Criteria

Table 5.5 presents criteria used by companies in selecting events and organizations to sponsor.

5.3.8 Successful Sponsorship and Cause-Related Marketing Applications

Unless actually requesting contributions, a cultural or artistic enterprise should promote the win-win aspect of sponsorship. Sponsorship applications or requests should take into account the benefits to the sponsor as well as the organization's need for sponsorship. To this end, it is important for cultural marketers to:

1. Think like a marketer: identify the marketable assets of the cultural or artistic enterprise; these may include name, board members, community, and public awareness of the organization and its programs.
2. Learn as much as possible about the company being approached: read the business press; check the company's annual reports; watch its ads and promotions.
3. Before approaching a company, try to identify its target market.
4. Address the needs of the potential sponsor: show the company that sponsorship will help it sell more products or services and at the same time benefit the arts organization.
5. Identify the primary decision-maker: for sponsorship and cause-related decisions, the person to approach may not be the head of the foundation but a marketing and/or sales executive.

Table 5.5
Relative Importance of Sponsors' Objectives

Objectives	Average (4 = very important, 3 = important, 2 = slightly important, 1 = unimportant)
Sales-related objectives	**2.93**
Increase sales	3.26
Make prospecting easier for sales force	2.58
Product-related objectives	**2.90**
Increase top-of-the-mind awareness of product	3.30
Identify a product with a market segment	3.07
Modify product image	2.67
Encourage customers to try product	2.50
Corporate objectives	**2.65**
Enhance corporate image	3.56
Increase awareness of firm	3.36
Increase long-term performance	3.34
Become involved in the community	3.13
Identify the company with a market segment	2.92
Impress opinion leaders favourably	2.88
Acquire new business contacts	2.81
Change public perception of firm	2.58
Improve employee relations	2.48
Keep up staff morale	2.37
Mark a special event	2.31
Counteract bad press (damage control)	1.98
Reassure shareholders	1.79
Facilitate recruitment of new employees	1.77
Personal objectives	2.09

Source: Godbout, A., N. Turgeon and F. Colbert. 1991. *Pratique de la commandite commerciale au Québec : une étude empirique.* Montreal: Chair in Arts Management, HEC Montreal. Research Report n° GA91-02.

While investment in sponsorship continues to grow, sponsors say the quality of sponsorship proposals is declining. And, increasingly, companies measure the impact of sponsorships in hard numbers. This means that sponsorships and cause-related marketing partnerships must be more carefully planned.[23] A successful proposal

1. Sells benefits, not features. Cultural managers tend to be very proud of their program, venue, or event. As a result, their proposals often describe the opportunity – the merits of the cause; the artistic excellence of the festival, concert, or exhibition; the economic impact of the event – rather than the benefits to the sponsor. Sponsors do not buy causes, events, exhibitions, or performances; they buy promotional platforms to help them sell products or services.

2. Addresses the needs of the sponsor, not those of the cultural organization. Many sponsorship applications focus on the organization's need for money. However, companies with an interest in sponsorship are not motivated by a cultural organization's need for funds; they want to know *what is in it for them.*

3. Is tailored to the sponsor's business category. Different sponsors require different benefits; for example, a proposal to an insurance company might focus on access to the arts organization's mailing list or board of directors, while one to a soft-drink distributor might describe on-site visibility and sales rights.

4. Includes promotional extensions. There are two types of sponsorship benefit. The first is automatic – benefits that come with the deal and require nothing further from the sponsor, such as sponsor identification on collateral materials and on-site signage. The second derives from the sponsor's ability to build upon the sponsored entity through trade, retail, and sales extensions. Today, automatic benefits rarely provide sufficient return to justify the time and expense of sponsorship. An effective proposal illustrates how a cultural property or event can be used as a unifying element or theme for media advertising and sales promotion. It is not sufficient to give companies a checklist of automatic benefits; proposals should include a menu showing prospective sponsors how to capitalize on their investment.

5. Minimizes the risk to the prospective sponsor. It is much easier for a corporate marketing or communications executive to authorize a media buy than a sponsorship. A proposal can minimize risk by including guaranteed media in the package and listing reputable co-sponsors; the existence of co-sponsors tells a prospective sponsor that the opportunity being offered has been favourably reviewed by other companies.

6. Includes benefits. The cultural organization or event should be presented in terms of its total contribution to meeting the sponsor's objectives – rather than one element, such as media coverage, being isolated (see Table 5.5); the idea here is that when it comes to benefits to the sponsoring company, the whole should be greater than the sum of the parts.
7. Offers the company the opportunity to form an alliance that provides access to resources that otherwise would not be available.

5.3.9 Negotiating the Sponsorship Agreement

When a sponsorship agreement is being negotiated, the business relationship established between the sponsor and the cultural or artistic enterprise must be kept in mind at all times. For the sponsor, the enterprise or event is primarily a promotional tool. For the sponsored organization, the sponsor is similar to a client who must receive a benefit in exchange for money. Both parties need to feel they are getting their money's worth. Therefore, a written contract is imperative. The contract should include:

1. The goals of the sponsoring company and the cultural or arts enterprise
2. Goods and services to be offered by both parties
3. The geographic area to be covered
4. Starting and ending dates
5. Creative specifications, such as use of the partners' logos, names, and images – for example, which partner will control advertising on broadcasts and the meaning of the term "official"
6. Details on how funds will be accounted for and the portion of sales that the arts enterprise will receive
7. The legal/financial system in place to track and distribute funds

5.3.10 During and after the Sponsorship

Cultural managers need to develop a system for examining and analyzing the sponsorship or cause-related marketing campaign from start to finish. The sponsored enterprise will have to keep track of the campaign's goals and the consumer's perceptions and communicate these to the sponsor. Sponsors follow up to see if their communications objectives have been met. They want as much information as possible. By providing such information, an artistic enterprise enables the sponsor to determine whether its investment has been worthwhile.

After the event or at predetermined intervals, evaluative meetings should be held with the sponsor to assess the results and the benefits accrued to each party. Finally, success should be celebrated and the sponsor thanked for its service to the arts enterprise and the community.

5.3.11 Pitfalls and Dangers of Sponsorships from the Perspective of the Arts Organization

It would be foolish to believe that a sponsorship or cause-related marketing campaign is risk-free. Arts managers should discuss sponsorship with their key stakeholders, including the board of trustees, staff, and artistic leadership. Possible negative repercussions will have to be discussed. In any sponsorship or cause-related marketing venture, the arts enterprise should focus first on it mission. Sponsorship and cause-related marketing generate income for the arts organization, while the corporate partner derives publicity, enhanced image, promotional assistance by volunteers from the arts organization, and increased sales.

The question most often posed about sponsorships and cause-related marketing is whether corporations profit unduly. With the controversy surrounding events such as the *Sensation* exhibition of works owned by Charles Saatchi at the Brooklyn Museum several years ago, there is much discussion about sponsorship and the possibility for conflict of interest. Simply stated, the issue is whether sponsorships and cause-related marketing partnerships are ethical.

From the perspective of the cultural manager, the reputation of the arts enterprise is a fundamental concern. The manager must determine whether the nature of the arts organization or its mission will be diminished or fundamentally altered through its association with a for-profit company.[24] In any case, managers must be careful not to affiliate with a sponsor that is a major competitor of a key stakeholder such as a major donor. Equally important is the need to think through "exclusions" – companies with products or services that may conflict with the mission of the artistic enterprise. For example, it would be inadvisable for a children's theatre to accept a sponsorship from a tobacco company.

Cultural enterprises should consider developing and adopting a policy on sponsorship. Such a policy should:
- Stress the partnership nature of sponsorship
- Define sponsorship as a business arrangement, distinct from a contribution
- State the arts enterprise's commitment to the concept in positive terms; companies like to know that arts organizations are enthusiastic about collaborating, as opposed to taking a "we'll take your money but we don't approve of you" approach

- Clearly state exclusions – those companies with which the cultural organization will not do business
- Spell out the rights of the sponsor and the arts enterprise
- Provide an escape clause, allowing the arts enterprise to cancel the arrangement should the sponsor's activities run counter to its mission[25]

The policy should be approved by the board of trustees. All sponsorship agreements should be in writing.

As governments throughout North America and much of Europe move to cut their support to arts organizations, corporate sponsors are moving in to fill the breach. Mega-sponsors have emerged, which sometimes results in the renaming of cultural venues.

As competition for support heats up, corporations are expecting greater recognition for their efforts. In fact, more and more companies are moving away from simple philanthropy to sponsorship with a marketing edge. Companies are taking greater care to target and select arts organizations that are well matched with their own demographics. In other words, sponsorship is not about having a good heart!

This does not mean that arts enterprises should respond by engraving the name of a sponsor on the stage floor or by referring to a sponsor during the course of a play. Rather, arts managers need to seek a balance between outright intrusion into the artistic product and mission and tasteful recognition of a sponsor's contribution.

Example 5.2
The Queen's Theatre: An Original Fundraising Story

The Queen's Theatre is a 500-seat "regional theatre" on the outer edge of London. It produces its own works – seven shows during the year, each running for three weeks (Monday to Saturday), as well as a six-week traditional Christmas pantomime. It also rents itself to amateur groups, schools, and community groups for one-night events, brings in touring work, from dance to talks to stand-up comedy, and runs Sunday lunchtime jazz events. The result of this busy program is that over a year the Queen's Theatre presents some 500 events, remaining open with public performances 363 days a year.

The theatre receives public subsidy – from its local authority, from Arts Council England, and from a confederation of outer London boroughs; unusually, as much as 70% of its income is earned income, leaving just 30% from subsidy.

Some four years ago, under a new director and management team, the Green Room was in desperate need of refurbishment. There was no money in the budget, and at that time no hope of raising business support nor any tradition of private giving. How to raise the funds? "We'll sell raffle tickets to the audience," suggested the director, Bob Carlton. "£1 per ticket, and you can win a bottle of Champagne. We'll announce the winner from the stage after the performance." Everyone, from board to staff, from front of house to backstage, attacked the idea. It would demean the theatre and the idea of theatre; end-of-show speeches were a thing of the past, a hangover from the bad old days of dreary unadventurous theatre; and anyway, no one would buy the tickets since they would be too busy reading the program, chatting, or being tempted to buy refreshments.

The director decided he'd go it alone. He went to the local supermarket and bought a single bottle of (cheap) Champagne, for around £10, and a book of numbered raffle tickets.

Then, as the audience came in that first night, Carlton simply walked up to them: "Buy a raffle ticket – only £1 and you could win a bottle of Champagne." He arranged to have the raffle announced over the foyer PA system before the show and again at the interval. He sold 50 tickets, walked on stage at the end of the show and announced the winning number. Profit: £40.

(continued)

Example 5.2 (continued)

Next night, same procedure. Profit: £70. The following night Carlton persuaded a member of the acting company to announce the winning number from the stage.

By now it was clear that the idea had worked. Tickets were selling. Indeed there was an extra buzz of excitement in the auditorium as the audience applauded the show and at the same time waited for the winning number to be announced.

At this point the general manager came on the scene. If the director could sell 70 tickets, she would do better. And she did. And a sense of competition set in and spread to the house manager, to the production manager, to the head of marketing, to the stage management team, who all (except for one person, who had to stay backstage) came out to beat each successive record number of per-night ticket sales.

In just a few weeks they had raised all the money they needed, wholly off budget so that even the board couldn't interfere in how the money was spent. There were other benefits. The exercise did wonders to bond the entire staff, by giving them a challenge, some fun – and something out of the ordinary to do. It gave the audience something of a thrill, adding to a lively evening's entertainment. And it brought staff of all kinds and at all levels into direct contact with members of the audience.

That kind of face-to-face, informal contact with an audience is something that usually only the box office and front-of-house staff can hope for, and even *their* contact tends to be formal and systematized. To act almost as market traders, as hucksters, runs counter to just about everything in the current customer service canon in the arts. And the curtain speech, totally out of character and addressing the audience from the stage, upset no one, perhaps because it was so removed from the historic "thanks for coming, see you next time" message. In fact it had the positive effect of bringing performers and the audience closer together – and, incidentally, tempting audience members to stay on in the bar after the show and meet the company.

And the Green Room? New furniture, kitchen equipment, lighting – a place to enjoy sitting in.

Source: Michael Quine, Senior Lecturer, City University, London, United Kingdom.

SUMMARY

The absence of government from the arts in the United States is offset by the fact that private enterprise and individual donors invest heavily in the arts.

Individual donors give to social causes based on their personal tastes and preferences, while in the case of a foundation the choice of a cause is determined by its mission and objectives. Corporations that engage in sponsorships, on the other hand, are seeking prestige and an alternative advertising vehicle.

Corporate sponsorship in the cultural sector has become a part of the communications strategy of the cultural or artistic enterprise. Throughout the 1980s, the proportion of the budget allotted to sporting events was gradually transferred to cultural events. Sponsorship is strictly a business decision for executives, who consider it a way to replace the traditional media as a promotional vehicle.

The success of a sponsorship is measured according to various criteria, the most important of which is that the sponsorship meet the objectives of the sponsor. An effective sponsorship involves mutual understanding and respect. The solicitation of sponsorships should aim for the establishment of a long-term business partnership.

QUESTIONS

1. How did the United States develop such a strong tradition of philanthropy?
2. What are the three forms of participation in the private sector market?
3. How important is the private sector in the budgets of cultural organizations?
4. Define the notion of sponsorship.
5. What is a cause-related marketing campaign?
6. How important is the cause-related market in monetary terms?
7. What are the objectives of a sponsor?
8. How is the decision to sponsor a cultural event made?
9. What are the main selection criteria for corporate sponsors?
10. How does one make a successful sponsorship application?
11. Why is the period following the event important for a sponsor?
12. What are the main risks associated with the sponsorship system?

Notes

1. Canadian Conference of the Arts/Conférence canadienne des Arts. *Useful Statistics.* http://www.ccarts.ca/en/advocacy/publications/toolkits/documents/UsefulStatsENG_000.pdf., p. 8.

2. Brown, M.S., ed. 2005. *Giving USA 2005: The Annual Report on Philanthropy for the Year 2004,* 50th ed. Indianapolis: Giving USA Foundation, p. 149–151, 90. See also Opera America, http://www.operaam.org/

3. See http://www.operaam.org/ and http://tcg.org/

4. Shuster, J., and M. Davidson. 1985. *Supporting the Arts: An International Comparative Study.* Cambridge, MA: Department of Urban Studies and Planning, Massachusetts Institute of Technology.

5. Brown, M.S., ed. 2005. *Giving USA 2005: The Annual Report on Philanthropy for the Year 2004,* 50th ed. Indianapolis: Giving USA Foundation, p. 23.

6. Ibid., p. 21.

7. Toppe, Christopher M., Arthur D. Kirsch and Jocabel Michel. 2002. *2001 Giving and Volunteering in the United States: Findings from a National Survey.* Washington: Independent Sector, p. 18, 106.

8. "Prologue." http:\\www.fundwell.com

9. de Tocqueville, A. 1840. *Democracy in America,* Vol. 2: *Relation of Civil to Political Associations.* http://xroads.virginia.edu/~HYPER/DETOC/home.html.edu/

10. Brooks Hopkins, K., and C. Stolper Friedman. 1997. *Successful Fundraising for Arts and Cultural Organizations,* 2nd ed. Phoenix: Oryx Press, p. xiv.

11. Ibid.

12. See IEG Network. http://www.sponsorship.com/forum/glossary.html

13. Ibid.

14. http://www.sponsorship.com/learn/growthadvertising.asp

15. *IEG Sponsorship Report,* Vol. 22, N° 24 (December 22, 2003).

16. Ibid.

17. *Cone Cause Related Marketing.* http://www.conenet.com/website/crm/index.htm

18. "Prologue." http:\\www.fundwell.com. See also the Field Museum Web site. http://www.field-museum.org/museum_info/press/press_sue_timeline.htm

19. See Romesch Ratnesar, "Doing Well by Doing Good." *New Republic,* January 6, 1997, p. 4.

20. *1999 Cone/Roper Cause Related Trends Report: The Evolution of Cause Branding.* Boston: Cone, Inc., 1999. http://www.roper.com/news/content/news115.htm

21. Fisher, V., and R. Brouillet. 1990. *Les commandites : la pub de demain.* Montreal: Éditions Saint-Martin, p. 15.

22. IEG Network. http://www.sponsorship.com/forum/FAQ.html

23. See Lesa Ukman, *Six Attributes of the Successful Proposal.* IEG Network, December 6, 2001. http://www.sponsorship.com/slearn/successfulproposal.asp

24. Hammack, D.C., and D. Young, eds. 1993. *Non-profit Organizations in a Market Economy.* San Francisco: Jossey-Bass, p. 300–301.

25. McClintock, N. 1996. "Why You Need a Sponsorship Policy and How to Get One." *Front and Centre,* Vol. 3, n° 5 (September), p. 12–13. Distributed by the Canadian Centre for Philanthropy. http://www.ccp.ca/information/documents/fc102.htm

For Further Reference

Fishel, D. 2002. "Australian Philanthropy and the Arts: How Does It Compare?" *International Journal of Arts* Management, Vol. 4, n° 2 (Winter), p. 9–16.

Grey, A.-M., and K. Skıldum-Reıd. 2003. *The Sponsorship Seeker's Toolkit,* 2nd ed. Sydney: McGraw-Hill.

Kelly, Kathleen S. 1998. *Effective Fund-Raising Management.* Mahwah, NJ: Lawrence Erlbaum.

Martin, P. 2003. *Made Possible By: Succeeding with Sponsorship. A Guide for Nonprofits.* San Francisco: Jossey-Bass.

Martorella, R., ed. 1996. *Art and Business: An International Perspective on Sponsorship.* Westport, CT: Praeger.

McNicholas, B. 2004. "Arts, Culture and Business: A Relationship Transformation, a Nascent Field." *International Journal of Arts Management,* Vol. 7, n° 1 (Fall), p. 57–69.

Mulcahy, K. 1999. "Cultural Patronage in the United States." *International Journal of Arts Management,* Vol. 2, n° 1 (Fall), p. 53–58.

Sauvanet, N. 1999. "Sponsorship in France." *International Journal of Arts Management,* Vol. 2, n° 1 (Fall), p. 59–63.

Skinner, B.E., and V. Rukavina. 2003. *Event Sponsorship.* New York: John Wiley.

PLAN

Chapter 6

Segmentation and Positioning

by Jacques Nantel

OBJECTIVES

- Understand fully the concept of segmentation and its application within the context of arts management
- Distinguish between segmentation bases and descriptors
- Comprehend the importance of segmentation to a manager in the arts milieu
- Understand the concept of positioning in terms of both competitors and target segments

INTRODUCTION

In order to gain a clear picture of what their consumers are looking for and to develop effective marketing strategies, marketing managers may resort to market segmentation. This chapter explores the principles of segmentation and highlights its different functions, while explaining how managers can identify the different market segments for their product.

The main strengths and weaknesses are described, as are the different segmentation techniques that allow marketing managers to define a clear position for their products as well as for the company as a whole.

6.1 DEFINITION OF SEGMENTATION

Segmentation is probably the most basic yet most misunderstood marketing principle.

While cultural enterprises target several markets, these markets have one characteristic in common: they are all composed of consumption units with similar although not identical needs. Consequently, it is nearly always possible, though not necessarily desirable, to analyze a market by breaking it down into subgroups. This separation of the units that make up a market is called segmentation. The needs of each subgroup are homogeneous but the various subgroups are heterogeneous in terms of their needs.

The book market, for example, could be considered a market made up of consumers who share an interest in reading. This interest is demonstrated by their purchasing of books. Although accurate, this description does not help the marketing manager very much. Indeed, the subgroups that form this market could be described using many different variables, including type of book sought (novel, biography, science fiction) and reason for purchase (studies, leisure, personal development, social visibility).

Weekly magazines and newspapers do not target the same clientele, yet they all try to meet similar needs (information or entertainment). The common trait, or common denominator, for these publications is adaptation to the needs of specific segments of the population. Magazines such as *Time*, *Paris Match*, and *Maclean's* and weekly newspapers such as Montreal's *Voir* or Toronto's *Now* do not necessarily reach the same readership. The readership of *Time* could be described as English-speaking and interested in international news, the readership of *Paris Match* as French-speaking and interested in national news in France, and the readership of *Maclean's* as English-speaking and interested in national news in Canada. *Voir* and *Now* are intended for people interested in the local cultural scene. This thumbnail sketch helps us to visualize what we mean by "market segmentation."

If we look at stage productions as a market, we see how it could be divided according to genre – for example, opera, ballet, and theatre. This classification may be justified from the producer's viewpoint, but it is not relevant in terms of target segments. Consumers will likely find Verdi's *La Traviata* more similar to a play such as *Romeo and Juliet* than to an opera such as *Wozzeck*! In other words, the first two works may target the same segment, which is different from the target segment of the third.

6.2 THE FUNCTIONS OF SEGMENTATION

Market segmentation can fulfil two important functions. The application of the principle of segmentation forces any company to analyze systematically the different needs expressed by its markets. In other words, here the function of segmentation leads companies to perform in-depth market studies to determine the degree to which the demand is really homogeneous. Using the results of this type of analysis, the marketing specialist may decide to attack one or several segments, or the market as a whole.

The second function of segmentation is to provide a strategy stemming from an analysis of the market structure. This strategy is called positioning the product. There are basically two types of positioning. The first is product differentiation, which seeks to define the position a company's product should have vis-à-vis the competitor's product. Quebec's summer-theatre market presents an interesting example of product differentiation. These theatres often perform the same repertoire yet are distinguishable by location or by special meal and/or accommodation packages. In this case, the target segment is often the same, so each company will try to outdo the others, even by just a little, to attract that clientele. The second type of positioning is of particular interest to us. This type of positioning is closely linked to the principle of segmentation and attempts to offer consumers within a particular segment a product that meets their needs as closely as possible. In short, this form of positioning strives to define its product(s) according to the demands expressed by one or several segments. An example of this form of positioning would be the variety and diversity of musical groups: a baroque quartet, a chamber orchestra, an electroacoustic ensemble, and a full symphony orchestra do not all target the same audience. In fact, a symphony will even offer several combinations of concerts in order to reach different segments.

> **Example 6.1**
> ## The River Run Centre: Targeting Schoolchildren
>
> Linamar for the Performing Arts began at the River Run Centre in Guelph, Ontario, in fall 2000, when one of the Centre's patrons suggested to general manager Rob Mackay that in order to achieve success, the theatre would have to bring in schoolchildren.
>
> With the support of a local corporation, Linamar, a theatre education program was developed for children in Grades 1 through 8. Each child living in Guelph attends the theatre twice a year for free.
>
> Over the course of each child's 16 visits, efforts are made to ensure that his or her experience at the River Run Centre is as broad as possible: classical music, theatre, world music, contemporary dance, spoken word, Aboriginal performances. Teachers' guides are designed with a view to helping children better understand why they liked or disliked a particular performance as well as what to expect when they enter the theatre, when to applaud, and how to leave to go to the bathroom. As a side benefit, many adults who had never visited the theatre before are now regular Linamar attendees with their children. Teachers have remarked that at each performance they gain a new idea for teaching the arts back in their classroom.
>
> *Source:* William D. Poole, Director, Centre for Cultural Management, University of Waterloo, Canada.

6.3 MARKET STUDIES AND SEGMENTATION

Although conceptually the principle of market segmentation may seem simple, in practice defining the segments can be problematic. Much of this chapter is devoted to the various approaches used in defining a market segment. Of course, no one can simply decide to "segment" a market. All that any business can do is see if the market is indeed segmented – that is, whether or not there are different types of needs. Only after the marketing manager has a good grasp of the company's market structure can decisions about appropriate marketing strategies be made. In this respect, an accurate reading of the market structure is vital, since a poor analysis may easily lead a company to commit two types of errors, which, if applied to a strategy, could spell corporate disaster.

The first error is to assume that the market is segmented when in reality it is not. This reading of the situation might prompt an organization to develop new products when the original product is sufficient, thereby mobilizing human and financial resources unnecessarily.

The second error is to consider the market uniform when in reality it is made up of various segments. Under this impression, a company might offer a product designed to please everyone and no one. Since the product is not really suited to anyone, it would end up at the bottom of the heap, under products better suited to the specific needs of target segments.

Conversely, an accurate definition of the target market structure will assist the manager in crafting the company's marketing strategy.

6.4 DEFINING SEGMENTS

It stands to reason that an effective marketing strategy is based on an excellent understanding of the target market's structure. In other words, a marketing manager asks the following questions in drafting the optimal strategy: Is the market segmented? If so, what are the segments? The answers to these questions should enable a manager to create better strategies.

There are five essential conditions to be met in defining segments:
1) The response to marketing pressures (current or potential) in the market must vary from one segment to the next.
2) The segment must be definable in such a way as to guide corporate strategies.
3) The segment must be quantifiable.
4) The segment must be profitable.
5) The segment must be relatively stable over time.

6.4.1 Variations in Response to Marketing Pressures from One Segment to Another

In order to test whether or not a market is composed of segments, a marketing manager must first ensure that all the consumers do not have the same needs and that the needs are expressed through different behaviours. In most markets, consumers react differently to the products offered. In this book, segmentation will be based on the different ways of dividing a market in order to group the various consumer reactions to market pressures.[1] The more segmentation is based on consumer behaviours, the more strategically useful it becomes. There are five basic determinants of market segmentation: the purchaser/non-purchaser dichotomy, frequency, loyalty, satisfaction, and preferred brand or product.

The Purchaser/Non-purchaser Dichotomy

This dichotomy is the most basic way of categorizing consumers. In fact, the purchaser/non-purchaser dichotomy could be said to reflect two segments, each having a different response to market pressures. All markets would therefore be composed of at least two segments. This way of looking at a market may help a company create new products.

Frequency or Rate of Consumption

Like the purchaser/non-purchaser dichotomy, the market for a cultural product can be divided according to the relative rate of consumption. In addition, there is a major difference in the demand among various competing prod-

---

Example 6.2
The Sydney Opera House: Micromarketing for Ethnic Groups

When presenting a play about an Indian-Australian growing up in Australia, the Sydney Opera House (SOH) wished to target the Indian community. The SOH knew little about this community (its location, its media, its social conventions) and, at the same time, had anecdotal evidence that many non-English-speaking communities knew little of the SOH (how to get there, how much it cost to attend). For example, even when community members knew about a relevant production they did not feel comfortable dealing with the SOH box office.

The solution was to employ a community leader (who was not a professional marketer) as a marketing coordinator for the community. This person placed notices in the local first-language press and in community centres, and, more importantly, spoke directly to community opinion leaders to inform them about the play and explain what it was about – and how to get to the theatre.

The coordinator helped to demystify the whole experience for the group, and, more importantly, "sold" tickets to a particular "community" performance by collecting names and money on behalf of both parties. The seats were reserved with the SOH box office and the sales were reconciled on the evening of the performance when the coordinator, along with the group, arrived at the theatre.

Source: Stephen Boyle, Associate Director, Arts and Cultural Management Program, University of South Australia and Craig Cooper, Assistant Producer, The Studio, Sydney Opera House, Sydney, Australia.

---

ucts as well as within the demand for each product in terms of frequency of purchase. For example, we can say that in terms of volume (frequency) of purchase, the theatre market is segmented. This statement alone would be of little use, though, without data on who attended the theatre, which theatre, and why. As we will see below, there is a second component to segmentation – descriptors. This component is vital to any serious discussion of marketing strategy.

Degree of Product or Brand Loyalty

The third way of dividing a market relates to the degree of loyalty consumers show for a specific cultural product – that is, for a particular company or troupe. The impulsiveness or consistency revealed by consumers through their purchasing behaviour often provides an excellent basis for segmentation, since it categorizes consumers according to their sensitivity to various marketing pressures. In terms of cultural products, subscriptions, especially regular subscriptions, allow for a greater understanding of consumer behaviour.

The Consumer's Level of Satisfaction

A fourth way of looking at segments is to consider variations in the level of satisfaction expressed by the consumer. This measurement is related to the first three, since the act of purchasing or not purchasing, the volume or frequency of consumption, and brand or product loyalty are all directly or indirectly related to the level of satisfaction expressed by the consumer.[2] This point is especially interesting when spin-off products are launched, since these products are designed first and foremost for consumers who are satisfied with the original product. An analysis of the clientele based on its level of satisfaction also allows for the creation and positioning of new products that meet the needs of consumers who are dissatisfied with products currently on the market.

The Preferred Brand or Type of Product

The last way of looking at market segmentation is to analyze variations in preference with regard to different products or brands. A study of preferences in musical styles (Table 6.1) published in the United States provides a good example of segmentation according to type of product. This approach is especially well suited to situations where there are several rival brands – for instance, movie theatres or different theatre companies. Unlike other approaches, this one is not limited to existing products, but extends to variations in the demand for a hypothetical product. The market study could also introduce the new product (as an idea, a suggestion, or a fait accompli) to consumers so that they can give their opinions. If need be, the study could also compare similar cultural products already familiar to the consumers.

6.4.2 Segment Description

Defining a segment according to an existing variation in demand is an essential step in segmentation; however, if that variation is non-existent, segmenta-

---

Table 6.1
Music Preferences (USA)

Type of music	Liked in 1997 (%)	Liked best in 1997 (%)
Country-Western	64.6	20.7
Rock	59.8	18.2
Hymns or gospel	57.6	13.8
No particular type	NA	7.7
Classical/chamber	47.5	6.7
Mood or easy listening	67.1	5.9
Jazz	48.4	4.9
Blues or rhythm & blues	62.7	4.8
Latin, Spanish, salsa	28.9	3.9
Big-band	45.0	2.8
Rap	16.8	1.9
Operetta or show tunes	44.2	1.8
New Age	30.9	1.5
Soul	40.0	1.4
Contemporary folk	37.6	1.1
Reggae	31.6	0.8
Ethnic/national traditional	30.6	0.8
Bluegrass	42.1	0.7
Opera	18.8	0.6
Parade or marching band	32.1	0.2
Barbershop	22.4	0.1
Choral or glee club	26.0	0.1

Source: National Endowment for the Arts. 1997. *Survey of Public Participation in the Arts: Summary Report.* p. 47.

tion is obviously impossible. Although defining a segment is essential, it is far from adequate. Defining segments by consumer profile alone would be redundant in terms of strategic planning. In other words, saying that a market may be made up of non-purchasers, loyal purchasers, or large-volume purchasers is not wrong, but limiting the description to a single system of classification is of little practical use. It is far more important to find descriptors for the different segments.

A descriptor is a variable that essentially characterizes a segment. Its first purpose is to answer the key questions of who and why. In other words, who is or is not going to the theatre, and why? Who regularly buys a season subscription to the opera, and who only occasionally buys a single ticket, and why? Why do some people go to the theatre often, whereas others go only once in a while? Which consumers are ready and which are not ready to take a risk by seeing an avant-garde work?

In short, descriptors help characterize and quantify segments. There are almost as many descriptors as there are adjectives in the dictionary; however, researchers tend to limit themselves to previously effective or revealing ones. These descriptors may be grouped as follows: geographic, sociodemographic, psychographic, and related to the benefits sought by consumers.

Geographic Descriptors

Geography is one of the most commonly used descriptors in market segmentation. Geographic differences often reflect cultural, climatic, or environmental differences. What makes geographic descriptors interesting is the fact that they enable marketing managers and researchers to develop and visualize the profile for various consumers. Joel Garreau, former publisher of the *Washington Post*, divides North America into nine large regions, each of which he considers a nation.[3] He believes that the cultural differences from one region to the next influence consumer profiles. According to Garreau, New England, including Canada's Atlantic provinces, is a region that has little in common with the region he calls Ecotopia, located west of the Rocky Mountains, and the Sierra Nevada (extending from Anchorage in the north to Point Conception in the south). One of Garreau's nine regions is Quebec province; another comprises parts of Canada plus that part of the United States that stretches from the Canadian border in the north to the Mexican border in the south and from Denver in the east to the Sierra Nevada in the west.

Geographic descriptors are appropriate tools for defining and estimating the segments that make up a market. Although easy to use – perhaps too easy – geographic descriptors are not problem-free. The main problem lies in the fact that many executives assume that their market is segmented and that this segmentation can be best described using geographic variables.

In the broad area of cultural products, the distinction between a large city and a region is commonly used. This distinction is accurate only if the urban market for the cultural product in question is characterized by a demand different from that in the surrounding region(s). Since many cultural organizations lack the resources to undertake a study of geographic descriptors, they may fall into the trap of assuming that there is a distinction between a city and its surrounding region(s) and basing their marketing strategies on that unfounded assumption. This potentially serious error in judgement could result in a company limiting its marketing efforts to a specific part of the territory and thereby completely overlooking a potentially rewarding market segment.

Sociodemographic Descriptors

Sociodemographic descriptors are all the variables used to describe or quantify the composition of a society, including age, sex, level of education, income, ethnic background, number of children, language, religion, type of dwelling, and profession. These descriptors are probably the most frequently used in segmentation, since they enable a company to personalize its clientele more easily. Not only do they describe segments in easily understood terms, but they also rely on national census data, which means they can give an idea of a market's potential.

Although easy to use, sociodemographic descriptors are not without drawbacks. Some find them inadequate for describing segments typical of certain markets, particularly in areas where inter-brand discrimination is involved. Winter[4] points out some of the main flaws in sociodemographic descriptors. First, many marketing managers rely on these easy-to-use descriptors, which do not always reflect the market. Second, sociodemographic descriptors only partially fulfil a descriptive function – that is, they describe – only who buys. Since they cannot explain why a large segment adopts a certain behaviour, they are of limited use in developing a corporate marketing strategy. For example, regardless of whether the studies are conducted in North America, Eastern Europe, Western Europe, or Australia, their findings consistently show that consumers of high art are better educated and more affluent than the average consumer; thus, for a company operating in this market, segmentation based on sociodemographic descriptors is not very helpful. All in all, sociodemographic descriptors are useful for "personifying" the targeted segment(s), but often they are unable to provide the marketing professional with all the information needed to develop a proper corporate marketing strategy. Other descriptors, such as psychographic ones, may fill the gaps.

Psychographic Descriptors

Some people decide to buy a new product as soon as it hits the shelves, while others are concerned about the image they will project by attending a particular event. Obviously, for some products, these people have a consumer profile unlike the average. However, their consumer behaviour cannot be attributed to age, sex, income, or region. Variations in preference or choice for many products simply cannot be explained using sociodemographic or geographic descriptors alone, but are related to variables that involve values and opinions. These variables have been named "psychographic descriptors."

Lazer[5] first introduced the concept of psychographic descriptors, which was later developed by Weels.[6] This type of descriptor can be divided into two broad categories. The first is linked to personality and draws upon the psychological research of Allport,[7] Cattel,[8] and Murray.[9] Certain personality tests are used in marketing to categorize consumers according to differences in their behaviour. In fact, many studies have tried to link the use of certain products to specific personality traits. For example, Tucker and Painter[10] observed that men who easily adopted new fashions in clothing were more sociable and had more influence on their peers than average. Similarly, many studies, including that of Robertson and Myers,[11] have used personality traits to group individuals in terms of the speed with which they would adopt a new product.

The second category of psychographic descriptors includes lifestyle analysis, which assumes that individuals can be grouped according to the activities they engage in, opinions they hold, and interests they show. Consumers are usually asked a battery of questions on activities, opinions, and interests. In fact, this test is often called an AOI test or inventory. The questions touch upon many subjects, ranging from shopping and leisure to economic and political views. Through general or product-specific questionnaires, several lifestyle analyses have been performed. Using statistical analysis, consumers are grouped by relatively homogeneous AOI profiles. These profiles are then tested to see if they enable researchers to pinpoint accurately the differences in levels of demand. These levels are usually evaluated according to preference in terms of competing brands.

In most cases, psychographic profiles are based on questionnaires given or sent randomly to a sampling of consumers. These questionnaires are very long and usually include a section describing the consumer profile in terms of numerous products, a media-consumption profile, a sociodemographic profile, and a psychological profile based on a series of questions related to consumer values in terms of activities, opinions, and interests.

Marketing professionals should always bear in mind that psychographic segmentation based on AOI and values does have certain weak points.[12] The first is a lack of clear definitions and an absence of a valid theoretical framework. The second lies in the fact that the questions asked are often formulated by the researchers. If the questions are changed, the profiles and groupings are automatically modified. The third is the way these profiles are drawn up using cluster analysis. Of all the multidimensional techniques available, this one is the weakest. Just one blip in the algorithm or a difference in computer capacity may completely upset the configuration of the profiles. A fourth weak spot lies in the length of the questionnaires normally used. One questionnaire can ask over 300 questions in the psychographic section alone. The extent to which the respondents are representative is questionable, since people who are prepared to spend over an hour on a survey may not reflect the general public. Although this last point may be said of all surveys, the problem becomes more serious if the researcher wants to establish a psychographic profile of the society. The fifth weakness is the survey's lack of discriminatory power. In this sense, the number of studies showing the rate of consumption for a product or brand as more or less equal from one lifestyle to another is especially important.

Descriptors Based on Benefits

Of all the descriptors, those based on benefits sought best describe buying patterns. These descriptors answer the question, Why are there different levels of demand in the same market? According to the principle that all consumers do not buy the same type of product for the same reason, this approach attempts to group consumers who want the same benefits from the same product. The market can therefore be divided into as many segments as there are benefits or combinations of benefits sought. From a strategic viewpoint, benefit segmentation is especially important since it often gives some shape to the notion of market positioning.

In the area of cultural products, several studies have attempted to define art consumer segments. Steinberg, Miaoulis, and Lloyd[13] have set out seven segments, four of which describe consumers who do not go to shows (consumers concerned about safety, consumers more involved with their children, hedonists, and pragmatists). The other three segments describe consumers who do go to shows ("culture vultures," those seeking entertainment, those looking for an aesthetic experience). In terms of cultural and artistic products, the greater the benefit segmentation, the more useful the segmentation is to marketing managers. In other words, a better grasp of the specific benefits consumers sought by leads to better marketing strategies.

This form of segmentation, first introduced by Haley,[14] remains useful for companies seeking their own niche in the marketplace. The main advantage of this form of segmentation is that it sets out the reasons behind different levels of preference in a market. Once a corporation has this kind of reading of its market, it can try to enhance its product so that it corresponds better to the benefits sought by consumers. A product-oriented company will seek to offer benefits on aspects other than the artistic product itself.

This chapter covers the most important ways of describing segments. Naturally, there are other descriptors, but those presented here are the most pertinent to any analysis of the cultural-product market. Of course, market segmentation may use a combination of descriptors. In practice, the most important decision is the choice of descriptors. Why is one type of descriptor selected rather than another? At first glance, the answer appears simple, since a marketing manager could simply choose the descriptors that describe most effectively the different levels of demand found in the particular market. In practice, however, choosing descriptors is not always so easy. An excellent knowledge of the target market is vital to any segmentation study. On the basis of this study, a company can always try to divide its market using specific descriptors and thereby try to discover the structure of the market and profitable market opportunities.

Many companies seem to work backwards in their segmentation studies. Rather than start by analyzing the various levels of demand for their product, they start by segmenting their market based on descriptors in order to see if the groups offer different levels of demand. There is nothing wrong with this approach as long as real differences in the levels of demand are found. In many cases, intuitive knowledge of the market may make this kind of approach desirable. However, it is fraught with weaknesses if there is no real difference in the level of demand. An executive may try out a lot of descriptors before realizing that none of them actually reveals differences in consumer behaviour. Moreover, some managers might even be convinced that the descriptors used are adequate when they do not describe the reality of the market at all. In these cases, companies often adapt their product to segments that are basically similar.

In terms of cultural products, creation plays a key role; as a result, a product can rarely be adapted to the needs or demands of a segment, and even less often to some average of several segments. Yet it is important for a marketing manager to look at the finished cultural product and consider the characteristics of whatever segment might be most interested in it.

6.4.3 Quantifying Segments

Describing the profile of each segment within a market is not enough; the size of each segment is also needed. Quantifying segments – in other words, determining the exact number of people per segment and the potential revenue per segment – is the third prerequisite for effective segmentation. Evaluating segments is easier if segmentation is based on sociodemographic descriptors.

Once the segments are defined in these terms, it is relatively easy to use secondary sources, such as a national statistics bureau (Statistics Canada, US Census Bureau, Australian Bureau of Statistics), to analyze the number of individuals or companies that make up the segments. It is a different story when starting with psychographic variables, which often require the marketing specialist to do market studies based on scientific samplings to determine the number of individuals in a given segment.

The segments formed must be not only quantifiable but also useful. Segmentation is effective only inasmuch as it enables a marketing manager to create a different and effective marketing plan for each segment. In this respect, sociodemographic variables are not particularly useful. Even though they may help to put a human face on a segment, they are limited in their ability to explain behaviour. Hence, descriptors related to benefits and to usage are probably the most useful.

The combination of the last two criteria demonstrates one of the paradoxes of segmentation studies. Often, a descriptor enables the researcher to quantify segments quite easily but the segments are not useful in developing sophisticated strategies. This is often true of sociodemographic descriptors. Conversely, descriptors related to the benefits sought may pinpoint accurate segments, but do not quantify them. Ideally, segmentation is based on a blend of several descriptors.

6.4.4 Profitability of Segments

An effective segment is a profitable segment. Profitability is the fourth essential condition for effective segmentation. As a rule, if a company is interested in a specific segment, it has seen some potential profit there. These varying levels of demand may, in turn, be expressed in terms of the probability of buying. Through a formula that multiplies the probability of purchase by the number of individuals per segment and by the expected average purchase, the marketing manager obtains the expected revenue per segment. Since adaptation of a corporate marketing strategy to a specific segment normally entails additional expense, product or service redesign, and adaptation of advertising and possibly distribution, the company must ensure that the earnings generated by that segment will exceed those expenses. Companies may occasionally integrate similar segments in order to ensure profitability. Of course, the dynamics of cultural markets are slightly different since corporate earnings do not come from consumers only, but also come from sponsors and government granting agencies.

Example 6.3
Mercadante Theatre of Naples: Defining and Targeting Two Audience Segments

In 2003 the management of the Mercadante Theatre in Naples asked itself what kind of audience it needed in order to sell tickets without losing sight of the theatre's mission. The answer was that there is no such audience.

The theatre then settled on different marketing strategies for two target audiences: middle-aged high school or university graduates with middle to high incomes; and young people under 30, including high school and university students.

For the first target segment, management decided not to modify its current marketing strategy. For the second target segment, it came up with a new system: the prepaid card.

This new system would replace the traditional subscription only in the case of young people, who tend to dislike the inflexibility of the subscription system.

During the 2004/05 season, the card allowed young people to attend five performances for €50, with the flexibility of not having to choose plays in advance: they simply had to call the box office and book a seat; the card could be used by anyone at any time, and by more than one person at a time.

The prepaid card represents policy innovation at three levels: (a) pricing – 50% discount on the ticket price; (b) availability – it is sold at the beginning of the season through the box office, over the Internet, or by telephone; and (c) promotion – it is modern, appealing, and newsworthy.

During the second season the theatre introduced two separate cards: one for adults and one for young people – the same concept but different prices.

The marketing strategies of the Mercadante Theatre have been remarkably successful. The prepaid cards sold out in just three days. The theatre has met a significant challenge: it has increased its advance sales and gained a new, young audience, yet without experiencing a decrease in its traditional subscriptions.

Source: Fabiana Sciarelli, Professor, University of Naples "Federico II" and University of Perugia, Naples, Italy.

6.4.5 Segment Stability over Time

The fifth and last condition for effective segmentation is the assurance (albeit relative) that the segments will remain stable long enough for the company to turn a profit on the additional investment that an adopted marketing strategy may imply. If market needs evolve quickly, some forms of segmentation may no longer be suitable. This is often the case with segmentation that relies upon descriptors related to benefits, especially in rapidly growing sectors like the fashion world. In these cases, a marketing manager must not only ensure that the segments exist and are indeed profitable, but also try to determine their life span.

6.5   SEGMENTATION TECHNIQUES

How do marketing professionals use the five essential conditions described above to define which segments make up their market? In this section, on segmentation techniques, it is important to remember that there are two broad categories: "a priori" and "cluster-based."

6.5.1 A Priori Segmentation

Using the a priori technique, a manager assumes that one or several descriptors will be adequate to explain variations in needs, preferences, or behaviours observed. In the market, the hypotheses behind these assumptions may stem from a range of sources that include gut feelings, secondary sources, and focus-group sessions. The marketing manager will use the results gathered during this first stage to determine whether or not the market is segmented and whether or not these segments may be described using the variables chosen. A scientific analysis of the market is necessary. Once the market has been divided according to the descriptors selected, the marketing manager can see if there really are different levels of demand. Should this be the case, the manager can decide which segment(s) to attack according to the five conditions presented above.

The advantage of this approach to segmentation is that it is analytically simple. In fact, it tests only specific hypotheses. For example, if a company believes that the levels of demand for a new symphony orchestra in a given city could vary according to age, benefits, and the novelty of the repertoire offered, the company could test its hypothesis before proceeding. The disadvantage inherent in this approach is that different levels of demand may be recognized but not explained by the descriptors the marketing manager has chosen, in which case the manager must develop new hypotheses regarding the descriptors which could explain these differences. The resulting hypothesis would then have to be tested, just as the previous one was.

6.5.2 Cluster-Based Segmentation

A manager using this type of segmentation must have some knowledge of the market structure, knowledge that is still based on either research or intuition. Nevertheless, it does not require strictly formulated hypotheses in terms of the nature of the descriptors that might help explain segment formation. In this approach, a market study is carried out to survey consumers on many aspects, including most of the segmentation bases and descriptors. Multidimensional techniques, such as cluster analysis or correspondence analysis, are then applied to define groups of individuals (thus the term cluster-based). Each group presents a certain internal homogeneity in terms of its level of demand, as well as a certain heterogeneity in terms of the other groups. Analysis follows, with some comparison of the groups that enables the marketing manager to ascertain whether these needs and behaviours are indeed different. If they are, some of the descriptors used in the market study are reused to further describe these needs and behaviours. The advantage of this approach is that it allows the marketing manager to discover innovative ways of defining segments without being restricted by predetermined patterns. The disadvantage lies in its length and cost in comparison with the first approach, which may give convincing results in the initial stages. Nevertheless, the cluster-based approach is particularly useful when applied to segmentation according to psychographic descriptors and descriptors related to benefits or usage.

6.6 FUNCTIONAL SEGMENT PROFILES

No matter which approach is used, the segments defined by a segmentation study must meet the five conditions given in section 6.4. Once a market is broken down into segments that 1) represent different levels of demand, 2) may be described using the questions "who" and "what," 3) are or may prove to be useful and quantifiable, 4) are or may be profitable, and 5) offer some temporal stability, those segments may be discussed in terms of their functional profiles. As a result, the challenges faced by a manager in the cultural milieu relate not to defining segments but to finding segments for a particular cultural product. Once this has been accomplished, the wise marketing manager will use positioning to implement a successful marketing strategy.

6.7 POSITIONING IN MARKETING

While market segmentation may be considered an analytical concept, positioning a product is seen as a strategic concept. In other words, once a market structure is well understood, a company may decide on its strategic positioning. Two types of positioning are possible and are not mutually exclusive. The first is positioning in terms of one or more segments; the second is positioning against the competition.

Figure 6.1 illustrates the way in which a company decides on the strategic positioning of its product. As we can see, the two principal factors guiding the company's decision are the structure of the market – the segments of which it is composed, and the positioning of the competition.

6.7.1 Positioning by Segment

As suggested above, a company may choose to adapt its strategy to the needs of one segment only. This kind of strategy, known as the "concentrated marketing strategy," is highly recommended for cultural organizations, which, given their limited resources and unique mission, are well advised to target one particular segment. This type of positioning requires an excellent understanding of the segmentation descriptors that explain consumer preferences and behaviours. In some instances, this type of positioning uses segments defined through sociodemographic variables, as is the case for troupes specializing in children's or teens' theatre. In other cases, this positioning is based on geographical variables. In fact, the term "Off Broadway" means just that. (The notion of a "fringe festival," in contrast, implies that the artistic product is at the margin or edge of mainstream theatre in a given city.) In most cases, though, cultural organizations are positioned by segments defined according to the benefits sought by consumers. For example, a survey conducted by the management of the Powerhouse Museum in Sydney, Australia, revealed that

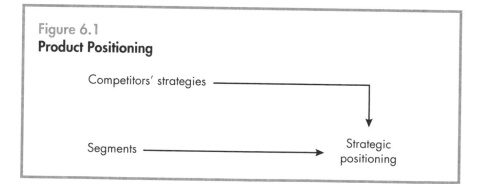

Figure 6.1
Product Positioning

Competitors' strategies

Segments ⟶ Strategic positioning

the public perceived the Powerhouse not as a traditional museum but as a place of discovery offering exciting, hands-on experiences [15]; to the extent that these attributes correspond to the benefits sought by consumers, they can be used in positioning the museum.

Using the data from a study of various cultural products, Nantel and Colbert[16] revealed the key benefits consumers sought from this type of product. Their research involved consumers matching up 16 cultural products and 13 adjectives commonly used by theatre and art critics. Figure 6.2 gives a perceptual map of the key benefits sought by show-going consumers. As we can see, the benefits selected have been divided into four broad categories along two main axes. The horizontal axis lists benefits sought along a continuum ranging from "entertaining" to "adds to my cultural knowledge," "enriching," and "prestigious." The continuum on the vertical axis runs from "relaxing" to "exciting." It is no accident that "change of pace" lies in the centre

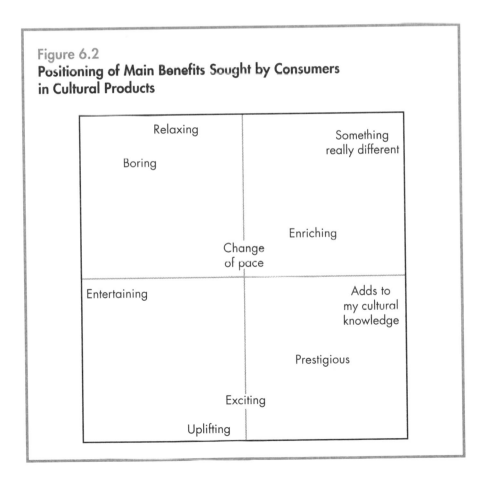

Figure 6.2
Positioning of Main Benefits Sought by Consumers in Cultural Products

Relaxing

Something really different

Boring

Enriching

Change of pace

Entertaining

Adds to my cultural knowledge

Prestigious

Exciting

Uplifting

of the illustration. This benefit is essential to every type of cultural product. This classification of benefits allows a marketing manager to define, albeit roughly, four segments based on the benefits sought. There are consumers who want relaxing and enriching activities and others who want relaxing yet entertaining activities. Still other consumers seek exciting and enriching activities, whereas others want exciting and entertaining activities. Of course, a single consumer may look for one benefit in one circumstance and another benefit in other circumstances. Some consumers may limit their choice systematically to activities offering the same benefits, while other consumers may prefer a variety of benefits. All of these possibilities reveal the sometimes complementary, sometimes competitive nature of various cultural products. Different producers offering similar benefits could form an association to provide a combination of activities for consumers wishing to concentrate their cultural activities in one area. Conversely, an association of products with different benefits would be more suitable for a segment of consumers seeking to diversify their range of cultural outings.

The 16 products analyzed were then positioned according to these benefits and the four segments described in the preceding paragraph. Figure 6.3 illustrates their positioning. Certain products, such as pop music and musical comedy, seem to offer similar benefits. On the other hand, ballet and stand-up comedy are in opposite corners, so to speak.

The positioning of a cultural product according to the benefits offered and, initially, the segments targeted enables a marketing manager to pinpoint which products are key competitors and which ones are potential allies. These examples reveal the extent to which a positioning strategy is the result of a keen understanding of the features and benefits sought by consumers. Without this knowledge, positioning becomes a theoretical exercise of little use in shaping corporate strategy. Once again, as seen in Chapter 4, it is very important to know which criteria consumers actually use in making their choices.

Once product attributes have been determined, positioning may take place using perception, preference, or behaviour. From a technical point of view, this type of positioning may be based on various strategic approaches. However, a manager must go beyond the type of positioning selected and remember that this exercise can be profitable only if it indicates the optimal way to market the product. This optimization can occur only if the manager knows which attributes or benefits require action.

6.7.2 Competitive Positioning

A good grasp of the segments targeted by a cultural product increases a manager's ability to position the product. Nevertheless, in many cases several

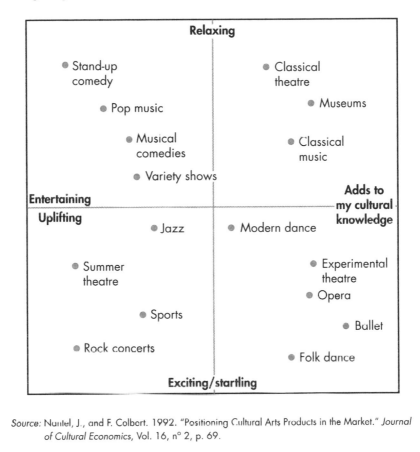

Figure 6.3

Positioning of 16 Cultural Products According to the Main Benefits Sought by Montreal Consumers

Relaxing

● Stand-up comedy

● Classical theatre

● Pop music

● Museums

● Musical comedies

● Classical music

● Variety shows

Entertaining

Adds to my cultural knowledge

Uplifting

● Jazz

● Modern dance

● Summer theatre

● Experimental theatre

● Opera

● Sports

● Ballet

● Rock concerts

● Folk dance

Exciting/startling

Source: Nantel, J., and F. Colbert. 1992. "Positioning Cultural Arts Products in the Market." *Journal of Cultural Economics*, Vol. 16, n° 2, p. 69.

cultural products may serve and target the same segments, hence the same benefits, at the same time. Here is where competitive positioning, also called "product differentiation," proves invaluable. In such cases, the regular consumer must be offered an additional benefit that sets the product purchased apart from the competition. This is a major reason for the success of the BBC Proms Concert, a festival founded in 1895 at London's Royal Albert Hall. From the beginning, the Proms have always focused on both aspects of a concert: the music and the social content. One of the things the spectators appreciate most about the Proms is the low-cost standing room in the arena and the gallery. The arena is the space in front of the orchestra pit where the most expensive seats are usually located. For the Proms, the seats are removed from this area and people are free to sit on the floor or remain standing. The seats are also removed from the gallery, which is located above the balcony and offers the advantage of allowing the consumption of food and beverages before the concert and during the intermission. "The Proms provide the audience with a high quality musical experience, but also an occasion for 'fun'."[17]

Some companies take the opposite tack: instead of trying to differentiate their products, they try to associate them with an existing product. This strategy enables them to benefit from the competitor's image. Movies with titles such as *Fatal Attraction* have bred "me-too" products such as *Fatal Seduction*. In a study on positioning in major Montreal theatres, the average consumer's perception was that two companies, the Rideau Vert and the Théâtre du Nouveau Monde, were very close. This kind of positioning is not necessarily bad if it serves the needs of most consumers and the market can support two competitors considered fairly similar by the average consumer.

SUMMARY

Segmentation plays a pivotal role in the marketing strategy of a cultural organization. Given that a market is not segmented but a market's segments are defined, the role of the segmentation bases and descriptors used should be carefully considered.

"A priori" and "cluster-based" are two broad categories of segmentation.

On a more practical level, segmentation involves the description of operational profiles of segments and the adaptation of segmentation theory to marketing strategy. Here, the notion of positioning comes into play.

In short, segmentation is an ideal conceptual starting point for the strategy-planning process. It is, however, the result of serious, in-depth market analysis, and not a strategy in itself.

QUESTIONS

1. What are the two main functions of segmentation?

2. What are the consequences, for a company, of a poor analysis of market structure?

3. Why would a new theatre troupe be interested in the concepts of segmentation and positioning?

4. Briefly describe the five conditions needed to define segments.

5. Briefly describe the five basic determinants of market segmentation.

6. As the marketing director of a new symphony orchestra in your city, you identify several segments in the market. If you decide to adopt a multiple-positioning strategy, how will your marketing decisions be affected?

7. What are the limitations to using sociodemographic descriptors in marketing?

8. What advantages are there for a publisher in using benefit descriptors?

9. Why is it often preferable to use a blend of descriptors when describing a market segment?

10. What is the difference between "a priori" and "cluster-based" segmentation? What are the advantages and disadvantages of each?

11. Under which circumstances is it better to use one overall marketing strategy? Use an example to support your answer.

Notes

1. Wind, Y. 1978. "Issues and Advances in Segmentation Research." *Journal of Marketing Research*, Vol. 15 (August), p. 317–337; Lilien, G.L., and P. Kotler. 1983. *Marketing Decision Making: A Model-Building Approach*. New York: Harper & Row.

2. Churchill, G.A., and C. Surprenant. 1982. "An Investigation into the Determinants of Consumer Satisfaction." *Journal of Marketing Research*, n° 19 (November), p. 491–504.

3. Garreau, J. 1981. *The Nine Nations of North America*. New York: Avon.

4. Winter, F.W. 1987. "Market Segmentation: A Tactical Approach." *Business Horizon*, Vol. 27, n° 1 (January/February), p. 57–63.

5. Lazer, W. 1963. "Life Style Concepts and Marketing: Toward Scientific Marketing." In *Proceedings of the AMA Winter Conference*, Boston, p. 130–139.

6. Weels, W.D. 1974. "Life Style and Psychographics: Definitions, Uses and Problems." In *Life Style and Psycho-graphics*. Chicago: American Marketing Association, p. 317–363.

7. Allport, G.W. 1961. *Pattern and Growth in Personality*. New York: Rinehart & Winston.

8. Cattel, R.B. 1973. *Personality and Mood*. San Francisco: Jossey-Bass.

9. Murray, H.A. 1960. "Historical Trends in Personality Research." In *Perspectives in Personality Research*, H.P. Davis and J.C. Brengelman, eds. New York: Springer.

10. Tucker, W.T., and J.J. Painter. 1961. "Personality and Product Use." *Journal of Applied Psychology*, Vol. 45 (October), p. 325–339.

11. Robertson, T.S., and J.J. Myers. 1969. "Personality Correlates of Opinion Leadership and Innovative Buying Behavior." *Journal of Marketing Research*, Vol. 6 (May), p. 164–168.

12. See "The Blood Bath in Market Research." *Business Week*, February 1991, p. 72–74; Nantel, J. 1989. "La segmentation, un concept analytique plutôt que stratégique." *Gestion, revue internationale de gestion*, Vol. 14, n° 3 (September), p. 76–82; Kassardjian, H.H., and M.J. Sheffet. "Personality and Consumer Behavior: An Update." In *Perspectives in Consumer Behaviors*, 4th ed., T. Robertson and H.H. Kassardjian, eds. Glenview, IL: Scott, Foresman.

13. Steinberg, M., G. Miaoulis and D. Lloyd. 1982. "Benefit Segmentation Strategies for the Performing Arts." In *An Assessment of Marketing Thought and Practices*, B.J. Walker, ed. Chicago: American Marketing Association, p. 289–293.

14. Haley, R.I. 1968. "Benefit Segmentation: A Decision Oriented Research Tool." *Journal of Marketing*, Vol. 32 (July), p. 30–35.

15. Scott, C. 2000. "Branding: Positioning Museums in the 21st Century." *International Journal of Arts Management*, Vol. 2, n° 3 (Spring), p. 35–39.

16. Nantel, J., and F. Colbert. 1992. "Positioning Cultural Arts Products in the Market." *Journal of Cultural Economics*, Vol. 16, n° 2, p. 63–71.

17. Kolb, B.M. 1998. "Classical Music Concerts Can Be Fun: The Success of BBC Proms." *International Journal of Arts Management*, Vol. 1, n° 1 (Fall), p. 16–24.

For Further Reference

Athanassopoulos, A.D. 2000. "Customer Satisfaction Cues to Support Market Segmentation and Explain Switching Behavior." *Journal of Business Research*, Vol. 47, n° 3 (March), p. 191–207.

Dussart, C. 1986. *Stratégie de marketing*. Boucherville, QC: Gaëtan Morin Editeur.

Kaufman, L., and P.J. Rousseeuv. 1990. *Finding Groups in Data: An Introduction to Cluster Analysis*. New York: John Wiley.

Kozinets, R.V. 1999. "E-tribalized Marketing? The Strategic Implications of Virtual Communities of Consumption." *European Management Journal*, Vol. 17, n° 3 (June), p. 252–264.

Nantel, J. 1989. "La segmentation : un concept analytique plutôt que stratégique." *Gestion, revue internationale de gestion*, Vol. 14, n° 3 (September), p. 76–82.

Statistics Canada. *Market Research Handbook*. Ottawa: Author. Catalogue no. 63-224 (yearly).

Struhl, S.M. 1992. *Market Segmentation*. Chicago: Research Division, American Marketing Association.

Waggoner, R. 1999. "Have You Made a Wrong Turn in Your Approach to Market?" *Journal of Business Strategy*, Vol. 20, n° 6 (November/December), p. 16–21.

Weitz, B.A., and R. Wensley. 1988. *Readings in Strategic Marketing: Analysis, Planning and Implementation*. Chicago: Dryden Press.

Wu, S.-I. 2000. "A New Market Segmentation Variable for Product Design – Functional Requirements." *Journal of International Marketing and Marketing Research*, Vol. 25, n° 1 (February), p. 35–48.

PLAN

Chapter 7

The Price Variable

OBJECTIVES

- Understand the components of the price variable
- Examine the objectives related to this variable
- Describe the main methods of price setting
- Understand the notion of elasticity
- Discuss dynamic pricing and other most common pricing strategies
- Introduce Baumol's Law

INTRODUCTION

This chapter, which deals with the price variable, focuses specifically on price from the perspective of the consumer market. We then look at how companies determine the prices of their products by considering the factors involved in the decision-making process, corporate price objectives, and certain methods that facilitate the decision-making process.

A brief review of the various ways of calculating product costs and profitability follows, with an emphasis on the highly specific context of the arts sector.

We then explain the economic notion of elasticity, which establishes a link between the variation in demand and price, and apply it to other variables within the marketing mix.

If we accept that the demand curve for a product is a combination of smaller curves, each one representing a market segment, we can relate the price variable to market segmentation. At the end of this chapter, the most common pricing strategies, along with the well-known paradox called Baumol's Law, are presented.

7.1 DEFINITION

From the consumer's perspective, price is the amount one must pay to purchase a product or service (including applicable taxes). However, the price paid by the consumer is not necessarily limited to this narrow definition. In calculating the price of a product, one must also take into account the various expenses related to its consumption (transportation, restaurant, babysitter, etc.), the leisure time invested, the risk associated with the purchase, and the physical effort expended by the consumer (travelling, parking, etc.) (see Figure 7.1). Even if a company offers free entry to an event, the consumer must "pay" for the outing in the form of various kinds of effort. Seen from this perspective, then, a product is never really free.

As we saw in Chapter 1, the amount of leisure time available to consumers is not increasing, and may actually be decreasing for certain categories of worker. Consequently, along with disposable income, time for leisure activities and outings has become a precious commodity. To some extent, consumers are required to allocate both their time and their money in accordance with their preferences and their budget.

The risk associated with a purchase is the equivalent of the psychological effort that the purchase requires (Chapter 4) – for example, the social risk of being identified with a particular group, the risk of not understanding or

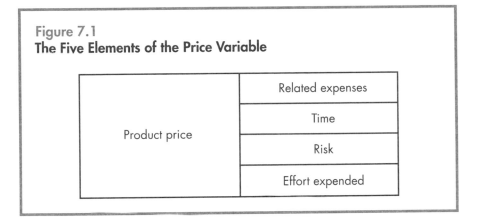

Figure 7.1
The Five Elements of the Price Variable

Product price	Related expenses
	Time
	Risk
	Effort expended

not liking the product, the risk of being upset. Risk, then, is the lack of certainty that needs or expectations will be met. It is based on personal perception, which varies from one individual to the next.

The better consumers know and understand a product, the less their risk, since they can use their own judgement. Conversely, the less consumers know, the more they must trust external sources of information in order to judge the amount of risk involved. For instance, a classical play directed and performed by well-known professionals at the Stratford Festival in Stratford, Canada, or the Lincoln Center in New York, two prestigious venues, represents less risk than an unreviewed avant-garde or alternative production that none of the consumer's peers has seen. Yet personal taste may prevent a consumer from appreciating the less risky, well-known classic and cause him or her to be pleasantly surprised by the riskier, unknown work. This perception of risk applies to every cultural product, whether it is a novel, a CD, a concert, or an exhibition.

Physical effort refers to the effort expended by the consumer to travel to attend a show or to purchase a product such as a book or CD. In each case, the consumer must come to terms with the travel required to make the purchase or to reach the venue. While the Internet can certainly reduce the physical effort required to purchase certain products (and hence the cost of those products), the company's Web site must be sufficiently user-friendly and efficient to facilitate the purchase.

7.2 PRICE SETTING

From the corporate viewpoint, setting a price is akin to sending a signal about product value to the marketplace. Price setting also determines the amount

Example 7.1
The Centre in the Square: Price Strategy for High School Students

On a road trip in eastern Canada, Centre In The Square general manager Jamie Grant mused about how to get high school students into his theatre in Kitchener, Ontario. This led to the founding, in 2000, of eyeGO to the Arts, a program based on the simple premise that high school students will encourage their peers to attend live theatre if the price motivates them to take a risk and if they are treated as valued patrons.

In its first year, the program had two partners and 637 tickets were sold. Over the next five years, 17,267 eyeGO tickets were sold in the program's home community – $86,335 spent by high school students to attend opera, dance, classical music, plays, and musical theatre. In fall 2006, at least 134 partners in five Canadian provinces will be participating in eyeGO.

eyeGO to the Arts allows high school students to buy $5 tickets when single tickets go on sale, for the best available seats for any performance presented by the eyeGO partner. The program is simple to access and simple to administer, and it involves no additional cost to the student.

The program can be successful by word of mouth, but when combined with an eyeGO Youth Council or Outreach Coordinator, it takes off. Marketing materials feature young people or designs by young people. Partners include community groups, professional arts organizations, and presenting theatres. Students are encouraged to become active participants and relate their experiences on the eyeGO Web site (http://www.eyego.org/).

Source: William D. Poole, Director, Centre for Cultural Management, University of Waterloo, Canada.

of effort an organization must supply to reach the break-even point and the acceptable level of financial risk.

The pricing decision must take several factors into account, including the potential reaction of customers, the competition, and, in some cases, even government authorities and regulatory bodies.

A company cannot rely on any simple formula when setting the price of its products, since pricing is the result of a multitude of compromises. The company must strive to set the best possible price given the circumstances.

7.2.1 Objectives Targeted

If the objective of the price variable is supposed to fit well with the other variables in the marketing mix, it must be based upon a corporate policy drawn from more general overall goals.

Price objectives can be divided into four categories: those related to profits or surpluses, sales, competitive balance, and corporate image.[1] Sometimes they can be complementary, depending on the segment targeted.

Profit-Based or Surplus-Based Objectives

Many companies in the arts sector strive to set their prices as low as possible, whether to encourage consumption, to make their product accessible to all, to expand their customer base, or, at the very least, to lower the perceived price barrier. For these companies, profit is not the first objective. Their main concern is to balance their revenues and expenses, without necessarily generating a surplus.

In contrast, those enterprises characterized in Chapter 1 as "market oriented" are concerned first and foremost with generating a high level of profit.

Other firms adopt a position somewhere between these two extremes: without seeking a high level of profit, they hope for at least a slight surplus that will allow them to set up a reserve fund for unforeseen expenses.

Sales-Based Objectives

One corporate goal may be to expand the company's sales or market share. By lowering its prices and thus reducing its profit margin, a company can expect to capture a percentage of the competitor's clientele and increase sales and hence market share. This strategy may, of course, cause the competition to lower its prices too. In keenly competitive sectors in which the consumer remains indifferent to brands, this strategy may start an all-out price war that, in the end, benefits only the consumer.

Another way to increase sales is to attempt to reduce the other components of the price variable, such as the amount of effort expended. Good customer service, for example, can reduce the physical effort required of the consumer.

This type of price policy can also help the company to meet objectives related to the development of new markets (if the target markets are price sensitive) or the building of customer loyalty (as in the case of subscriptions).

Goals Related to Competitive Balance

In sectors at the maturity stage in their life cycle, companies may at times wish to maintain the competitive balance and avoid a price war. The competitors within the market then align their prices behind the market leader and rely on strategies related to other variables in the marketing mix to hold on to their market share.

The performing arts are currently in this situation. Companies in this sector set ticket prices at the same level as others in the same category. The maximum price is generally that of the company considered the biggest or most prestigious. The same phenomenon can be observed in the film and DVD industry.

Goals Related to Corporate Image

A company may set its prices according to the image it wishes to project. As we saw earlier, price can represent a highly symbolic dimension in the consumer's eyes. An organization wishing to project an image of quality may set its price high (this is the case for firms with a strong, prestigious brand image), whereas an organization wishing to convey the message that its product is accessible to most people will set its price lower. Some organizations may choose to project an image of both prestige and accessibility. A theatre company, for example, might charge a high regular price while offering a discount for students and seniors. In all of these examples, the objective will be reached only if the price corresponds to the policies applied to other variables in the marketing mix and if the consumer sees this price in the same way as the manufacturer does.

7.2.2 Method Used

The goals related to price setting dovetail with the various methods that may assist the marketing manager in making a decision. Three methods are given in this chapter. The first method is based on consumers, the second on competition, the third on costs.

The Consumer-Based Method

According to traditional marketing theory, the best price is the one the consumer is willing to pay. The consumer is, in fact, the ultimate judge of price-related matters. Setting a price lower than what the customer is willing to pay means lost profits; however, setting a price higher than what the consumer is willing to pay may mean lost sales. The most reliable way to know the consumer's price threshold is to ask. Since there are various ways of asking, marketing-research techniques can be very helpful. Studies have shown, for example, that certain consumers are willing to pay more for an orchestra seat[2] or would be prepared to pay 25% more for a ticket to a show whose run has been extended.[3]

It should be noted that the consumer-based method suffers from one major limitation: prices set by the competition rein in a company's freedom in

Example 7.2
An Exercise in Pricing

The Queen's Theatre in Hornchurch, an outer suburb of east London, was facing the problem of low revenues for its productions – low revenues caused by low audience levels.

The theatre achieved around 19% of tickets sold for the three-week run of each show, or around 1,500. Those who came liked the work, built on a talented group of actor-musicians who formed a semi-permanent company.

To achieve higher revenues, management decided to increase prices. There were three ticket prices, and they were increased: the two rows that people actively chose to sit in took the biggest price increase, while there was a guarantee to keep the bottom price at £8.00. The result of this adjusting of price and of seating areas was a small increase in revenue. The average yield per ticket was about £12.00.

The management team decided on a significant change. There were three shows in the season, each running for three weeks, with the season starting in September. In May they offered a deal: "Buy your tickets before the end of August, and it's three shows for £15.00. You get vouchers which you can exchange for tickets when you know which night you want to come – if there are seats left."

This deal was offered from May through the summer. The result: more than 4,000 tickets sold, a huge increase over previous numbers and more than enough to wipe out the fantastic discount. After all, for the people who had been paying the top prices, this was three shows for the price of one. And even setting aside the cash up front, those who later read the reviews and decided to buy single tickets had less choice.

The theatre became, again, a bright, buzzy place – and good-humoured to boot. Not only did everyone working there find themselves excited by the growth path, but the fabulous increase in sales brought media coverage. The real proof of success was when a couple complained: they'd tried to exchange their voucher for tickets for the last night of a show – and on the very day of the performance. But it was sold out. "Your fault," they were told with a smile. "That's fine," they replied. "See you next time: we just thought we'd complain to see how you reacted."

That was four years ago, and the scheme continues – albeit at increased prices – bringing a critical mass of sales and allies to the flexibility that so many subscription schemes cannot offer.

Source: Michael Quine, Senior Lecturer, City University, London, United Kingdom.

this area. Even if a consumer claims to be prepared to pay more for a company's product, if competitors set their prices considerably lower, that company must take note or risk losing sales and reducing its market share.

The Competition-Based Method

In opting for this method, a company sets its prices according to the competition's. Since no market research is required, this method is simple and inexpensive. Unfortunately, it lets others decide how much the consumer is willing to pay for the product. In other words, the distinctive features that a company's product may have are ignored, and any potential for positioning through price is lost. If consumers perceive competing products as similar and their perception cannot be changed, basing a price on the competition's price is the most appropriate method, since shoppers are sensitive to price changes. It is therefore important to monitor prices on the market in order to react swiftly to a competitor's price change.

The Cost-Based Method

The cost-based method is simple, since it involves setting a price which enables manufacturers to generate what they consider to be a fair profit. Setting this price requires some calculation of the cost price per unit produced. Another amount, or profit margin, is then added.

The main advantage of this method lies in its simplicity. There are, however, two disadvantages. First, the method does not take into account consumers' reactions. Second, it may be awkward to apply if unit costs vary in direct reaction to the product level (economies of scale based on the amount produced) or if it is difficult to spread out certain costs absorbed by the company through the manufacture of other products.

Executives usually use one of the three methods described above to set their prices, while keeping in mind the general principles underlying the other two methods. For example, a pricing decision is not made solely on the basis of the competitor's price; a firm must examine its costs and anticipate the consumer's reaction.

7.3 CALCULATING COSTS AND PROFITABILITY

Regardless of the method used, corporate executives must always take into account the total of all costs incurred in manufacturing a product.

There are, to put it simply, two types of cost calculated in the total cost of any product: fixed costs and variable costs. Fixed costs remain unaffected by the number of units produced. Such costs include rent, permanent payroll, general insurance, and any costs unrelated to the company's production level. Variable costs are directly and proportionally related to the number of units manufactured. These costs include primary materials (e.g., the paper used to print a book) or transportation costs (e.g., additional transport costs for cities added to a theatre company's tour).

Classifying costs may prove difficult, however. Some costs vary not proportionate to the level of corporate activity but according to the steps in the manufacture of product units. The movie-theatre owner may assign additional staff to the ticket booth not on a per-customer basis but once a certain number of spectators is reached. For example, only one person may be necessary to look after the ticket booth as long as the number of patrons per evening is fewer than 500, two people once the number ranges from 500 to 1,000, and three people when the number rises above 1,000.

Once the fixed and variable costs which make up the total production cost are known, the break-even point can be calculated. The break-even point is an important concept in any pricing decision. Breaking even depends on the number of units sold, the selling price per unit, and the level and distribution of fixed and variable costs. This figure can be obtained by dividing the total of fixed costs by the gross margin or marginal contribution, which simply represents the selling price per unit minus the variable costs per unit. This concept is expressed in graphic form in Figure 7.2.

$$\text{Break-even point} = \frac{\text{Fixed costs}}{\text{Gross margin}} = \frac{\$50,000}{\$50 - \$25} = 2,000 \text{ units}$$

In this example, if the total of all fixed costs is $50,000, the selling price is $50, and the variable cost per unit is $25, the break-even point is reached when 2,000 units are sold. This means that the company will face a deficit if fewer than 2,000 units are sold, and will make a profit (or surplus) if sales exceed 2,000 units (Figure 7.1).

An executive may use this technique to appraise the risk of launching a new product according to some hypothesis related to different price levels. The risk is then expressed in terms of the number of units that have to be sold to reach the break-even point, as illustrated in Capsule 7.1.

7.4 STATE AND PRIVATE SECTOR FINANCIAL CONTRIBUTIONS

The earnings generated through the sale of the basic product and spin-off products are generally considered to be only one of the company's four

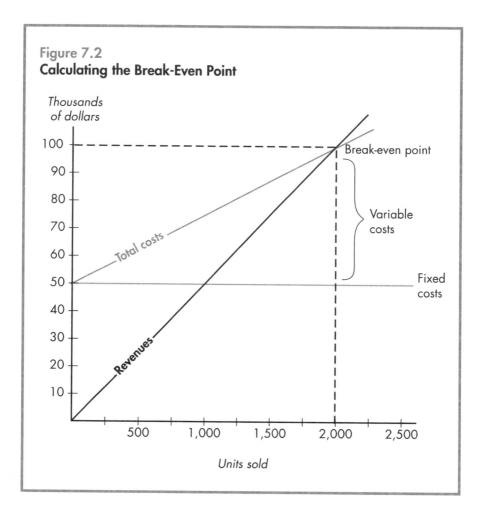

Figure 7.2
Calculating the Break-Even Point

sources of revenue. Governments, the private sector, and partners also contribute financially. Through grants or subsidies, the private sector, governments, and partners finance a decrease in the price paid by the consumer. The purchaser of a ticket to a performance pays only a fraction of the real cost of the product purchased. Government support and private money are designed to encourage the price-sensitive segment of the market to buy a product that interests them.

An increase in market demand, as the result of an overall reduction in price, may be seen as one of the feasible goals of government participation in the arts. There are, however, limits to its effectiveness, as the next section will show, since the demand for cultural products is generally inelastic in terms of price.

Capsule 7.1
Different Break-Even Points According to the Theory of Price Applied

The promoter of a show knows that the fixed costs per performance are $10,000, including artists' salaries. It costs $2 per ticket in variable costs – program, insurance, ticket handling, and credit-card commissions. The average ticket price will be set at a level that, multiplied by the number of tickets to be sold, will cover all of the promoter's expenses. At $30 a ticket, 357 units must be sold; at $25 a ticket, 435 units must be sold; and at $20 a ticket, 555 units must be sold. If the venue seats 1,000 people, the minimum capacity to be reached would be 35% (350 seats occupied out of the 1,000 available), 43.5%, or 55.5%, based on the respective ticket price.

If the promoter thinks that 1,200 seats could be sold at a ticket price of $20, the performer may appear for just one night. This means taking a loss on the potential 200 tickets that could be sold only on another night. Given the cost structure, the one-night-only theory would generate $8,000 in profit:

($20/ticket – $2 variable costs/ticket) × 1,000 tickets
– $10,000 in fixed costs.

The two-night theory generates a $1,600 profit:

($20/ticket – $2 variable costs/ticket) × 1,200 tickets
– 2 × $10,000 in fixed costs.

The first theory, or one night only, turns out to be more profitable financially, not to mention the impact of a full house rather than a hall at only 60% capacity. The promoter could decide to raise prices so as to attract only 1,000 people and increase profits. On the other hand, by lowering the ticket price, it might be easier to attract more consumers. In any event, the lowest possible price would be $12, since that is the break-even point for a 1,000-seat hall:

($12/ticket – $2 in variable costs/ticket) × 1,000 tickets
– $10,000 in fixed costs.

7.5 THE NOTION OF ELASTICITY

According to economists, there is a relationship of cause and effect between the set price of a product and the number of units sold. In a nutshell, the higher the price, the smaller the number of units sold. Conversely, the lower the price, the higher the number of units sold.

In simple terms, this theory maintains that the consumer wants to buy an article for the lowest price possible. On the other hand, a firm is inclined to produce an amount as large as the price is high. Obviously, for the firm, mass production allows for significant economies of scale that will increase the profit margin per unit. Not only do the sales figures increase, but also the profit margin per sale.

In Figure 7.3, equilibrium is achieved where the curves representing supply and demand intersect. If, in fact, the price that consumers are willing to pay is very high, manufacturers are ready to produce more. If the price were lower, manufacturers would be less interested in making the product, even though more consumers would be prepared to buy it.

Equilibrium is reached at point A, the intersection of the curves in the example given in Figure 7.3. The $1 selling price translates to the consumption of 100 units (point B) and leads to a supply of 500 units (point C); in other

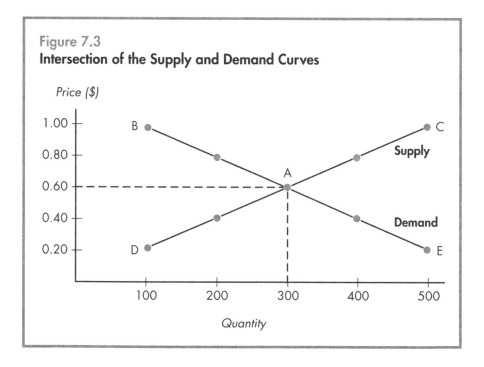

Figure 7.3
Intersection of the Supply and Demand Curves

words, the companies are prepared to manufacture this number of units, given the profit potential. Conversely, a selling price of 20¢ would generate a supply equal to 100 units (point D), whereas consumer interest could generate demand equal to 500 units (point E). Equilibrium corresponds to the optimal point at which the greatest number of companies and the greatest number of consumers are satisfied. In this case, that would be 300 units at 60¢.

Price elasticity is the term used to describe the relationship between the price and the quantity purchased. Since the quantity or amount purchased varies inversely and proportionally to the price, demand is considered elastic if, after a price change, the number of units or products consumed varies more than proportionally to this price change.

Conversely, demand is considered inelastic if, in the case of a price change, consumption varies less than proportionally to the price. Ideally, perfect elasticity implies that even a minimal price shift would generate an infinite increase in the amount consumed. A perfectly inelastic demand would imply that for any price variation, the demand remains the same (see Figure 7.4). Demand can be either elastic or inelastic to varying degrees. Elasticity may even be neutral, if the change in price and in quantity are equal.

Today, price is still an important factor in the decision to buy a product, but there are now variations in the type of product and the individual consumer's financial status and comfort, and so it is useful to apply the concept of elasticity to other variables in the marketing mix in order to explain variations in demand – product elasticity, promotion elasticity, and distribution elasticity. Indeed, an advertising campaign, an improved service, or a more suitable distribution network can affect demand (Figure 7.5). It is therefore possible to increase product sales by providing more points of sale, halls, or travelling

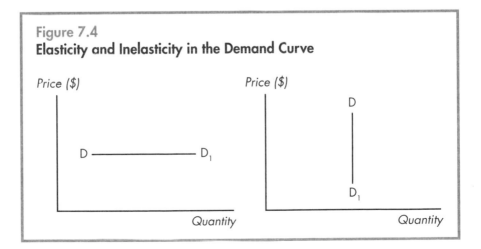

Figure 7.4
Elasticity and Inelasticity in the Demand Curve

Price ($)

D ——————————— D₁

Quantity

Price ($)

D

D₁

Quantity

exhibitions, or by improving sales techniques such as accepting credit cards or selling through automatic tellers, by telephone, or by catalogue. Another way of attracting customers is to offer complementary products of a cultural or educational nature (children's workshops, guided tours, lectures, conferences, membership cards), as most museums now do. These examples show how modifying a particular variable can have a positive effect on the quantity consumed. On the other hand, it is obvious that a decrease in promotion or in the number of points of sale will lower product demand.

Unlike their commercial counterparts, artistic enterprises usually choose not to modify the product as a strategy to increase demand. This way, artists retain their creative (artistic) integrity, or the unique quality that makes them interesting. This is not necessarily true of the cultural industries, in which product elasticity may be used as a strategic variable. Of course, this presumes that modifying the product will indeed bring positive consumer reaction.

Elasticity in terms of demand, according to the different variables of the marketing mix, varies with the product and the target market. Ads or critics may rave about the virtues of a symphony orchestra, but not everyone will be interested in the benefits described. An opera company may offer student prices, but not all students will be interested in attending. A recording

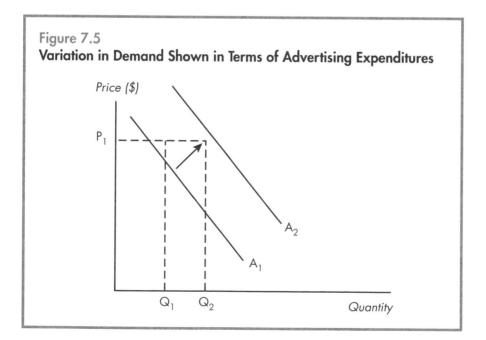

Figure 7.5
Variation in Demand Shown in Terms of Advertising Expenditures

or a handcrafted object may be displayed at several points of sale with little increase in consumption.

In fact, the variables of the marketing mix must form an extremely coherent whole. As previously stated, a poor choice regarding one variable can jeopardize an entire strategy. Demand for a given product may be elastic according to some variables in the marketing mix and inelastic according to others. Moreover, some markets, such as those comprising students and senior citizens, react more to the price variable than others. In short, any attempt to estimate the demand or explain variations in past sales must take into account the effects of elasticity on the four variables that make up the marketing mix.

7.6 PRICE AND MARKET SEGMENTATION

So far, demand has been represented here as a continuous curve. In reality, however, it is a set of several small curves representing the demand for each segment of a market. Figure 7.6 illustrates this concept.

For example, in the theatre market, some people are prepared to pay a high price for an orchestra seat (segment 1), some are looking for low-cost tickets anywhere in the theatre (segment 3), and some want a moderately priced ticket (segment 2). For each segment, the price may vary slightly without necessarily translating to lost sales. Beyond a certain point, however, theatre-goers may opt for a lower-priced ticket for a poorer seat rather than miss enjoying the product completely.

The link between the notion of segmentation and the price variable helps explain the two main factors given by survey respondents when asked what prevents them from attending performing arts events more often: lack of time and high prices. Similar results have been obtained in studies conducted in the United States,[4] Australia,[5] and Canada.[6] Actually, these two factors correspond to two different market segments. The professionals and white-collar workers who account for a large proportion of performing arts audiences lack the time to attend the shows they would like to see, and are even willing to pay more for a flexible subscription or for a guarantee that they will enjoy the performance (as in the case of shows with an extended run). Students and those with low incomes, in contrast, are interested in cheaper tickets because they are often on a tight budget. By offering an across-the-board price reduction for all audience categories, the company would be unnecessarily depriving itself of revenue without obtaining the desired effect, since a segment of its audience is insensitive to price.

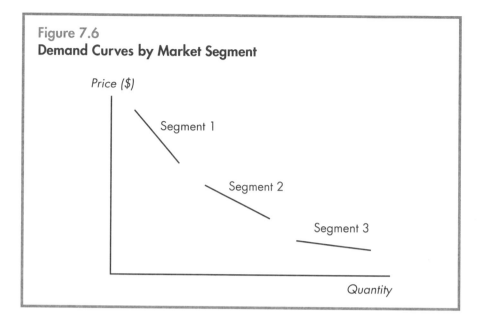

Figure 7.6
Demand Curves by Market Segment

Price ($)

Segment 1

Segment 2

Segment 3

Quantity

The demand curve actually represents the overall demand for a given product, considering each segment of the market and thus the average trend in terms of demand for that product.

7.7 PRICING STRATEGIES

In setting prices, a company must choose among several strategies, each of which is likely to influence consumer perceptions and, hence, the level of product consumption.

7.7.1 Skimming and Penetration

Skimming and penetration strategies are used primarily in the launching of new products by companies that reproduce a prototype.

A company that opts for the skimming strategy is introducing its product at a high price in order to earn the maximum profit per unit sold. This strategy targets a public prepared to pay a high price for a specific product. The vendor sells fewer units but at a higher price, in order to benefit from the substantial earnings generated initially by skimming. The company may later lower its prices gradually in order to reach more price-sensitive consumers. This strategy can be applied if the product is unique, has unique attributes, projects prestige, or enjoys a near monopoly. An example would be the re-

Capsule 7.2
International Price Setting in the Cultural Industries

Several variables influence the setting of prices for cultural products in the international market. Here are two examples of price setting for cultural exports.

The sale of drama series to foreign markets. U.S. distributors are well versed in this business, as American television programs are sold in nearly every market in the world. How are prices for drama series determined? First of all, the price set represents a weighting of a country's total population, GDP (gross domestic product), television penetration rate, and number of available channels (competitors). Thus, prices can fluctuate greatly from one region to another. In addition, trade magazines such as *WorldScreen* publish annual price lists for television programs in all international markets (http://www.worldscreen.com/priceindex.php).

The sale of TV program formats. Selling the format of a television program in a foreign market is common practice. The distributor sells a formula that has already been applied successfully in its home market. The client buys the title, the music, scripts, and an approach. Examples of formats that have been sold in foreign markets are the reality show *Survivor*, originally presented in the United States, *Tout le monde en parle*, distributed in France and Quebec, and *Un gars, une fille*, which has been exported to 25 countries. Here, too, the cost can vary widely from one country to the next. Production of the same concept might have a budget of $1 million in the United States and $250,000 in Canada.

release of a deluxe-edition novel in paperback format. Obviously a market segment that is not price-sensitive yet is likely to buy the product is essential.

The market-penetration strategy, on the other hand, consists of selling as many units as possible by setting the price as low as possible. The company realizes a relatively small profit per unit, but counts on the number of units sold to generate substantial profits. This strategy targets large market segments and budget-conscious consumers. The penetration strategy usually allows a company to cover its product design and launching costs more slowly than does the skimming strategy.

Although these strategies are usually applied to the launching of new products, skimming may sometimes also apply in the growth stage of a product. For example, a new show may be so popular that it is held over. In this case, when announcing extra dates, the company may choose to increase its ticket prices, since the show's popularity makes the audience less price-conscious.

7.7.2 Prestige Pricing

Price has a psychological influence on the consumer's evaluation of the product. A high price tag raises expectations and, paradoxically, reduces the perceived risk. In fact, a high price usually reassures shoppers and even represents a "gold seal" of quality.

Although quality is almost always associated with high prices, the latter are not always associated with quality. At one time or another, every shopper learns this expensive lesson through personal experience. The association of high prices with quality is based only on subjective criteria and is not necessarily believed by all consumers. This association depends largely on their past experiences, their knowledge and awareness of the product, and their trust in the company promoting the product.

The link between quality and price does, however, enable a company to set relatively high prices by highlighting the prestige associated with the consumption of certain products. This is the strategy used when an organization solicits donations from wealthy citizens or when it holds a benefit gala.

Prestige pricing actually increases the value associated with consuming a product, thus lending it an "added value" and reducing the perceived risk while generating greater profit for the company. The value-added component attracts a certain category of consumers who are label- or designer-conscious. This segment of the market may not have been tapped previously through strategies based on other variables in the marketing mix. In a strategy based on prestige pricing, real psychological or physical advantages sought by the targeted clientele must be offered. If not, the strategy may backfire. For example, the directors of the Ravinia Festival in the United States decided to open a private restaurant carrying a membership fee of $5,000 and offering members private parking near the main entrance to the Festival; company presidents can entertain guests at the restaurant prior to the concert and are offered a brief presentation of the evening's program; after the concert, members can mingle with the artists over dessert and refreshments.[7]

As Figure 7.7 shows, the number of units consumed, or the demand, increases as the price decreases until point A is reached. After that, the relationship flips and the demand decreases along with the price. One explanation for this phenomenon lies in the fact that consumers seeking a prestige product want to stand out in a crowd. Of course, once all and sundry can have

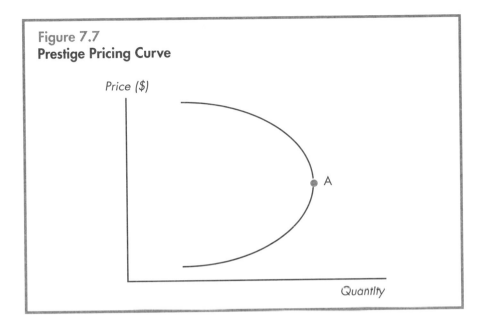

Figure 7.7
Prestige Pricing Curve

Price ($)

A

Quantity

the product, the reason for buying it disappears. Conversely, those who do not want to be identified with another social class by their consumer behaviour may refuse to buy the same product even when it becomes readily affordable.

7.8 DYNAMIC PRICING *(BY PHILIPPE RAVANAS)*

"The cynic," wrote Oscar Wilde, "knows the price of everything and the value of nothing." Matching price and value has always been difficult, particularly in the arts. The aesthetic value of a cultural product is eminently personal and subjective. As we saw in part 7.6 above, demand/price elasticity for the same cultural product can vary from one consumer segment to another. Demand for the product can also vary from one time period (a day, a week, a month) to another. Finally, price itself influences the perceived value: since all that is rare is expensive, we often assume that what is expensive is rare (see part 7.7.3).

Setting a fixed, standard price for all customers prevents organizations from taking advantage of these variations. If a cultural organization wants to maximize profits or surplus, it has to develop a *dynamic pricing* policy. With dynamic pricing, different prices are set for the same product, according to each consumer segment, consumer behaviour, or time of consumption – not according to the cost of producing the product. The organization can set in advance the different prices at which it will sell the same product to different customers. This is called *segmented pricing*. Alternatively, the organization can negotiate the price with each individual customer during the transaction. This is called *negotiated pricing*. Thanks to information technology, each consumer can instantly compare the quoted price with the price of comparable products and make an informed decision.

7.8.1 Segmented Pricing

If an organization observes demand/price elasticity variations from one consumer segment to another, it should try to determine what consumer preferences might be behind the variations and structure its prices accordingly. For example, a performing arts organization can scale its prices for a given show using the following parameters:

- *Placement of seats relative to the stage:* Orchestra, balcony, or loge seats can be sold at vastly different prices. The price differences are not necessarily correlated to variations in acoustic or visual quality from one seat to another.
- *Time and date of the show:* During a season, demand for a given show can vary based on three factors: time of day (matinee or evening), day of the week (mid-week or weekend), and time of year (season, during school holidays). A price scale could reflect this variation.

The organization could then divide its inventory into seat allotments for each price category, allowing customers to purchase the ticket that best suits them given their budgetary or time constraints. This way, the organization can improve attendance and its revenues.

After analyzing past sales, the organization might decide, before the start of the season, to change the seat allotment or the price for each category, based on demand. For example, if the orchestra seats in the first 10 rows sell better than those in the next 10, the company could either raise the price of seats in the first 10 rows or move rows from one category to another.

The company could also entice its customers to buy early by lowering the price for tickets purchased before a specified date. These anticipated sales will serve to improve the organization's cash flow.

This approach to pricing is far removed from the traditional "one price fits all" approach.

7.8.2 Yield Management

Until recently, it was almost impossible to change the number of seats or the price of each category *during* a season. This is now feasible, however.

Advances in information technology and online distribution, the accumulation of consumer information in large databases (see part 8.7.3: Database and Modelling), and the manipulation of data with powerful mathematical tools have given rise to a new scientific pricing technique called Yield Management (also called Revenue Management or Real-Time Pricing).

According to Optims,[8] a French software company, this technique "calculates the best pricing policy for optimizing profits generated by the sale of a product or service, based on real-time modelling and forecasting of demand behaviour per market micro-segment. It offers an excellent solution to the problem of comparing supply and demand thanks to differentiated pricing and systematic control of the inventory for sale in each price category. All players benefit from using this concept: the producer gains in increased turnover and revenue; the end-user enjoys lower prices for the same quality of service."

This pricing technique was developed for the airline industry but has spread to other industries, such as tourism and the hotel industry, that have the following characteristics:

- Production capacity is fixed but demand for services fluctuates
- Variable costs are low
- Inventory is perishable: unsold services cannot be stored
- Services can be sold through reservation before the date of production and consumption
- Demand/price elasticity varies from one consumer segment to another, which calls for segmented pricing

Many cultural organizations, particularly performing arts organizations, fit this model and can therefore use the Yield Management pricing technique.

Chicago's Steppenwolf Theatre Company uses this technique. It combines past sales data with information collected through customer surveys after each première of a show to build a mathematical model that accurately forecasts sales for the whole season. This enables Steppenwolf to adjust its marketing strategy immediately. If the sales forecast is lower than the budget, the company can increase promotional spending and lower ticket prices to improve attendance. If the sales forecast is higher than the budget, the company can lower promotional spending and increase ticket prices to maximize income.[9]

The implementation of Yield Management requires careful planning. The organization must take care to ensure that consumers do not respond negatively to the price variations.

7.8.3 Negotiated Pricing

Theoretically, the maximum profit is reached when each product is sold at the highest price possible, dictated by supply and demand. This point cannot be reached when the price structure is set in advance. To achieve this goal systematically, the enterprise must negotiate the price of each product with each customer, in order to reach each customer's reserve price (the maximum price he or she is prepared to pay for that particular service).

Negotiating prices for cultural products is hardly a new phenomenon. Christie's and Sotheby's, the world's two leading auction houses, have been doing it for more than two centuries. In the performing arts, "scalpers" have mastered the technique. Until recently, though, negotiated pricing could not be used profitably for most cultural products; it was limited to rare and expensive items and relegated to the resale, or grey, markets.

The Internet has opened up a new era: online auction sales are growing exponentially. Any cultural organization can now use an auction site such as eBay, the world leader in the field, to sell its inventory, or it can plug auction software to its own Web site. This is already common practice in the field of sports and could be extended to culture and the arts.

7.9 BAUMOL'S LAW

No chapter on price as a variable would be complete without some mention of what is now called Baumol's Law. Baumol is an American author whose seminal articles[10] examine the structural problems experienced by companies in the performing arts in terms of rising production costs. Baumol defines the problem as follows. First, performers' salaries rise more slowly than the income earned by other workers throughout the economy. Second, performers' salaries constitute the largest part of production costs in the performing arts. Lastly and paradoxically, production costs for a live show increase faster than those in the overall economy. Let us look at the reasons for this state of affairs.

Commercial enterprises set their prices according to the expenses they incur. In order to produce a good or a service, another amount, the mark-up, is added to this price to ensure a profit. Mass production lets the commercial firm save substantially by spreading its fixed costs and a percentage of the salaries over a larger number of units. This lowers unit costs considerably. What is more important, however, is that these firms are in a position to benefit from increased productivity through technological advances or reduced manufacturing times. By enhancing productivity, they can both lower their prices and raise their employees' salaries. Salary increases do not raise total production costs; they simply spread the decrease in production costs between a price reduction and a salary increase.

Production costs for works in the performing arts cannot be lowered by increasing productivity, which is essentially linked to labour costs that cannot be shrunk any further. A Shakespearean tragedy requires the number of actors scripted. Beethoven's symphonies always require the same number of musicians playing for the same amount of time as when the symphonies were first composed. Logically, it would follow that an increase in salaries cannot be compensated for by a decrease in labour costs. Neither the number of employees nor the amount of time needed to assemble the product can be reduced. In other words, productivity cannot be improved. Therefore, a company in the performing arts cannot increase artists' salaries without increasing revenues. According to Baumol's research, American companies in the arts give lower pay increases than their counterparts in other sectors. Unlike other sectors, the arts see production costs rise more sharply, since artistic enterprises cannot take advantage of a gain in productivity.

This paradox helps to explain why the price of tickets to live performances must increase faster than the overall consumer price index. Inflation actually represents the average of the prices asked by firms with high productivity gains and firms that cannot gain such productivity. The sectors that experience gains in productivity and lower their prices accordingly produce a decrease in the inflation rate, while others that cannot declare productivity improvements cannot lower their prices. But if the latter do not increase salaries, employees suffer a reduction of their revenues because of the increase in the cost of living. In order to be able to raise employees' salaries, these companies must increase their ticket prices to be able to cover these extra costs; in so doing, they put pressure on the price index. Organizations that can gain in productivity do not have to increase their prices in order to pay their staff better, since they can do that by sacrificing a portion of these productivity gains.

Baumol concludes that for companies in the performing arts to have the financial resources needed to increase performers' salaries at the same rate as organizations in other sectors, ticket prices – or public subsidies and private donations – would have to increase at a rate well above that of inflation.

In a nutshell, the greater the productivity gains in the overall economy, the more the arts sector suffers. Conversely, the lower the productivity gains, the healthier the arts sector will be.

Example 7.3
The Swiss Museum Passport: A Collective Pricing Strategy

Switzerland, with a population of 7.5 million, has one of the highest museum densities in the world. It boasts nearly a thousand museums, 40% of which are regional museums; 20% art, historical, or archaeological museums; 20% natural science or technology museums; and 20% museums devoted to various other themes.

In 1997 the Association of Swiss Museums, Swiss Tourism, and the Federal Office of Cultural Affairs joined forces to create the Swiss Museum Passport (SMP) (www.passeportmusees.ch) and establish a foundation to administer the scheme. The aim of this initiative was to diversify and increase the museum going public and to forge supply-side links between the tourism industry and museums through a tariff community structure similar to that existing for public transit in Switzerland.

The SMP gives the holder unlimited access to participating museums for a limited period. Consumers can choose an annual passport, a monthly passport, or books of tickets. There are different price categories for adults, the unemployed, the disabled, retirees, children accompanied by an adult, and individual children. A passport holder is admitted to any museum that is a member of the tariff community (420 museums in 2006). The foundation signs a contract with each museum determining its average admission price. Each SMP visit is registered and the museum is reimbursed for up to 80% of the average price. Participation in the SMP scheme is voluntary and the museums must agree to provide the foundation with accurate figures.

In 2000, on the occasion of its 100th anniversary, the Raiffeisen Bank declared that its VISA, MasterCard, and EC Direct cardholders would henceforth be able to use their card as a museum passport. Raiffeisen mounted a successful advertising campaign using the print media, television spots, and its own newsletter, which generated over 105,000 entries in the first year alone. Not surprisingly, the partnership was renewed, and in 2004 nearly 220,000 people visited museums using a Raiffeisen card. According to people in the museum community, the customers of this bank are generally not frequent museum visitors.

(continued)

Example 7.3 (continued)

Among the other partnerships that have been negotiated, since 2000 the SMP Foundation has been recognizing REKA vacation rental contracts as valid museum passports. This partnership generates close to 13,000 tourist entries each year. As of 2006, moreover, Swiss Travel Pass holders can combine train, tramway, and bus travel with museum visits, leading to an estimated 40,000 entries.

In 2005 a total of nearly 350,000 museum entries using the passport were registered, triggering the transfer of close to three million CHF to participating museums. Over a period of 10 years, the SMP has succeeded in attracting new publics to Swiss museums, including Raiffeisen customers, tourists, and young people. According to the Link Polling Institute, between 1998 and 2006 regular museum-goers increased the frequency of their visits and more than one in two people are now familiar with the museum passport.

The SMP Foundation has been approached by cities in France to extend the passport's territorial reach beyond the borders of Switzerland. In July 2006 European Union culture ministers discussed the possibility of creating a European museum passport, basing their deliberations on the Swiss experience. Watch for further developments.

Source: François H. Courvoisier, Professor, Haute École de Gestion Arc, Neuchâtel Business School, Switzerland.

SUMMARY

For most pricing decisions concerning cultural products, the marketing manager or executive must consider not only the money associated with the good or service, but also the expenses related to the purchase and even the consumer's effort, which may be physical or psychological or both and which includes the notion of perceived risk.

Price elasticity is a term used to describe the relationship between the set price and the quantity of goods bought by consumers. This relationship is elastic if, with a price change, the number of products consumed varies more than proportionally to the change. The opposite occurs when, after a price change, the amount consumed is less than proportional to the price change. The notion of elasticity also applies to the other three variables in the marketing mix.

Consumers do not base their decision to buy a product on price alone. Other factors affect their thinking. These psychological factors influence the demand curve, which leads to different levels of demand according to market segment and product. In some extreme cases, this curve rebounds through "prestige pricing."

Pricing decisions must be made according to the objective a company targets through its pricing strategy. There are four main objectives. They are related to profits, sales, competitive balance, and corporate image.

There are also several price-setting methods available, including customer-based, competition-based, and cost-based pricing.

Price may be used as a strategic tool. A firm may use the skimming strategy (relatively high price, lower sales) or the penetration strategy (relatively low price, high number of units sold). There are a whole range of price-reduction strategies as well: functional reductions, quantity discounts, seasonal reductions, discounts, and indemnities. In the cultural sector, there are also reductions for seniors and for less desirable seats.

A cultural organization can also use a dynamic pricing policy. With dynamic pricing, different prices are set for the same product, according to each consumer segment, consumer behaviour, or time of consumption – not according to the cost of producing the product.

Lastly, the arts sector suffers from an inherent structural weakness expressed eloquently in Baumol's Law. Baumol shows why it is impossible to increase productivity and how labour costs dominate in the performing arts. As a result, commercial and non-commercial enterprises within the arts sector find themselves in a vicious circle whereby admission fees must rise higher than the consumer price index.

QUESTIONS

1. Why should we associate the notion of risk with the price of a product?
2. Compare and contrast the four categories of price-setting goals.
3. What are the advantages and disadvantages of each price-setting method?
4. Briefly describe the notion of elasticity in pricing.
5. How is the demand curve a combination of several curves related to different market segments?
6. What are the objectives of the penetration strategy
7. What roles do price-reduction strategies play?
8. What is the prestige price?
9. Explain what "dynamic pricing" means?
10. Can you describe Baumol's Law?

Notes

1. Desormeaux, R., et al. 2006. *Gestion du marketing*. Boucherville, QC: Chenelière Éducation Éditeur.

2. Scheff, J. 1999. "Factors Influencing Subscription and Single-Ticket Purchases at Performing Arts Organizations." *International Journal of Arts Management*, Vol. 1, n° 2 (Winter), p. 16–28.

3. Colbert, F., C. Beauregard and L. Vallée. 1998. "The Importance of Ticket Prices for Theatre Patrons." *International Journal of Arts Management*, Vol. 1, n° 1 (Fall), p. 8–16.

4. National Endowment for the Arts. 1997. *The 1997 Survey of Public Participation in the Arts: Summary Report*. http://www.arts.gov/pub/Survey/SurveyPDF.html

5. Roy Morgan Research. 1997. *Theatre Audience in Victoria*. South Melbourne, Australia: Author (p. 6).

6. Colbert, F., C. Beauregard and L. Vallée. 1998. "The Importance of Ticket Prices for Theatre Patrons." *International Journal of Arts Management*, Vol. 1, n° 1 (Fall), p. 8–15.

7. Cardinal, J., and L. Lapierre. 1999. "The Ravinia Festival under the Direction of Zarin Metha." *International Journal of Arts Management*, Vol. 1, n° 3 (Spring), p. 70–84.

8. For more information about Optims, see www.optims.com

9. Ravanas, P. 2006. "Born to Be Wise: The Steppenwolf Theatre Company Mixes Freedom with Management Savvy." *International Journal of Arts Management*, Vol. 8, n° 3 (Spring), p. 64–73.

10. Baumol, W.J. 1967. "Performing Arts: The Permanent Crisis." *Business Horizons*, Vol. 10, n° 3 (Autumn), p. 47–50.

For Further Reference

Dhalla, N.K. 1984. "A Guide to New Product Development Pricing Phase." *Canadian Business* (April).

Felton, M.V. 1989. "Major Influences on the Demand for Opera Tickets." *Journal of Cultural Economics*, Vol. 13, n° 1 (June), p. 53–64.

Ford, N.M., and B.J. Queram. 1984. *Pricing Strategies for the Performing Arts*. Madison, WI: Association of College, University and Community Arts Administrators.

World Screen. http://worldscreen.com/priceindex.php

PLAN

Chapter **8**

The Distribution Variable

OBJECTIVES

- Know the three components of the distribution variable
- Describe the elements of a distribution channel
- Look at the main distribution strategies
- Define physical distribution
- Introduce the basic principles used in selecting a commercial location
- Describe the different modes of international distribution

The Distribution Variable 199

INTRODUCTION

In the first section of this chapter, we define place as a variable and look closely at the distribution context for cultural products.

We start by studying the commercial ties among businesses and intermediaries along the distribution channel. Our focus then shifts to the major strategies available to manufacturers whose marketing objectives are being met primarily through the distribution variable. We also examine the logistics involved in circulating goods within a network of "partners" – that is, physical distribution.

Lastly, we define the main elements to be considered in choosing the location of a business or cultural establishment.

The concepts discussed in this chapter apply to both the cultural industries and organizations active in the arts sector. In reality, application may vary according to the specific features of the products involved.

8.1 DEFINITION

8.1.1 The Three Elements of the Distribution Variable

The distribution variable, as it relates to the consumer market, includes three distinct elements: distribution channels, physical distribution, and commercial location.

Distribution channels, or networks, include all those who play a role in the flow of goods from producer to consumer; they can include agents, distributors, presenters (concert halls), bookshops, record stores, exhibition centres, movie theatres, and so on.

Physical distribution is the function that guarantees the flow of a product from one intermediary to another and, ultimately, to the consumer. It involves decisions related to the logistics of product distribution.

Location is the choice of a physical site, such as the store where the product can be bought (in the case of a book or CD, for example) or the place where the product can be consumed (in the case of a play, movie, or museum, for example).

When seen in relation to the cultural enterprise's other three markets – the state, the private sector, and partners – the distribution variable can usually be summed up in the direct contact between the producer and the players in each market. There is little or no need for intermediaries, there is no physical distribution of the product, and there is no store, theatre, or museum.

This chapter thus focuses on the distribution variable as it relates to the consumer market.

8.1.2 Distribution of Cultural Products

In the cultural milieu, the consumer's form of consumption determines the product's mode of distribution.

There are products designed for collective consumption – products to which consumers gain access by gathering in one place for a set period of time. A show, an exhibition, and a film screened in a movie theatre are a few examples. There are also products designed for individual consumption, which consumers can enjoy whenever and wherever they please. Recordings, books, and visual works of art owned by the consumer fall into this category. In the first category, there is a sequential distribution concept in touring shows and travelling exhibitions. In the second category, the product may be distributed in the same fashion and even through the same network as any other consumer good.

This system for classifying products according to form of consumption reveals the important role played by the time, place, and duration of consumption (see Table 8.1).

Naturally, for some products the consumer has total control over when, where, and how long to consume. For example, a consumer may elect to read a novel at home, on the bus or subway, during lunchtime, and so on. The same consumer can decide when and how fast to read, whether to reread a passage, and so on. The theatre-goer, on the other hand, is not free to decide at any given time to attend a performance. For this consumer, travelling time, curtain time, and other factors must be known in advance.

Table 8.1
The Consumer's Role in Determining the Place, Time, and Length of Consumption Activity

	Show	Exhibition	Film	Recording	Video-cassette	Book	Work of art
Place	−	−	±	+	+	+	+
Time	−	±	±	+	+	+	+
Length	−	+	−	−	−	+	+
Possession of technical dimension	−	−	−	+	+	+	+

There are also situations in which the consumer has a choice in two of the three aspects. For example, although a film may be presented for collective consumption, the same film may be playing at several movie theatres but at slightly different times. The consumer can thus pick the most convenient place and time. The museum-goer must visit the museum while it is open, but, with the possible exception of blockbuster exhibitions, the exact day, time, and length of the visit remain individual choices.

In some areas, such as film and radio broadcasting, the Internet has given consumers the freedom to choose when they want to consume works, where previously the time of consumption was imposed on the consumer.

Besides place, time, and duration of consumption, there is the aspect of possession. Possession of the technical dimension of a product obviously gives the individual consumer greater flexibility.

From a managerial viewpoint, these different situations affect the pressures that a cultural organization experiences. In fact, the greater the consumer's choice in terms of place and time of consumption for a cultural product, the broader the marketing manager's range of distribution possibilities. Conversely, if product features restrict consumption, the manufacturer has less room to manoeuvre. For example, a publishing house can vary distribution routes or use more bookshops in order to offer its product to the widest possible potential readership. The promoter of a stage show, on the other hand, must necessarily tour regions in a certain order with a single version of the product. Since the latter situation often means being in the right place at the right time, a promoter's or marketing director's error in judgement is difficult to correct.

Risk also varies according to whether the choice of place and time depends on the consumer or the producer. When the consumer has some control, as is the case for recordings, books, and videos, the product can be consumed after purchase. This is not the case for products whose consumption cannot be postponed, such as stage shows or exhibitions. In this case, consumers must choose among the products offered at that time. This distribution restriction increases the risk for live-performance products.

In short, the form of consumption unique to many different cultural products necessarily implies management of the distribution variable, which, in turn, is affected by the product. Hence distribution channels, physical distribution, and the location where the customer buys or consumes the product may need to be adapted to the product. In the case of products intended for collective consumption, the enterprise accompanies the consumer throughout the consumption process, whereas in the case of products designed for individual consumption, the contact between the company and the consumer ends with the purchase of the product.

8.2 DISTRIBUTION CHANNELS

A distribution channel includes all of the different agents who bridge the gap between the producer, or manufacturer, and the end consumer. These are paid intermediaries who may never actually take possession of the product yet intervene in the production and consumption process. In the cultural milieu, this description would apply to all the intermediaries who make works accessible to the consumer. The producer of a good or a service and the consumer are part of this channel. The total number of agents, and hence their functions, may vary from one company to the next.

Any decision related to the choice of a distribution channel and the various agents involved is important, since the company is simultaneously establishing business relationships with a number of "partners," and the quality of those relationships can spell the success or failure of future marketing strategies. Moreover, once a company signs a distribution agreement with agents, it loses some flexibility, so that modifying marketing strategies later on becomes more difficult. On the other hand, the choice of distribution channel influences the other variables of the marketing mix. Pricing, for instance, is a result of the number, quality, and size of the intermediaries used. The type of promotion required also depends on the channel selected.

However, it is not always the producer who selects the intermediaries with whom he or she will do business. More often than not, it is the presenter who decides. In the case of a festival, for example, producers cannot just impose their shows; it is the festival that chooses what shows it will present. Similarly, regardless of what the publisher thinks, a bookshop may refuse to put a particular novel on its shelf, either because it has no space available or because it believes the book will not sell.

In the case of a touring show, the theatre company may find that there is only one presenter in town, and therefore has no choice but to do business with it. In a situation such as this, the presenter's monopoly position gives it a strategic advantage over the producer in negotiating the contract. The tables are turned, however, once a star is involved. A well-known artist represents a "sure bet" for the local presenter, whose customers may insist on seeing the star, thus giving the artist's agent the upper hand in negotiating the terms of the contract. In this case, the presenter becomes a market for the producer (see Chapter 1).

However, a manufacturer is not forced to use agents and intermediaries. There is always the possibility of selling directly to the end consumer. Direct distribution is not always feasible, however, in the performing arts. A touring company, for example, rarely has the human and financial resources required to produce its show in all the cities visited. Record companies and publishing firms face the same situation. Put simply, intermediaries fulfil a number of key functions. This explains why producers entrust intermediaries with the distribution of their product. In doing so, however, producers relinquish a share of their power over the actual sale of the product and also distance themselves from their clientele. This loss of power may create friction among the various members of the distribution network.

8.2.1 The Functions of an Intermediary

Intermediaries do more than reduce the number of contacts among the various players within a market; they perform several other important functions. Table 8.2 presents these functions in three categories: logistics, commercial, and support. Not all functions are fulfilled by all members of the channel, however. For example, a concert hall does not normally take on a warehousing function.

All along the distribution channel, various agents handle some of the logistics involved in distributing a product. Not only do they look after transportation and warehousing, but, more importantly, they enable a company to adjust the quantity and variety of the product. This point is significant, since consumers usually buy small quantities of products produced by different manufacturers – for example, one or two compact discs, a couple of novels. Manufacturers may, however, release a large quantity of a few products so as to benefit from the economies of scale described in Chapter 7. As mentioned above, intermediaries allow a company to make adjustments in the quantity

Table 8.2
The Functions of a Distribution Channel

Logistic function	Changes • in quality • in variety
Commercial function	Product purchasing Negotiations Promotions Contacts
Support function	Risk-taking Financing Research

and selection of products sold by offering a specific number of products from different companies. As a result, consumers can find what they want in one place and manufacturers or producers can respect their standards of quality.

The distribution channel is valuable in terms of commercial as well as logistical functions. When agents negotiate and sign agreements, they take possession of the product – if not physically, at least legally. They also handle product promotion and deal with customers. The producer of a show, for example, may provide some of the advertising material needed but also assigns to the presenter or theatre owner the task of advertising the artists performing that season. The presenter actually communicates with the consumer and provides customer services, such as reservations, tickets, and coat check. The producer benefits from the presenter's experience, knowledge of the local market, and corporate image. The producer who does not use the services of an intermediary must take on all these responsibilities and tasks without necessarily having the appropriate infrastructure. Of course, producers do not always entrust other members of the channel with crucial functions such as promotion. Sometimes they take it upon themselves to draw customers into stores by means of aggressive advertising.

Support services allow a company to delegate other important responsibilities to an intermediary. In agreeing to sign a contract with a producer, the presenter takes on some of the risk associated with an artist's performance and, at the same time, assumes some of the financing involved – for example, promotional expenditures. By virtue of being more "in touch" with the consumer, the presenter can often provide a wealth of information.

The different functions carried out by intermediaries vary according to the type of distribution channel used. In some cases intermediaries assume all the functions described above, while in other cases these functions are fulfilled by the producer. This is the case with Cirque du Soleil, which produces all of its touring shows itself. In some instances, the distribution functions are shared between the different partners along the channel. For example, large publishing houses often establish subsidiaries abroad instead of using agents.

8.2.2 Types of Distribution Channels

The number of different intermediaries per level along the distribution channel determines whether or not it can be called complex. Figure 8.1 describes the different types of distribution channels. The simplest is obviously the producer selling directly to the consumer. In the arts, this form of distribution could be a theatre company that owns its own venue or a publisher that sells its products over the Internet. Longer channels could be the film producer using a distributor that deals with movie theatres or a string quartet that uses an agent to find a presenter.

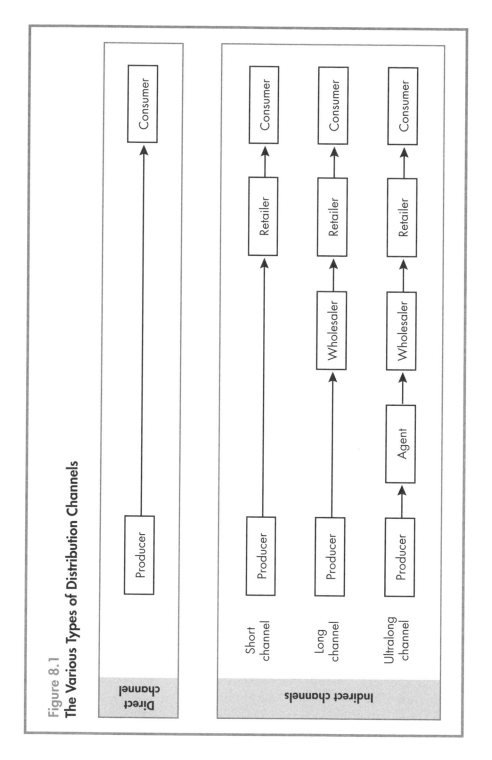

Figure 8.1
The Various Types of Distribution Channels

The use of a direct distribution channel does not necessarily mean, however, that the company is content to distribute its product at a single venue. For example, the Royal Armouries Museum in London, England, which has been housed in the Tower of London since its founding in the 15th century, decided to adopt an alternative approach to reaching a broader public.[1] In partnership with private enterprise, the museum opened two additional sites, one in Portsmouth and the other in Leeds. This expansion has allowed the museum to display more of its collection while reaching a wider audience.

Figure 8.1 covers all the realities of the cultural milieu; it should be noted that the partners at each stage of distribution may be assigned different titles and functions in specific sectors. In the performing arts, for example, there are often a producer, an agent, and a presenter; however, this is not the only network possible. A producer may decide to deal directly with the presenter without an agent. In fact, a firm may decide to distribute its product via several different distribution channels. In the publishing world, for instance, books are sold through a variety of channels, including the traditional bookstore, mail-order book clubs, and the Internet. In the film industry, it is only when the end consumer is about to view the product that distribution becomes fragmented. Distributors receive the film from the producer, then use one of several different ways to reach the consumer (movie theatre, video club, pay TV, traditional TV, not-for-profit network, Internet, telephone, etc.). In the recording industry, consumers can turn to record shops, department stores, or mail-order clubs.

The more intermediaries in the distribution network, the higher the price of the product, since each intermediary collects a margin to cover its costs, thus driving up the price of the product. It follows logically that the firm that manages to take over one or more steps in the distribution process can increase its profits or surplus, or offer a lower price to consumers.

The main disadvantage of the long distribution channel is lack of flexibility. This disadvantage is a result of the large number of intermediaries, which essentially reduces a manufacturer's ability to manoeuvre. Another disadvantage is lack of control over the way the product is sold. The greater the number of intermediaries, the more distant and less influential a manufacturer becomes. On the other hand, the producer's costs are lower with a long channel. For example, the sales force is generally reduced to a minimum, since the company deals with a limited number of agents.

In short, the advantages of a long distribution channel correspond to the disadvantages of a short one, and vice versa. The smaller the number of intermediaries, the greater a company's influence on the marketing of its product. On the other hand, the shorter the channel, the higher the producer's costs.

8.2.3 Managing the Distribution Channel

Mallen[2] outlines the main aspects of distribution management using four objectives and six strategic decisions.

In general, manufacturers use a distribution channel to optimize their profits. In order to do so, they must keep the various intermediaries along the channel motivated.

Optimizing profits means first maximizing sales (objective 1), then minimizing costs (objective 2). A firm must consider its optimum profit margin over both the long and the short term, since in some situations it may be preferable to sacrifice immediate profits for the long-term betterment of the firm. Hence the firm's destiny is tied to that of the intermediaries. Since the intermediaries have a stake in the company's future, they develop a relationship similar to a partnership. Here, the idea of maximizing motivation takes on its full meaning, since motivating the distribution agents, or "partners," has a definite impact on the manufacturer's financial health. A bookseller, for example, may decide to showcase one particular publisher's books. Similarly, a distributor may promote one artist more than another. In other words, maximizing motivation among the members of the distribution channel meets two more of the manufacturer's objectives: maximize cooperation along the route (objective 3) and maximize the manufacturer's influence on the members (objective 4). If the manufacturer obtains maximum cooperation from each member, the place-variable functions are handled efficiently. Nevertheless, the manufacturer must maintain a healthy level of influence over the various partners.

The company seeking long-term optimum profits or the not-for-profit group striving for long-term financial stability must build up a distribution network that meets six criteria, presented here as a series of choices. These basic criteria deal with the choice and length of the distribution channel and the distribution strategy (intensive, selective, exclusive), as well as the number and selection of intermediaries overall and at each stage of distribution.

The first decision is exemplified by a classical-music ensemble that must choose between hiring an agent and using its own sales force to organize a tour. The choice depends on the sales objectives set by the ensemble, the costs involved, and the amount of cooperation and influence (real and desired) it expects. Obviously it is easier to exert influence on an employee who is seen daily than on an outside agent who has other clients. On the other hand, the set cost that an employee's salary represents is higher than an agent's commission, which often depends on that agent's productivity. In fact, distribution at the international level frequently requires the use of a foreign agent well acquainted with both the local market and potential customers.

A company must also decide on a distribution strategy: Is it better to use as many distribution partners as possible, or to select only those which meet specific criteria (see section 8.3)? The exact number of intermediaries (agent, wholesaler, retailer) at each of the different stages of distribution can then be set.

Once a company has decided on the distribution strategy, the length of the distribution channel, and the number of intermediaries at each level, it must decide which type of intermediary is most likely to meet its corporate objectives. The ideal intermediary will fulfil the functions set out by the company. For example, a record company or book publisher may opt for distribution in department stores, where musical expertise or literary advice is almost non-existent, rather than be associated with a chain of specialized shops where sales clerks might be able to offer advice to the customer.

The producer must also decide how many routes to use. Should the latest film be marketed right away in movie theatres and in video clubs? Should another distribution possibility, such as pay TV or the Internet, be included? All of these questions (and possibly more) should be raised during the decision-making process.

Once these four decisions have been made, the manufacturer or producer must decide how much help to give the various partners – for example, the kind of promotional material to give them, and how much.

Lastly, the firm must decide on the individual intermediary. For example, if a large museum wishes to hold an exhibition in several different regions, it must select the appropriate venues with the necessary technical equipment or capacity (size of halls, standard display conditions, etc.). The firm can then decide on the various candidates according to whatever museological and marketing criteria it chooses.

8.2.4 The Behaviour of Distribution-Channel Members

One of the fundamentals of distribution management is controlling the behaviour of the members along the channel. The distribution channel should not be seen simply as the flow of merchandise from producer to consumer, since it is also a social network in which interpersonal relations play an important role in the overall dynamics. Rosenbloom[3] describes four key dimensions in this social network: conflict, power, roles, and communication.

Misunderstandings in distribution should be considered normal, unless, of course, they turn into conflicts that could paralyze channel activities. Conflicts can arise in various ways – for instance, the parties may have poor communication methods, a different definition of each partner's role, diverging views on the responsibility inherent in certain decisions, or even contradictory objectives. The distribution manager must always be on the look-out for potential "hot spots," be able to judge their impact on the firm, and be able to resolve problematic situations in the best interests of all concerned.

Any company using partners to bring its product to market seeks to influence the different members of its distribution channel so that certain tasks are accomplished properly. The following means can be used to that end. Partners may be rewarded, monetarily or otherwise, or penalized, especially when the company is larger than the other members. Legitimacy granted by the members at the previous level is also required here; otherwise the whole system falters. Some agreement on the outcome is also needed so that everyone feels like a team player. Lastly, corporate expertise is needed so that the members conform to the company's will.

The knowledgeable distribution manager will also have a definite idea of the roles each member along the channel should play. Once each member knows what to expect from the others, relations generally run more smoothly. Naturally, the producer or manufacturer must also convince the various partners to accept their own role and that of the others.

As in any other human enterprise, communication and information are fundamental in distribution management. Conflicts between two different partners can arise from a simple difference of opinion caused solely by poor communication. The absence of vital information can actually poison the marketing of a product.

8.3 DISTRIBUTION STRATEGIES

Below is a description of two major types of distribution strategies: intensive, selective, and exclusive strategies; and push and pull strategies.

8.3.1 Intensive, Selective, and Exclusive Distribution Strategies

The intensive distribution strategy involves the maximum distribution of a product through as many points of sale as possible. In this strategy, the producer makes no selection among retailers interested in carrying its product. The recording and publishing industries provide numerous examples of intensive distribution.

Selective distribution involves selecting retailers according to specific criteria. This form of distribution prevents retailers from all offering the same product. The selection process corresponds to specific objectives often linked to corporate image. Companies using the selective distribution strategy are actually trying to control their image and ensure that their retailers or partners have a positive image or enjoy a reputation for credibility in the milieu. This strategy can also create a certain sense of product uniqueness or rarity by limiting the number of points of sale, so that the consumer must shop at specific, carefully chosen places to obtain or consume the product.

In the visual arts, some artists choose the galleries with which they wish to do business. In doing so, they exclude competing galleries that would like to sell their works. Once manufacturers select the retailers with whom they will do business and grant them exclusivity, they are said to be using the exclusive strategy. In this case, the retailer enjoys the monopoly for a given product within a specific territory. Film producers often use this strategy when granting exclusive distribution rights for a film to a distributor in a specific region or territory.

8.3.2 Push and Pull Strategies

The push strategy consists of offering a higher profit margin to retailers so they will work harder to promote and sell a given product to their customers. Manufacturers can offer this additional margin by reducing their advertising budget. They assume that a retailer earning higher profits on a particular brand will work harder to sell that brand.

The pull strategy, on the other hand, involves huge investments in advertising to generate such high demand that retailers want to carry the product in order to satisfy their customers. This is the strategy used by producers who take advantage of the approaching holiday season to release a CD of Christmas songs backed up by an advertising blitz.

Both strategies may be applied to cultural products. The pull strategy is used by some record distributors, such as K-Tel Records, or various American record companies handling stars like Michael Jackson. Most producers, however, tend to use the push strategy.

Many manufacturers have turned to push tactics by strategic default rather than design. As a strategy, pull requires a hefty initial outlay, which small firms cannot always afford. In the performing arts, for example, touring companies usually do not have the resources to launch a vast promotional campaign to attract an audience. Only the company's renown or reputation earned through previous products may incite promoters to buy a product. It would seem that in the case of a well-known performer or group, the producer necessarily returns to the pull strategy. Major media coverage in a large city often acts as a pole attracting provincial or regional audiences. The success of a touring Broadway show, such as *Cats*, *Les Misérables*, or *Miss Saigon*, depends on both its Broadway success and its ongoing success.

8.3.3 How the Strategies Interrelate

The two main types of pricing strategy (Chapter 7) and the two main types of distribution strategy (section 8.3) have been presented separately; however, in reality they are closely linked.

By using the skimming strategy, a company sells its product at a price higher than the competitor's. As a result, it sells fewer units yet generates a higher profit margin per unit. The strategy is successful only if the company earns a fine reputation or projects a prestigious image. This type of reputation or image is easier to achieve using selective or exclusive distribution strategies, which are generally associated with a push strategy. The penetration pricing strategy, which consists of selling as many units as possible at the lowest possible price, goes hand in hand with the pull strategy or the intensive distribution strategy.

8.4 PHYSICAL DISTRIBUTION

Physical distribution consists of all the logistics and transportation involved in bringing a product to market. Key distribution questions are: Where will the product be sold? How will it be shipped there? The various components of physical distribution are shipping, warehousing, inventory management, order processing, and merchandise handling and packaging.

The way in which a company manages its physical distribution is very important. Wise decisions involving the logistics of product distribution can reduce marketing costs significantly. Conversely, poor decisions can lead to major expenses and actually alter the image consumers have of the company. Distribution management is all the more delicate since the two physical distribution objectives – minimize costs and maximize customer service – are contradictory.

The general condition required to maximize customer service is a short ordering cycle with no product shortages and no shipping errors. This umbrella condition implies that a company must maintain a large inventory and therefore rent or own substantial warehousing facilities. Obviously, these facilities represent an equally substantial cost. Also needed are delivery facilities, qualified staff, and order and inventory-control systems capable of handling customer orders efficiently. Often, the corporate decision-making process hinges on the following two questions: What is the optimal inventory level required to avoid exceeding x number of shortages during a given period? What degree of quality is required, in terms of the labour and inventory-management systems, for the ordering cycle not to exceed x number of days? Both questions are extremely important strategically, especially in a highly competitive market.

The conditions described above are applicable in the cultural industries, in which a large number of physical units, such as recordings or books, are distributed. In other sectors, however, the idea of customer service, a fundamental aspect of physical distribution, applies even though stocking, warehousing, and ordering cycles are not involved.

Although their goods are not material, producers in the performing arts do have to determine how the product will be distributed to the public. The many parameters to consider include choice of cities on a tour, selection of venues, performance times, and ticket-sales techniques (mail order, automated ticket counter, Internet). These decisions must be made according to the company's distribution strategies. The company must strive for quality in suitable and diversified modes of distribution, such as ticket sales, since quality and diversity are two key aspects of customer service.

In large cities, where competition is fierce, the quality of customer service can play a crucial role. Potential audience members trying to reach a theatre company's box office may give up if the line is always busy, and may even call another theatre. If there is only one acceptable alternative, their second choice is obvious. However, if consumers can choose among three, four, or five acceptable theatres, they may hesitate, since they may well be indifferent to the alternatives. In this case, ticket accessibility may be the determining factor. If tickets to their first choice are unavailable, they will opt for their second choice.

8.5 COMMERCIAL LOCATION

Physical distribution consists of making a product accessible to the consumer. Location is the physical site where the product is bought or consumed. Points of sale or showrooms must be accessible, since consumers' effort is directly proportional to their interest in the product.

Consumers are generally prepared to expend greater effort for specialized products such as artistic products. However, the amount of effort a consumer will expend is limited. If the physical location is off the beaten path and difficult to reach or if the product is offered at inconvenient hours, the potential consumer will react. Montreal's Musée d'art contemporain provides an excellent example of the power of location. Until moving downtown and adjacent to Place des Arts (a performing arts centre), this museum struggled at Cité du Havre, a location off the Island of Montreal, far from the city's other cultural venues and poorly served by the public transit system. Not long ago, most museums were open weekdays only, from nine to five; now, museums cater to their clientele by remaining open evenings and weekends. Ticket offices that are closed until noon, the absence of a Web site, and the lack of parking have become key factors affecting attendance figures. Various geographical and physical features, such as a bridge, a railway crossing, or an industrial park, can also play a psychological and decisive role in limiting a consumer's choice of leisure activities.

The status and size of a city also influence the consumer. Consumers living in a suburb of a large city and even in nearby towns will travel downtown to attend a show. The opposite, however, is not necessarily true.

Several factors come into play in choosing a location. Access by public transit, parking, food and beverage services, and other factors must all be considered.

In both retail and the arts, the best location is one near several other establishments. The appeal or attraction of a group of businesses has a synergizing effect that an isolated enterprise simply cannot achieve. Large shopping centres in North America rely on this principle to draw their clientele. The downtown Toronto lakefront area provides the example of Ontario Place and Harbourfront Centre, joined in summertime by the Canadian National Exhibition. Another obvious example is the concentration of theatres in the Broadway district of New York.

Example 8.1
MuseumsQuartier in Vienna: Marketing and Branding – Conflict or Cooperation?

MuseumsQuartier is a "brand name" for a cluster site, the Imperial stables, which at present comprises some 40 diverse cultural organizations and cultural activities. It occupies 53,000 square metres and includes two new museum buildings and two discrete theatres with a seating capacity of 1,200.

Additional exhibition space is available for rent, along with offices, workshops, and studios. These rental spaces are grouped together under the brand name Quarter 21. Many small cultural organizations rent space in Quarter 21, which MuseumsQuartier describes as "a structure of self-responsible, constructively competing content-entrepreneurs, a modular-action platform for independent small institutions, culture offices and temporary initiatives." It could also be described as a vehicle for a cultural industry cluster with a focus on creativity and new and multimedia technology.

Common facilities are incorporated into the overall scheme. These include signposting, an information centre (infopool), lavatories, sitting areas, and courtyards.

(continued)

Example 8.1 (continued)

In addition to institutions, there are private tenants, restaurateurs, and shopkeepers, as well as long-time tenants who have their homes there.

MuseumsQuartier's one area of common interest and mutual benefit for all concerned is marketing, including branding. MuseumsQuartier is responsible for marketing and branding the site, both nationally and internationally. However, the marketing of programs is an individual matter left to each tenant.

The company has set out to "arouse the curiosity of old and new target groups" (MQ Company Marketing Plan, 2001). It expects to draw 1.1 million visitors annually, with the Leopold Museum as the star attraction at 250,000 to 300,000 visitors.

The MQ Company (location and branding marketers) and the tenants (specific brand image/communication concept marketers) are developing a shared approach to producing marketing literature for the site. MuseumsQuartier's logo is described as "simple, practical, effective, and consciously non-artistic" (MQ Briefing Information, 2001).

Many of the organizations mount temporary exhibitions and tour them nationally and internationally along with a program of lectures and education services for children, all of which require marketing.

There is consensus that the MuseumsQuartier and its marketing activities will increase visitor numbers for the tenants, largely in terms of foreign tourists. Much of the data on current audiences are derived from tenant ticket sales. For example, the Museum of Modern Art Ludwig Foundation Vienna attracted between 110,000 and 150,000 visitors to its two Viennese sites in 1999, and anticipates at least 150,000 visitors to its new premises in the MuseumsQuartier, with a larger proportion of tourists from overseas. The Vienna Festival is well established, and with the new and expanded facilities predicts a paying audience of around 200,000.

The smaller organizations largely serve local, regional, and national cultural markets often associated with practitioners, critics, and curators. MuseumsQuartier is expected to act as a "honey pot" for practitioners and as a visible focal point for international collaboration.

Source: Simon Roodhouse, Professor, University Vocational Awards Council, Bolton Institute of Higher Education, United Kingdom.

8.5.1 The Trading Area Principle

A trading area may be defined as "the geographical space from which a sales outlet draws its clientele and sales."[4]

The appeal of a particular point of sale is far from uniform within any territory. In fact, the further away the consumer goes from the point of sale, the lesser the attraction of that location. This variation in intensity of attraction leads to a threefold division within a trading area. The three subdivisions are called primary, secondary, and tertiary trading areas.

8.5.2 Definition of the Three Trading Areas

The primary trading area includes customers from the main population served by the sales unit – in other words, the densest part of the overall area in terms of number of customers reached. Depending on the type of business, the geographic features of the location, or the sociodemographic profile of its residents, this area can represent up to 80% of the clientele. For a shop, the primary trading area is the most important geographic sector, since most of its business relies on the area that includes the most loyal customers.

The secondary trading area includes the second most important consumer population. Here, sales hover between 20% and 40% of the sales volume. This is the geographic sector in which a business is most vulnerable to aggressive competition.

The tertiary trading area is essentially a residual zone holding 10% to 20% of the clientele. These customers shop only occasionally at the store or visit it only by chance – for example, tourists. Every shop has a tertiary area, over which it has little or no influence.

To determine the trading area for their sales unit, managers need only take a sampling of their clientele, note the addresses of the customers in the sample, and draw a dot representing each customer on a map of the city or area. The result is a graphic representation of the location of their customers, which they can then analyze. Trading areas have irregular shapes, and competitors' areas may be superimposed according to the geographic features of a city or neighbourhood and the power of attraction of each competitor (see Figure 8.2).

The configuration of a trading area depends largely on the type of product offered. A presenter with a varied program may find that some products reach a specific clientele and that a comparison by product category could reveal different contours for the trading areas.

8.5.3 The Usefulness of the Trading Area Concept

The outline of a trading area is useful since it allows a business to achieve the following eight goals.

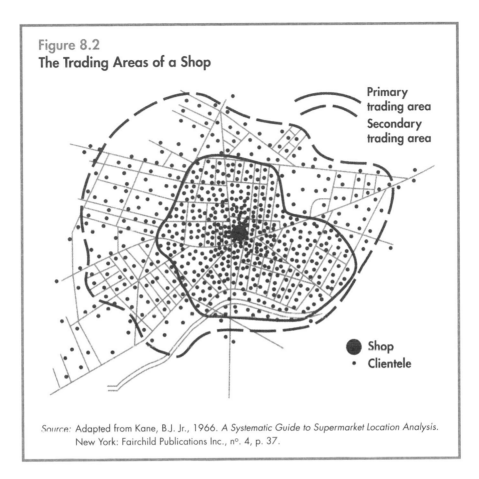

Figure 8.2
The Trading Areas of a Shop

Primary trading area
Secondary trading area

● Shop
• Clientele

Source: Adapted from Kane, B.J. Jr., 1966. *A Systematic Guide to Supermarket Location Analysis.*
New York: Fairchild Publications Inc., n°. 4, p. 37.

1) Estimate the demand in dollars within the geographic territory covered and compare the demand to the sales figures already in hand. The resulting calculation is the firm's market share.

2) Estimate future demand and its impact on store sales figures, especially if residential construction is planned within the area.

3) Decide on long-, short-, and medium-term market shares and sales objectives.

4) Measure the impact of competition in the territory and within each of the three trading areas vis-à-vis the competition.

5) Gain a better grasp of the socio-economic profile of the population living in the "attraction" area of the sales unit in order to adapt the marketing mix to potential customers.

6) Plan promotional campaigns according to potential consumers and the geographic limits of the attraction area. It could be that the firm is

wasting time and money by distributing print ads in a territory larger than the trading area or, conversely, that the firm could improve its coverage.

7) Compare outlets of a chain and, through rigorous planning based on the potential trading area, open new units. If, for example, the future location has characteristics similar or identical to those of an existing outlet, a company might forecast its volume, the size of the territory, and even the size of the new store.

8) Plan expansion by either enlarging the current store or opening other outlets.

8.5.4 Factors Determining the Extent and Configuration of the Trading Area

The three main factors determining the extent and configuration of the trading area are the product, the company's marketing strategies, and the consumer's perception of the company or the product.

Concert halls, museums, art galleries, bookstores, record shops, and movie theatres are all in the specialty category and normally have extensive commercial zones.

The other variables in the marketing mix play a role in determining the extent and configuration of the trading area. A certain pricing policy or an exciting promotion may encourage some consumers to patronize one shop rather than another. The fact that one firm is targeting a specific market segment will bring a specific category of consumers who live in a certain neighbourhood and thus give the trading area its own particular shape. This is the case for most museums, art galleries, and concert halls, which generally attract an educated, well-heeled clientele. An analysis of where this clientele lives usually reveals a concentration within postal codes where the income is higher than average.

The extent and configuration of a trading area depends on how consumers perceive certain factors. Distance, for example, may be evaluated in terms of real or psychological barriers found en route to the shop.

Some physical obstacles may actually change consumer behaviour. A river with a bridge, railway lines, highways, industrial parks, and public parks, to name a few obstacles, combine to shape the trading area. Shoppers will not cross a busy street, railway track, river, or industrial zone if they can avoid it. They will even travel a considerable distance further to shop elsewhere.

The type of street or the location of a shop influences the extent of the trading area. For example, a bookstore located within a subway station has a trading area that may be vast but is limited to commuters, while a bookstore located within a shopping centre benefits from the attraction of the centre as a whole.

8.6 INTERNATIONAL DISTRIBUTION

For prototype products, such as live shows, the type of intermediary used to arrange international distribution (or an international tour) is often a local or foreign agent. In some instances, producers of live shows will communicate directly with potential presenters. Museums, on the other hand, negotiate contracts directly with their counterparts in foreign countries when seeking to acquire the rights to a touring exhibition.

In the cultural industries, which deal mainly in the reproduction of prototypes, several distribution channels may be envisaged. The company may use an agent or distributor to export its product, or it may choose to sell the

---

Example 8.2
The Amadora International Cartoon Festival: Relocating a Facility

The Amadora International Cartoon Festival is Portugal's premier cartoon event. Since Amadora, a suburb of Lisbon, is a city known for its social and racial problems, this festival is one of the few events capable of attracting visitors to the area.

In 2005 the festival was faced with the need to relocate. It had several options, and after a careful assessment of parking facilities, security, access to public transportation, the dimensions and physical characteristics of the various spaces, costs, and so forth, the festival's management settled on a vacant commercial facility adjacent to Amadora's new subway station.

This decision proved to be an excellent one, as the new location not only allows visitors to use the subway as a means of transportation, but also reduces the perceived risk of visiting the festival. This location has the added advantage of bringing in Metropolitano de Lisboa as a major sponsor of the festival for a three-year period; the transport company uses its network of stations and trains to promote the Amadora International Cartoon Festival.

Source: Jorge Cerveira Pinto, General Manager, Evcom Lda, Lisbon, Portugal.

product directly, without an intermediary. Other options available to the company are described below.

8.6.1 Licensing

Licensing is the granting of permission by one company to another to use its intellectual property in return for royalties. Intellectual property can be a brand, copyright, technology, know-how, or even specific marketing skills. Different types of licensing agreement include the broadcasting rights to a television series, feature film distribution rights, adaptation rights for a program format or a book, or translation rights.

Licensing is a market entry or penetration strategy that applies only to the start of the exporting activity. While it is a strategy that involves little financial risk, there is no guarantee of significant future market penetration.

Licensing agreements often contain restrictions on the duration and territory of copyright use, the determination of royalties (percentage of sales, payment upon signing), commitments, dispute resolution and contract termination provisions, mutual guarantees, description of the rights granted, a confidentiality clause, and accounting aspects such as bookkeeping and auditing. The screenplay for the feature film *Louis XIX* was sold to the American producer Ron Howard, who adapted it for American audiences. The new version of the film was given the title *ED TV*. The contract granted Howard the right to use the screenplay of the original film.

8.6.2 Franchising

Franchising is a form of licensing agreement whereby one company sells another company the right to operate a business according to a specific format. It may involve the right to sell the franchise's product or to use its name, production methods, or marketing techniques. One of the benefits of a franchise arrangement for the franchisee is that it minimizes risk by providing a proven concept and a blueprint for conducting business. Franchising is also an excellent way for the franchisor to develop competence abroad with relatively little risk – although the franchisor does lose some control over the quality of the product, image, and work methods.

8.6.3 Direct Investment in a Company

In order to create or develop a permanent stake in a foreign country, a Canadian firm may decide to invest in a company abroad or to establish an office or subsidiary in a foreign country. Foreign investment allows the company to exercise greater control over the activities carried out in the country in question.

8.6.4 Joint Ventures

A joint venture, or strategic alliance, is formed when two or more partners invest in a company together, with shared responsibility for its management. Because many countries have strict regulations governing business ownership, strategic alliances are often the only way for companies to gain a foothold abroad. An example of a joint venture would be a Canadian firm that forms a partnership with a distribution company already established in South America.

8.6.5 Company Acquisition

Direct investment can also take the form of the acquisition of an existing company within a given territory. One of the advantages of this strategy is that, since the company is already established, the acquiring firm need not go through the process of finding office space, hiring staff, and so forth. Acquisition is thus a fairly rapid means of foreign expansion.

8.6.6 Subsidiaries

A company wishing to exercise greater control over its operations or to facilitate its growth may choose to open an office or a subsidiary abroad. By having a subsidiary in the foreign country, the company is in a better position to manage its production activities and ensure its expansion in the chosen territory. It may also be eligible for government assistance or subsidies in the foreign country. However, while the potential benefits can be very attractive, the financial risk is very high.

SUMMARY

The distribution variable includes three distinct elements: the distribution channel, physical distribution, and commercial location.

Distribution channels include all those who play a role in the chain bringing the product from the manufacturer to the end consumer. A distribution channel can be short, as in the case of a museum dealing directly with the public without any intermediary whatsoever, or long, as in the case of a recording company using agents who sell to wholesalers who then sell to retailers. The distribution route enables a manufacturer to reduce its total number of operations, by fulfilling a number of logistic functions, such as shipping and warehousing, and commercial functions, such as promotional support, financing, and inventory.

The main aspects involved in the management of a distribution channel correspond to four objectives and six strategic decisions. The four objectives are: maximize profit (or reach the break-even point) by maintaining maximum motivation within the distribution channel; maximizing profits means maximizing sales and minimizing costs. The six strategic decisions involve the length of the distribution channel, the distribution strategy deployed, the type of intermediaries, the ratio of routes to intermediaries, the degree of cooperation offered to intermediaries, and the selection of those intermediaries.

A distribution channel should not be considered simply the flow of merchandise from producer to end consumer. It is a social network in which interpersonal relationships play a role and influence the dynamics. The four key dimensions within this social network are: conflict, power, roles, and communication.

There are two broad types of distribution strategy: intensive, selective, and exclusive; and push and pull. The first type corresponds to the number of points of sale a firm wishes to use. If the firm is using the intensive distribution strategy, it wants to maximize the number of points of sale used. If the firm is using the selective distribution strategy, it chooses retailers according to specific criteria and, with an exclusive strategy, grants additional territorial protection. The second type of strategy involves the use of a profit margin earned by the intermediary and is based on the effort the manufacturer wants the intermediary to expend. If the agent or intermediary promotes the product, the margin will be greater, and vice versa. The producer or manufacturer uses this margin to balance the cost of an advertising or promotional campaign.

Physical distribution is made up of all the logistics and movements involved in bringing a product to market – that is, shipping, warehousing, inventory management, order processing, handling, and packaging. Physical distribution must meet two contradictory objectives: minimize costs and maximize customer service.

Location is the choice of a physical site where the product will be bought or consumed. By studying where consumers come from, it is possible to determine three trading areas based on the distance from the sales outlet and the concentration of the clientele. The extent and configuration of these trading areas are called primary, secondary, and tertiary. They are determined by the following factors: product (generic sense of term), corporate marketing strategies, and consumer perception.

In the cultural industries, which deal mainly in the reproduction of prototypes, there are six main modes of international distribution: licensing, franchising, direct investment, joint ventures, company acquisition, and subsidiaries.

QUESTIONS

1. The way a cultural product is consumed influences the distribution of that product. How?
2. What is a distribution channel?
3. Why are decisions about the choice of a distribution channel important?
4. What is the main reason for having intermediaries?
5. What are the main functions of a distribution channel?
6. What does complexity means in terms of a distribution channel?
7. Why must a company consider long-term maximum profits when managing its distribution channel?
8. What are the six basic questions a manufacturer must ask before setting up a distribution channel?
9. Explain the concept of a social network within a distribution channel.
10. Explain how the following strategies are interrelated: skimming and penetration; intensive, selective, and exclusive; push and pull.
11. Describe the different components of physical distribution.
12. What are the factors to be considered in choosing a good location?
13. How is the concept of a trading area useful to a manager?
14. Identify and describe the six modes of international distribution in the cultural industries.

Notes

1. Roodhouse, S. 1999. "A Challenge to Cultural Sector Management Conventions – The Royal Armories Museum." *International Journal of Arts Management*, Vol. 1, n° 2 (Winter), p. 82–90.

2. Mallen, B. 1977. *Principles of Marketing Channel Management*. Toronto: Lexington Books.

3. Rosenbloom, B. 1983. *Marketing Channels: A Management View*, 2nd ed. Chicago: Dryden Press.

4. Colbert, F., and R. Côté. 1990. *Localisation commerciale*. Boucherville, Quebec: Gaëtan Morin Éditeur.

PLAN

Chapter **9**

The Promotion Variable

OBJECTIVES

- Define promotion as a variable
- Identify the main functions of promotion
- Look at various promotional tools
- Learn how to select the most appropriate promotional tools
- Study a communications plan

INTRODUCTION

Promotion, the fourth variable in the marketing mix, is vital to the marketing strategy of any company. Promotion bridges the gap between the company and the marketplace.

In this chapter, we look at promotional tools, their functions, and selection criteria based on the objectives already set out for the consumer market. We then define the various components of a communications plan and take a closer look at direct marketing and media relations.

The solicitation of the cultural enterprise's other markets is not addressed in any detail in this chapter. Solicitation in these cases usually takes the form of direct contact between the cultural enterprise and the various players in the government, partner, or private sector market. The basic principles of communication apply equally to these markets.

9.1 DEFINITION

Marketing, advertising, and promotion are regularly confused. The following succinct definition should clarify matters. Advertising is actually a promotional tool, whereas promotion is a variable in the marketing mix. The marketing mix is one part of the overall marketing model.

Promotion is first and foremost a communications tool, an instrument for transmitting the official corporate message and image to the four markets of the cultural enterprise. Companies have direct control over corporate communications and can decide how to manage their image and the content of their message. Of course, other variables within the marketing mix can also reflect the company's image, and, in the cultural milieu, the critics also send a message to its different potential markets.

Cultural enterprises project an image to the general public as well as to other markets. Their image derives from consumer perceptions based on others' opinions, critics' reviews, experience, promotional campaigns, and so on. Although companies may not be able to control the consumer's perception based on messages received from other variables in the marketing mix, they can nonetheless influence public perception. In fact, pricing policy, choice of distributors, and promotional technique used can create or modify image. A high price level usually reflects a prestigious image, as in the case of a concert in a famous hall. Conversely, a concert advertised in the daily newspaper with a low ticket price reflects a more popular image.

Promotion is also a tool of change, enabling a firm to modify consumers' perceptions, attitudes, knowledge, and awareness. Therefore, promotion can educate the consumer about a product to varying degrees. It can also adjust consumer attitudes by turning indifference into desire or transforming negative perceptions into positive ones.

In other words, the function of promotion is to inform, persuade, and educate existing and potential customers.

9.2 PROMOTIONAL TOOLS

The four main tools used in promotion are advertising, personal selling, public relations, and sales promotion. The weight given to each may depend on the company's budget or the traditions within a particular industry. Also, certain tools are more appropriate for some markets than for others. Advertising, for example, is rarely used with governments, while contact with the private sector usually requires one-on-one communication (personal selling).

9.2.1 Advertising

Advertising can be defined as the impersonal means by which a company pays to communicate with its target market. Visibility obtained through

---

Example 9.1
Photography: An Important Promotional Tool

Photography is of the utmost importance in theatre and dance. A theatre should have an excellent relationship with a photographer who specializes in theatrical work. Images of exceptional quality have a better chance of being reproduced in nationwide publications.

A promotional shot must be set up in such as way that it "looks like theatre." A theatrical photograph should feature theatrical lighting, set, costumes, and make-up so that it is easily distinguishable from a photograph that is static and not theatrical-looking. This photograph will be instrumental in creating a branding image for the company. We look for a photograph that represents our organization (theatrical, edgy, contemporary, intriguing, etc.) and then use the image in our season ticket ad campaign, banners around town, on the side of our theatre, on the side of buses, and so forth. This image will become an identifiable icon for the entire season.

Source: Tad Janes, Producing Artistic Director, Maryland Ensemble Theatre, USA.

press releases or media coverage is considered publicity rather than advertising. Publicity is one element of the public relations function, which generally includes media relations.

An advertising message may appear in different electronic and print media. Common examples are television and radio commercials, newspaper and magazine ads, posters, billboards, advertising within the public-transit system, Weblogs (or "blogs"), and official Web sites.

In order for an advertisement to appear, payment is made to an advertising support vehicle, such as a radio or TV station, magazine, newspaper, or billboard.

The advertising message, whatever its medium, has a limited life span. In fact, ads are developed for a specific medium and may target both the general public (mass advertising) and a highly specific public (targeted advertising). The executive's challenge is to find out which advertising vehicles are the most appropriate. Here, a profile of the public reached by the various media that the firm is considering would prove useful.

The poster is used extensively by cultural enterprises. It is, however, merely a support for the other advertising tools used. In fact, potential customers may not always see a poster and, if driving, cannot stop to read the information given. Moreover, the average amount of time spent reading a poster is very short. The life span of a poster itself is brief, especially in large cities, where the practice of covering or removing posters has become fierce. As well, the amount of information that can fit on a poster is limited. A poster should be designed to attract attention and generate interest among prospective customers. Usually, it acts as a reminder of the message given in the main campaign.[1]

9.2.2 Personal Selling

Personal selling consists of transmitting a message from one person to the next through direct contact. This technique enables the seller to deal with the customer's reasons for not buying. Personal selling may be face to face, over the telephone one on one, or in groups.

Advertising is an extremely potent means of persuasion if the message to be transmitted is simple. For more complicated messages, personal selling is more effective, since the representative of the company can adapt the advertising message to the consumer and respond to his or her questions or reasons for not buying. Personal selling is the preferred variable for selling an idea. A funding or sponsorship request can be regarded as a form of personal selling in which the applicant attempts to convince the client that it will obtain the benefits sought if it "buys" the idea being proposed.

Besides using persuasion to sell a product, a salesperson also conducts research and provides information. Sales representatives learn all about customers' needs, problems, and reservations in order to respond to their expectations, and they supply services related to sales activities, maintain cordial interpersonal relationships with customers, and provide friendly assistance and advice during the purchasing process. They may also coordinate consumer needs with the company's other products or services.

9.2.3 Public Relations

Public relations (PR) has been defined as "the management function that evaluates public attitudes, identifies an individual or an organization with the public interest, and plans and executes a program of action to earn public understanding and acceptance" (*Public Relations News*, 27 October 1947). One of the main weapons in the PR arsenal of a cultural organization is publicity, which serves to promote a product or company in the media without paying to advertise. Media relations is part of the public relations function. Press releases and press conferences, speeches and presentations, free air time on radio or TV, and general media coverage are all examples of publicity.

For financial reasons, many cultural and arts groups are obliged to use publicity, particularly media relations, as their main vehicle to inform potential customers (see Capsule 9.1). The main disadvantage of this approach is that, since the company does not control all aspects of the coverage (message, frequency of publication, etc.), publicity cannot fulfil all the functions of the other variables in the marketing mix. Of course, the media also benefit from this relationship, since cultural activities attract a sizeable audience.

Cultural enterprises have tremendous power in terms of publicity, but the media do have the final say in deciding whether to air or print information and in which format. Hence, there is always some risk involved.

While it is important to distinguish clearly between the public relations function, which deals with a variety of the organization's publics (employees, board members, volunteers, audience members, the media, governments, sponsors, and donors), and the publicity function, which deals almost exclusively with media relations, it should also be noted that since many cultural organizations focus the bulk of their PR activity on the media, they have a tendency to equate public relations with publicity.

9.2.4 Sales Promotion

Sales promotion encompasses all of the efforts deployed to keep the name of the company or the product in the consumer's mind beyond the consumption experience.

Capsule 9.1
Basic Principles of Media Relations

The job of journalists working in the cultural milieu is to disseminate news; they are not in the service of cultural organizations or artists. Therefore, it is important for cultural groups to develop a relationship of trust with the media and to try to make their job easier.

The main tool used by the PR officer is the press list. A good press list has three essential characteristics: it can be broken down according to type of media; it contains the names of several journalists working in the same media; and it includes the organization's stakeholders, such as funding bodies, sponsors, and board members.

Media relations involves six steps:
- Formulate your news
- Prepare communications tools (press releases, photos, etc.)
- Target specific media and send your message out to them
- Follow up with the media to ensure that your news is published or broadcast
- Collect articles and reports following the release of the news item
- Analyze impacts and adjust your strategy

Source: Translated from Courville, N., "Les relations de presse dans le secteur culturel." http://www.gestiondesarts.com/index.php?id=383

It can take the form of a simple logo or succinct message printed on a small object (matchbook, pencil, badge) that is given away free of charge.[2]

As we saw in Chapter 1, spin-off products are an element of the company's main product. They serve to increase the company's overall independent revenue[3] and to prolong the consumption experience. A spin-off product can also help to disseminate the company's image, and thus can be an effective promotional tool. Museums and large organizations in the performing arts often use this form of promotion.

Sales promotion is usually applied to consumers, but it may also be used with retailers and distributors. When sales promotion is used with consumers, reductions might be given on the purchase of a certain number of tickets, for example. The same reduction technique can be used to encourage retailers to offer the product or to promote it more. Bonus points per unit sold, which can be exchanged for valuable prizes such as airline tickets or holiday packages, is a typical means of sales promotion.

9.2.5 The Promotional Mix

As stated above, promotion uses four main tools: advertising, PR, sales promotion, and personal selling. Every organization has its own recipe or scale for deciding on how much of each ingredient is needed. Some groups may be able to afford only the free promotion PR/publicity offers. Small artistic enterprises fall into this category: they often run print ads or produce posters but concentrate their efforts on obtaining media coverage. The ad or poster thus supports the other promotional tools and projects the group's image. Other groups may base their promotional strategy on the purchase of advertising in media that target specific segments. Some try to strike a balance among the four tools available. In the end, the promotional mix depends on the organization's goals and means.

Direct marketing can be described as a combination of several promotional tools. For example, telemarketing, which is one of the methods used by cultural enterprises to solicit donations from their subscribers, can combine personal selling, advertising, and sales promotion: an employee phones the potential client directly, then sends the person a brochure by mail or e-mail and encloses or attaches advertising elements (sales promotion) (see section 9.7 for more details).

9.3 THE FUNCTIONS OF PROMOTION

Promotion has two main functions: to communicate a message and to produce a change in the consumer.

9.3.1 Communicating a Message

The message a company wants to communicate may use one or any number of codes (pictorial, visual, graphic, written, symbolic, or even colour), which must be properly perceived and understood by the consumer.

Communication is truly a bilateral process that involves the active participation of both sender and receiver. It enables the sender to analyze gaps in understanding and to adjust accordingly so as to reach the receiver in a more efficient and suitable manner.

The communication process described here applies to individuals as well as to mass communication. In any event, for a message to be transmitted efficiently, the sender must know the identity of the receiver and which codes the receiver will understand.

9.3.2 Producing a Change in the Customer

Besides conveying a message, promotion acts as an agent of change. As such, it tries to generate positive consumer attitudes toward the product and, ultimately, product sales.

The function of promotion may be defined as a series of four steps: attract attention, create interest, generate desire, provoke action. These four steps are known by their mnemonic name AIDA (attention, interest, desire, action).

Of course, promotional campaigns are not conducted in a vacuum. One company's message is in competition with a staggering number of other messages produced by a host of other companies throughout the different sectors of the economy. Estimates have shown that the average consumer is exposed, consciously or unconsciously, to somewhere between 250 and 3,000 messages daily. The exact number depends on the individual's media-consumption habits. These messages are received while the consumer reads the morning paper, listens to the car radio, watches TV, or glances at a poster or billboard. Out of all those messages, approximately 75 will actually be perceived and only 12 will be retained. In other words, there is a constant barrage of messages and stimuli coming from all directions, and the average consumer must develop various mechanisms to filter out some messages. Obviously, any company trying to attract the consumer's attention faces an arduous task, especially given the number of messages and the number of consumer defence mechanisms.

Defence Mechanisms

Psychological processes called "defence factors" play a role in diminishing and even blocking messages transmitted by the mass media. These factors act as filters and enable the consumer to select messages. The selection process is linked to exposure and attention as well as understanding or retention.

Consumers looking for a product choose the messages they want to see or hear (selective exposure). For example, a consumer who wants to see a play willingly looks at the ads placed by theatre companies in the daily newspaper.

Selective perception implies that the consumer notices only certain messages because of the urgency or importance of personal needs. If those needs are very strong, the customer will be more receptive and possibly interested in buying. This mechanism explains how a consumer seeking one title can find it in the window without even seeing the other books displayed there.

Selective comprehension is another filter that comes into play when decoding an ad. The consumer interprets the signs (colour, symbol, shape, etc.) according to his or her needs and values. For example, red or orange is usually associated with warmth in people's minds, whereas deep blue is associated with cold. Signs or symbols must be selected carefully or the potential customer might misunderstand the message. It is also important to keep in mind, particularly in the case of international marketing, that cultural differences can play a huge role in the symbolic value associated with colours.

Another mechanism is selective retention, which enables the consumer to retain only part of the message received and perceived. Novelty, repetition, and interest do have a significant influence on retention, but the consumer's needs and values also have a definite influence on which messages are retained.

Subliminal Advertising

The obstacles encountered in persuading consumers to buy have encouraged researchers to search for ways to avoid the filters described above. Their research has led to experiments in subliminal advertising. In theory, subliminal advertising allows a message to break through the consumer's defences and reach the subconscious without the consumer's knowledge. In the consumer's subconscious, the desire to buy the product is then provoked.

An early experiment in subliminal advertising carried out in 1959 at a movie theatre started the American trend of ads using elements of subliminal advertising. The principle behind the experiment was quite simple.[4] The researcher had inserted one image of Coca-Cola among the 24 images projected per second on the big screen. As a result, viewers saw an unequivocal message, "Drink Coca-Cola," every second without knowing it. At intermission, sales of the famous soft drink rose by 52% over previous sales figures. The same experiment using popcorn generated an 18% increase in sales.

Further experimentation never yielded such convincing results, and nothing proved conclusively that the increase in sales during the 1959 experiment could be attributed solely to the subliminal messages projected on the movie screen. Other external factors not even considered by the researchers, such as room temperature, promotion at point of sale, and sheer chance, could have played a role.

Various individuals and lobby groups considered subliminal advertising dangerous and condemned it as a manipulative practice akin to brainwashing. As a precautionary measure, several countries have outlawed subliminal advertising.

9.4   THE CHOICE OF PROMOTIONAL TOOLS

9.4.1 The Parameters of Influence

In addition to the market that is targeted, the company's choice of promotional tools depends primarily on two parameters of influence: the complexity of the message, and the target market's knowledge of the product (referential dimension).

Since the choice of promotional tools varies according to the complexity of the message, a simple message can be delivered easily through advertising, whereas a complex message requires a far more personal approach.

The complexity of the message is often related to the complexity of the product as perceived by the customer. For example, a true opera buff immediately sees a reason for buying tickets to *Madama Butterfly*, while someone who does not know opera or even has a negative bias toward opera might see no reason whatsoever to do so. Although an advertising campaign can encourage the opera fan to buy tickets, personal selling would be far more effective in interesting the potential opera-goer in tickets to a performance of *Madama Butterfly*, or could at least deal with the consumer's arguments or modify perceptions.

There are six stages in the process that leads a potential buyer from ignorance to action: ignorance, knowledge, understanding, conviction, decision, and action.

The true opera devotee may be at stage 4, conviction. This is usually an individual who knows the repertoire, understands the significance of the works, can appreciate the content, and might be led to the decision stage more easily than the consumer starting out at stage 1, ignorance.

The more advanced the consumer is along the ignorance–action continuum, the less complicated the promotional campaign. The loyal readers of an established author launching a new book or the current subscribers to a series of concerts are part of a market segment near the action stage. Conversely, promotion is more complex when the potential consumer hovers around the ignorance stage or has a negative bias toward the product.

A promotional campaign should therefore guide consumers from wherever they may be along the continuum through the stages of the buying process up to the actual purchase of the product.

9.4.2 A Practical Model

The model presented in Figure 9.1 shows how the complexity of the product, the market size, and the choice of promotional tools are related.

The model is presented as a sequence of pyramids that represent the product, the market, advertising, and personal selling. Each pyramid forms a continuum. The tip and the base act as poles reflecting the importance of certain characteristics; for example, the tip of the product pyramid demonstrates a low level of complexity, while the base reflects a high level.

Example 9.2
University of New Orleans Musical Excursions Concert Series: Promotion in Troubled Times

When it became possible for the University of New Orleans to reopen in January 2006 following the devastation caused by Hurricane Katrina, the manager of the university's Musical Excursions concert series was faced with a daunting task. He was able to rebook his performers, and the concert hall was damaged and unusable although he had the permission of the theatre department to use its space. The only problem was how to find an audience.

Management knew that traditional marketing methods would not work. Many audience members were older and did not have e-mail; many others had had their computers damaged or destroyed. They also knew that the only way to find an audience was to go to the places that people frequented in post-Katrina New Orleans. Luckily, they had plenty of posters and flyers, which they supplemented with postcard-sized notices.

Students were sent into the three areas of the city that were still functioning – the French Quarter, the Central Business District and the Garden District – armed with materials to deposit with any business that was open. The response was positive. Most merchants were surprised to learn that the university was functioning. Most of the places that would normally be a natural for flyers and posters, such as museums and libraries, were closed or empty. By far the greatest response came from restaurants. Many of the people who had returned home were unable to cook because they had no gas or because the supermarkets were closed. Those eating establishment that were open, therefore, were packed every night, and customers waiting for tables had plenty of time to pick up promotional materials.

New Orleans residents were looking for places to go during that difficult time, and many thanked Musical Excursions for continuing the series instead of cancelling it for the season. The house was not filled every night, but attendance was always respectable and management was proud to be able to bring its concerts to the community. And the whole city knew that, during that time of rebuilding, the University of New Orleans was up and running.

Source: Harmon Greenblatt, Arts Administration Program, University of New Orleans, USA.

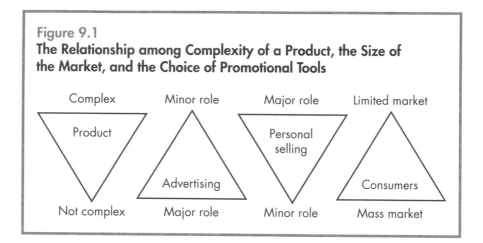

Figure 9.1
The Relationship among Complexity of a Product, the Size of the Market, and the Choice of Promotional Tools

The tip of the consumer pyramid indicates that the consumer market is limited and not very extensive, while the base portrays a much larger market, often called the "mass market."

The personal selling and advertising pyramids illustrate the order of importance of one or the other of these tools based on the complexity of the product and the market segment. Thus, the tip indicates limited recourse to promotional tools, while the base corresponds to extensive use of promotional tools.

As a rule, complex products are designed for a limited market. As we saw in Chapter 2, a product may be complex in terms of its technical specifications or in terms of the customer's product knowledge. Similarly, if a market segment has a negative attitude toward a product, that product may be considered complex to the consumers within that segment. The more complex the product, the more detailed the sales pitch and the higher the level of information used to convince the consumer. In this instance, personal selling is the most suitable tool, since advertising does not convey very complex or dense information. For example, a concert of electro-acoustic music is a simple product for experts in this type of music. A poster will therefore be adequate to inform fans and encourage them to buy a ticket. On the other hand, the sales pitch will have to be stronger for the consumer who has never heard of this art form and is not even a music fan. A poster and a newspaper ad will not be powerful enough to convince the latter consumer to attend. Personal selling is needed in this instance.

Conversely, since there is a vast market for simple products, personal selling is not necessary or even desirable, given the high cost involved. Advertising as a promotional tool works better in this case, since it allows for much broader market coverage.

9.5   THE RECEIVER

The process that consumers use to purchase a product may include several "players" who must be considered when developing a marketing strategy. They are the initiator, the influencer, the decision-maker, the buyer, and the user. Several messages must be created to reach the various players intervening in the purchase process.

In the market for children's theatre within the school system, various decision-makers have the final say as to whether the show will be presented. The many individuals involved have different roles in the decision-making process. The home and school association or parents' committee plays the role of influencer. The teaching staff is the initiator of the process, and the school principal usually plays the dual role of decision-maker and buyer. Lastly, the pupils are the users of the product. Each individual school may have its own decision-making procedure, and the number of players and their corresponding roles may double or shift at different stages in the process. For example, sometimes the parents or the teaching staff will trigger the process.

Any arts enterprise must know how the consumption units within the target market make decisions and examine the purchasing process.

9.6   THE COMMUNICATIONS PLAN

Once the marketing manager has determined which groups to target, it is time to develop a strategy based on the objectives set and the target segments to be reached. Marketers can use a series of basic questions to guide them in this process.

9.6.1   The Basic Questions Any Communications Plan Must Address

This plan is a practical tool used in reaching objectives and specific market segments. It forces a company to reflect upon which approach to adopt within several key parameters. In simpler terms, this plan can be considered an exercise that answers the questions Who? What? To whom? How? When? With what results? Table 9.1 lists the basic six questions.

Who?

First, in order to run an effective promotional campaign, a company must know the image it projects – that is, the consumer's perception of the company (positioning). The marketing manager or team should ask the following questions:

- How does the public perceive the company and the product?

- How does the company measure up in terms of the competition?
- Does the image projected accurately reflect the image desired?

What?

The company must then decide what kind of message to send. Key questions include the following:
- What advantages does the product have?
- What motivates the consumer to buy the product?
- What are the company's intentions in terms of communications?
- Can the image be changed?
- Is it enough just to make a product known, or do potential customers need to be led up to the buying stage?

To whom?

The company must segment its market and decide who actually receives the message. In other words, the questions are as follows.
- Which segment should be targeted?
- Who are the decision-makers?
- What is the profile of the target market?

How?

The company must then determine the optimal way of reaching the target segments. The following questions should be posed:
- Which media are usually consulted by the target segment(s)?
- Should written or electronic media be the focus?
- Which media should be used to reach the majority of target groups?
- Which promotional tools should be used most (personal selling, advertising, PR, or sales promotion)?
- Which codes should be used (colour, symbol, etc.)?
- Which unique features should be highlighted (renown, prestige, accessibility, novelty, exclusivity)?

When?

Naturally, the company must decide when the message should be transmitted, given the various objectives and limits implied by the choice of a particular channel. A number of questions arise:
- When should the subscription campaign be launched?
- What are the media and ad-placement deadlines?
- Which day is best for advertising (Saturday, Thursday, or another day)?
- What are the target market's shopping or purchasing habits?

With what results?

The company must have measurable objectives that enable it to judge promotional efforts. The following questions should give an idea of how effective a communications plan has been.

- By what percentage did sales increase?
- How did attitudes change?
- Is there a gap between the objectives targeted and those achieved? If so, why?
- Did the company draw upon all the resources at its disposal?
- Did it overuse its resources?
- Did the communications plan reach the target groups who did not know the product existed?
- Finally, the bottom line: Did the consumer actually buy the product?

9.6.2 The Content of a Communications Plan

A communications plan can be viewed as "an ordered series of decisions and operations designed to structure the channel of communication, to determine which elements to include in a campaign, and to evaluate the amount of money needed." A communications plan requires some prior analysis to enlighten this ordered series of decisions.

The Stages of a Communications Plan

After analyzing the situation, the marketing manager or team must set communications objectives, draft a budget, and create the overall promotional strategy with specific strategies for each component of the marketing mix. Three key decisions must be made for each component: determine the concept, determine the means or tools, and determine the budget. Lastly, the strategies must be implemented and monitored.

Setting Communications Objectives

Any promotional campaign needs clearly defined communications objectives, which must conform to the objectives of the marketing strategy. Marketing and communications objectives are somewhat different in nature.

Marketing objectives are expressed in terms of market share or sales volume. Communications objectives are related to changes that a company wishes to make in the customer's consumption process. Communications objectives usually include increasing awareness, maintaining the current rate of intention to buy, or modifying the consumer's preference.

These objectives must be expressed quantitatively in order to facilitate measurement of the results achieved. For example, a company might wish to increase its market share by 10% (marketing objective). It must therefore increase the intention of buying by 50% among potential consumers (communications objective) or achieve 80% capacity.

Drawing up a Promotional Budget

Drafting a promotional budget is usually a delicate matter in any company. Unfortunately, there is no miracle cure or secret recipe that enables a marketing manager to determine the optimal amount to invest in a promotional campaign.

There are, however, three basic principles that should be followed when setting the upper limit of the amount to be invested:

1) Each additional dollar invested must contribute to corporate profits or surplus.
2) Each additional dollar that generates at least one cent of profit or surplus is worthwhile.
3) The cost of a sale must be less than the revenue generated by that sale.

These three principles are both economically and logically obvious, but rarely does a company have the information needed to calculate down to the penny a budget that corresponds to them.

9.7 DIRECT MARKETING *(BY PHILIPPE RAVANAS)*

Traditional communication tools were developed to promote fast-moving consumer goods and have proven less efficient for cultural organizations. In the field of culture, targets are usually too small, products too complex, and budgets too limited to fully take advantage of mass communication techniques. Moreover, the impact of advertising is undeniable but difficult to precisely measure. One can never be sure that an advertisement has been seen, understood, and remembered, since communication is one way: from the organization to its target. Separating the effect of advertising from other factors influencing consumers is particularly arduous.

Last, promotional spending for consumer goods has been growing steadily and tends to overpower products with smaller budgets. Because of this constant growth, the multiplication of media, and the resulting advertising omnipresence, consumers tend to develop an immunity to this type of marketing and shield themselves from the communication avalanche by ignoring most advertising messages.

Direct marketing can address all of these concerns.

9.7.1 Definition

Direct marketing "consists of direct connections with carefully targeted individual consumers to both obtain an immediate response and cultivate lasting customer relationships."[5] In a direct marketing campaign, an organization sends a specific, usually time-limited, promotional offer directly to individual customers via mail, telephone, or e-mail and not via mass communication media such as billboards, press, radio, and television. This generates a direct and rapid response in the form of an order, a subscription renewal, a request for further information, or a visit to a retail outlet or a Web site.

Direct marketing often leads to direct distribution. Since the consumer responding to the offer orders the product directly from the company, the latter can do away with intermediaries and resellers. This model fits cultural organizations whose mission is to host live audiences (theatres, symphonies, museums) because tickets can be easily mailed or printed from the Internet.

Direct marketing is not new: catalogue sales have been around for a long time. However, the evolution of information technologies (particularly database management and the Internet) have breathed new life into this tool. Thanks to these technologies, it is now possible for an organization to forge a dense customized relationship with each individual customer with the goal of better meeting his or her needs.

Direct marketing offers several advantages:

- More accurate targeting than traditional advertising, since only the consumers whose buying potential has been identified will be contacted with a customized offer. With traditional advertising, targeting is only as precise as the audience of a given media. For example, an advertisement in a newspaper will be seen – and perhaps read – by its readers, who are not all actual or potential customers of the product promoted in the advertisement.
- Accurate return-on-investment measurement of a promotional campaign, since the rate of response to the offer and the cost per contact is known. For example, if one sends 1,000 letters with a specific offer and 20 people who received the offer respond to it, one can calculate the return on investment of the campaign by dividing the amount of the 20 sales by their total cost (time spent formulating the offer and drafting the message, costs for paper, printing, envelope, stamp, and handling).
- A more personalized, two-way communication stream with the target, since the latter is encouraged to respond directly. This consumer feedback is essential to improve the service offered and customer satisfaction.
- The possibility of sending dense messages and complex offers without the space limitation of traditional media.

- Reduction in lead time between the initiation of the offer and its reception by the customer, since the offer can be sent at any time, independent of the formal publication schedule.

For all these reasons, direct marketing is widespread and is becoming the main means of communication and distribution for many cultural organizations.

9.7.2 Direct Response Media

The media most commonly used for direct marketing are mail, telephone, and the Internet.

- *Mail:* this traditional medium for direct marketing is still very much in use, despite competition from the Internet. Mail offers many formats for direct, individual communication: letters, postcards, brochures, catalogues, samples, tapes or CDs. In many countries, the postal service offers discounted prices for mass mailing.
- *Telephone:* Telemarketing (i.e., using the telephone for direct marketing purposes) is faster and more interactive than mail, but also more expensive. Calling people is time-consuming and labour-intensive. Telemarketing is regulated in some countries: individuals can have their phone number de-listed to avoid receiving sales and marketing calls.
- *Internet:* e-marketing (i.e., using the Internet for direct marketing purposes) has some key advantages. It is as fast and interactive as telemarketing but much less expensive: an e-mail message costs a fraction of what a phone call or a stamp costs. Access to the Internet is growing rapidly; the vast majority of consumers of cultural goods are already connected or soon will be.

  However, the flood of "spam" (unauthorized commercial e-mails) has tainted the image of e-marketing. In reaction, several countries have adopted restrictive legislation to curb the flow of undesired e-mails.

  For example, Chicago's Steppenwolf Theatre Company[6] asks every ticket buyer for an e-mail address and has already gathered a database of 50,000 e-mail addresses. This database is an excellent tool for promoting ongoing or forthcoming shows, and allows for quick corrective actions in the case of lower-than-anticipated attendance. It takes only a couple of hours for Steppenwolf to define a promotional offer, draft a message, source the database for prospects, and e-mail them the offer at a very low cost.

If the organization chooses to use all these media, it needs to integrate them in a coherent direct marketing strategy. In turn, that strategy should be integrated in the overall marketing strategy and coordinated with all other communication tools used.

9.7.3 Databases and Modelling

To prepare for a direct marketing campaign, an organization must first collect all available and accessible information about each customer: contact information (name, address, phone number, and e-mail address) and information to assess his/her interest in the promoted product (sociodemographic and psychographic segment descriptors presented in Chapter 6, consumer behaviour data, etc.).

The organization can ask its customer for this information during direct transactions. Alternatively, it can buy the information from a third party or get it from an organization targeting the same audience, in exchange for information about other consumers. Consumer information is then consolidated in a computerized database for easy access and updating – particularly after each transaction with the customer.

The organization can then source the database for a specific type of consumer and offer them tailor-made services. It can also analyze past consumption patterns for each customer and follow the evolution of his/her relationship with the organization. This evolution is often called "the consumer life cycle". From all the information gathered, the organization can also extrapolate a series of standard consumer profiles: this process is called "modelling." By comparing the life cycle of one customer to several consumer profiles, the organization can forecast when, how, and how much a customer will buy. With such knowledge, it can contact him/her and offer them exactly what they want.

9.7.4 Direct Marketing and Relationship Marketing

This deep knowledge of each customer, the capacity to understand his/her taste and preferences and to predict future transactions, has transformed the marketing function. It announces the end of traditional mass marketing – the primary objective of which was to sell products to unidentified consumers using the same rationale and message for every consumer – and opens a new era of relationship marketing – the primary objective of which is to deepen the relationship between the organization and each customer in order to increase purchases.

This customized one-on-one relationship[7], is a source of wealth for an organization. It builds customer loyalty by tailoring services to consumer profiles, by offering these services when they are wanted, and by allowing the customer to critique the offer made. However, it necessitates significant investments in software and hardware, ongoing information gathering, and the ability to customize offers. To be profitable, it also requires the prioritization of high-potential clients.

All this is not always possible – or desirable – for cultural organizations.

Example 9.3
The Adelaide Symphony Orchestra: Segmentation and Audience Development

When the Adelaide Symphony Orchestra realized it had no programs directly targeting the 16-to-24 age group, a particularly important market segment for the future growth of the audience, it held focus groups with people in this age group and asked them what they would like or would expect to see when attending a live music performance.

These focus groups gave birth to a concept called The Edge, a series of orchestral concerts playing a repertoire of "indie style" bands such as Muse, Wolfmother, The Scholars, and Radio Head. The music is arranged by a professional composer, also in the 16-to-24 age bracket. The atmosphere of the concerts is enhanced through special public address and lighting systems, bar facilities, and having the entire audience stand for the performance.

Promotion is targeted directly to the 16-to-24 age group through the use of specific artwork styles, identified by the focus groups, printed on posters and bar coasters that are distributed to live music venues and clubs, merchandise such as T shirts, and promotion on local indie radio stations. Most significant has been the orchestra's use of social networking Web sites such as My Space to promote and build interest in the concept.

The Edge has been a huge success, with all concerts selling out more than two months before the event.

Source: Stephen Boyle, Associate Director, Arts and Cultural Management Program, University of South Australia, Adelaide, Australia, and Michelle Richards, Director, Marketing and Development, Adelaide Symphony Orchestra, Adelaide, Australia.

9.7.5 Ethical and Legal Considerations

Gathering more and more detailed information about actual and potential clients raises some concerns for privacy, particularly when an organization seeks to collect financial, medical, or personal information. Gathering this information through the Internet is even more problematic, since the open nature of the Internet does not guarantee confidentiality.

In many countries, these concerns have led to the creation of laws regulating this gathering process in order to protect consumer privacy – particularly the privacy of minors.

To fully exploit the potential of applying direct marketing principles to new information technology, an organization must not only conform to all regulations in place, but also define and publish a clear code of ethics, in order to reassure its customers. Each consumer should have the right to know what type of information has been gathered by the company about him/her and what it plans to do with this information, to refuse to have this information shared with any other organization, to have full access to it, and to be able to modify it. If an organization breaches this code of ethics, the organization will lose the trust of its customers.

SUMMARY

Promotional tools are advertising, personal selling, PR (which includes publicity), and sales promotion.

The functions of promotion are essentially to communicate a message to the consumer and bring about a change in the consumer. The change is particularly important if the customer is near the ignorance stage. If a great deal of change is needed or if the product is complex, personal selling is the most appropriate tool. If the change or product is relatively simple, advertising should be used, with the other tools used to support it. In the cultural milieu, limited budgets make PR/publicity the most widely used tool.

In any form of commercial communication, knowing the various players involved in the purchasing decision is important. There are normally five players: initiator, influencer, decision-maker, buyer, and user. The next step is to draw up a communications plan that answers six questions: Who? To whom? What? How? When? With what results?

As a rule, there are eight steps to follow in drawing up a communications plan. The first three are related to the corporate marketing strategy: analysis of the situation, setting marketing goals, and developing the marketing strategy. The five steps specifically involving the communications plan are setting objectives, drawing up a budget, developing strategies, and implementing and then monitoring such strategies.

Cultural enterprises often use relationship marketing (or direct marketing) as a way to target individual consumers. While the telephone and mail are the traditional media used for direct marketing, the Internet has given companies a valuable new tool for reaching consumers directly.

QUESTIONS

1. What is promotion?
2. What distinguishes the four promotional tools?
3. What are the main functions of the promotion variable?
4. When is personal selling better than advertising?
5. Where does public relations fit into the promotional strategy of an artistic enterprise?
6. Give examples of a situation in which the consumer is near the ignorance stage and a situation in which the consumer is closer to the action (buying) stage.
7. Who are the decision-makers involved in buying a ticket for a children's show? Why?
8. What purpose do the basic questions behind a communications plan serve?
9. Do critics play an important role in the cultural consumer's decision-making process?
10. What is the difference between a marketing objective and a communications objective?
11. What are the advantages of direct marketing?
12. What is the main advantage of relationship marketing?

Notes

1. Berneman, C., and M.-J. Kasparian. 2003. "Promotion of Cultural Events through Urban Postering: An Exploratory Study of Its Effectiveness." *International Journal of Arts Management*, Vol. 6, n° 1 (Fall), p. 30–40.

2. d'Astous, A., R. Legoux and F. Colbert. 2004. "Consumer Perceptions of Promotional Offers in the Performing Arts: An Experimental Approach." *Canadian Journal of Administrative Sciences*, Vol. 21, n° 3, p. 242–254.

3. "Independent revenue" is the revenue generated by the company itself, in the form of admission fees or sales of tickets, spin-off products, and so on. This type of revenue is exclusive of any grant or subsidy from the public sector.

4. McConnell, J.V., R.L. Cutter and E.B. McNeil. 1958. "Subliminal Stimulation: An Overview." *American Psychologist*, Vol. 13, n° 1, p. 229–242.

5. Kotler, P., and G. Armstrong. 2005. *Marketing: An Introduction*, 7th ed. Upper Saddle River, NJ: Prentice-Hall.

6. Ravanas, P. 2006. "Born to Be Wise: How Steppenwolf Theatre Mixes Freedom with Management Savvy." *International Journal of Arts Management*, Vol. 8, n° 3 (Spring), p. 64–73.

7. Peppers, D., and M. Rogers. 1996. "The One to One Future: Building Relationships One Customer at a Time." *Currency*, 14 December.

For Further Reference

Braun, M. 2000. "Courting the Media: How the 1998 Spoleto Festival USA Attracted Media Coverage." *International Journal of Arts Management*, Vol. 2, n° 2 (Winter), p. 50–58.

Colbert, F., A, d'Astous and M.-A. Parmentier. 2005. "Consumer Perception of Private versus Public Sponsorship of the Arts." *International Journal of Arts Management*, Vol. 8, n° 1 (Fall), p. 48–61.

d'Astous, A., A. Caru, O. Koll and S.P. Sigué. 2005. "Moviegoers' Consultation of Film Reviews in the Search for Information: A Multi-country Study." *International Journal of Arts Management*, Vol. 7, n° 3 (Spring), p. 32–46.

d'Astous, A., and F. Colbert. 2002. "Moviegoers' Consultation of Critical Reviews: Psychological Antecedents and Consequences." *International Journal of Arts Management*, Vol. 5, n° 1 (Fall), p. 24–36.

Fishel, D. 2002. "Australian Philanthropy and the Arts: How Does It Compare?" *International Journal of Arts Management*, Vol. 4, n° 2 (Winter), p. 9–16.

Kolb, B. 2001. "The Decline of the Subscriber Base: A Study of the Philharmonic Orchestra Audience." *International Journal of Arts Management*, Vol. 3, n° 2 (Winter), p. 51–60.

Pope, D.L., J. Apple and P. Keltyka. 2000. "Using an Integrated Ticket Donation Program to Increase Subscription Sales and Reach Underused Markets: A Strategic Marketing Approach." *International Journal of Arts Management*, Vol. 3, n° 1 (Fall), p. 39–46.

Van der Burg, T., W. Dolfsma and C.P.M. Wilderom. 2004. "Raising Private Investment Funds for Museums." *International Journal of Arts Management*, Vol. 6, n° 3 (Spring), p. 50–60.

PLAN

Chapter 10

Marketing Information Systems

OBJECTIVES

- Define internal sources of data
- Present and examine secondary sources of data
- Define and analyze the main primary sources of data
- Discuss the main methods of gathering data
- Outline the steps to follow in any research plan

INTRODUCTION

The marketing information system (MIS) is a fundamental part of the marketing process, since it provides the information needed to make enlightened decisions. The MIS represents an arsenal of tools useful in the decision-making process. Of course, no tool ever invented can replace good judgement!

An MIS uses three types of data: internal, secondary, and primary. Internal data represent all the information obtainable from within the company, such as sales and financial reports. Secondary data are published by public or private organizations in the form of reports made available to the public through the publishing organization, the Internet, or the library system. Primary data are obtained directly from the consumer. This information is usually collected through a market study, a poll, a survey, or business research. The company itself may do the work, or it may hire a specialized firm for the purpose. In this chapter, we will examine all aspects of the process, especially the sources and gathering techniques used for secondary and primary data.

10.1 INTERNAL DATA

The term "internal data" is used here to denote any information useful to the decision-making process found within the company. Internal data are usually derived from six sources: the accounting system, sales reports, the client list, a Web site "hits" report, company staff, and previous studies. It should be pointed out that a survey or study performed by the company is considered primary data gathering at the time of the study, but that the report retained as a file then becomes part of the internal data. These are all valuable tools for measuring the performance of cultural organizations.

While this chapter focuses on how the MIS functions in Canada, a similar approach can be taken for the international market. Appendix 1 presents examples of the sale of movies and television programs in foreign markets.

The accounting system can furnish a great deal of interesting information – for example, the break-even point for the company as a whole or for each company product individually. It also enables the marketing manager to measure how profitable corporate marketing efforts have been. An analysis of the data supplied by the accounting system can orient the firm and the gathering of primary and secondary data.

Companies can also use data drawn from sales reports generated by the box office or customer billings. Box-office data enable the marketing manager to plot the sales curve of a particular event, compare it to previous years, and decide, if necessary, what measures to take. These measures may affect one or several variables in the marketing mix. For example, if there is always a drop in sales a few weeks after the start of an event, it might be worth increasing the promotion budget for this period in order to maintain or increase attendance figures.

Such data enable a company to correct a strategy, based on the results obtained. Over the years, company standards may develop as guidelines not only for analyzing or forecasting sales figures but also for enhancing the marketing planning process.

The client, subscriber, or donor list of an organization, be it commercial or not-for-profit, is a mine of interesting information. The geographic location of customers, for example, is actually a company's trading area. As seen in Chapter 8, this is a simple method used to measure a company's penetration in a specific region or neighbourhood.

For other useful information, the marketing manager need look no further than the staff members who actually come into contact with the customers. These include telephone operators, ticket agents, ushers, security guards, guide-interpreters, and restaurant and bar personnel. Employees in communications or sales can collect data that may prove highly relevant to those making the final decisions.

Of course, every analyst must be well acquainted with previous studies or surveys. Although the information may be outdated, it can provide important clues on how to analyze the current situation. It might even be worthwhile repeating the experiment to compare the new data with the old.

Finally, thanks to the proliferation of Web sites, it is relatively easy for a company to obtain information on a particular industry. For example, all professional associations in the arts and cultural sector have an Internet site, many of which provide direct links to the association's member organizations.

10.2 SECONDARY DATA

10.2.1 General Considerations

Secondary data are those published by governmental organizations or by private groups. This kind of data is particularly useful to the marketing manager, since it provides the information needed to measure the size and evolution of product demand, the size and make-up of the product market, and even the structure of the industry itself.

The main advantage of using this type of data is the low cost, in terms of both time and money. Access to these documents involves few expenditures and the data can be gathered in a relatively short period, whereas several weeks or months may be needed to gather and collate similar information from a market study.

Example 10.1
The Stratford Festival: Using the Marketing Information System to Segment Patrons

After years of collecting, aggregating, and analyzing data on its audience, the Stratford Festival of Canada (a repertory theatre festival located in Stratford, Ontario) has developed a sophisticated Marketing Information System in order to better allocate its marketing resources and to make more informed, wiser decisions.

It has segmented its database of 400,000 patrons by using two criteria: value (how much a patron buys) and behaviour (why, what, when, where, and how he/she buys).

The value segmentation variable ranks patrons according to their purchasing pattern. For instance, *Preferred* patrons have attended the festival each year for the past four seasons and are in the top 10% of the spending bracket. The company devotes a significant amount of attention to them, contacting them by mail with expensive items, by phone, and by e-mail. *Conversion* patrons have attended the festival once during the past five seasons and have no history before or after that visit. They are usually contacted only via low-cost methods, such as e-mail.

The behavioural segmentation variable allows the company to better understand what offer a patron might respond to. For instance, *Standard Fair* patrons seek entertainment and attend only the musicals and popular Shakespeare plays, whereas *Non-standard* patrons seek artistic stimulation and attend more experimental productions on smaller stages and the lesser-known Shakespeare plays. Because of this information, the festival is able to develop VPOD (variable printing on demand) mailings by printing customer-specific text and/or images onto the materials sent to a patron, according to the segment to which he/she belongs. It allows the company to develop a personalized relationship with each patron by acknowledging what he/she saw last and presenting what he/she might enjoy seeing next.

By cross-examining and correlating the two variables, the company can identify which patrons have the potential to move to a higher spending bracket, and what type of promotional incentive or discount they should be offered.

Source: Philippe Ravanas, Professor, Arts, Entertainment and Media Management Department, Columbia College, Chicago, USA.

Secondary data also generate questions and hypotheses that orient primary-data research.

Secondary data include all information gathered for specific purposes from a perspective foreign to that suggested by the research problem set out by the company. Sometimes, the data provide a partial answer to the research problem or question. Sometimes, however, there is no pertinent information available on the specific issue or problem that the company has raised. Existing information may be out of date. In this case, the methodology used in the past to correlate data is an invaluable tool for the researcher wishing to repeat and update the study.

It should be pointed out that the more specific the set of problems is to the company and the more restricted the field of interest, the less information the secondary data will provide. In this case, primary data must be used.

10.2.2 Public-Sector and Private-Sector Data: Strengths and Weaknesses

Secondary data may come from either the private or the public sector. Such data can be found in documentation published by various public

---

Example 10.2
Opera Australia: Internal Data, Ticketing, and Customer Relations

Ticketing for arts events has moved from a transaction of simply selling a ticket to an opportunity to build a relationship with customers. Opera Australia has recognized this change and has adopted the Metropolitan Opera Company's ticketing system, which permits the company to keep up-to-date databases on its audiences. The database is an excellent tool for relationship management. It allows Opera Australia to promote upcoming shows and take remedial action on lower-than-average sales for current shows. It has changed the face of ticketing. Arts companies had long complained about the inadequacy of their ticketing systems, which did not allow for the development of a database of single-ticket purchasers and had limited ability to track subscribers. If traditional ticketing companies do not move with the times and view ticketing as a relationship rather than as a transaction, they will lose business to newer systems that see an opportunity to serve a growing market.

Source: Ruth Rentschler, Executive Director, Centre for Leisure Management Research, Deakin University, Australia.

Example 10.3
Queensland Theatre Company: Monitoring Patterns and Trends to Build Strong Customer Relationships

Season ticket holders are the Queensland Theatre Company's most important market segment, representing approximately 60% of all ticket sales annually. In 2002 the company introduced plastic, credit-card-sized season tickets printed with the company's logo and branding imagery. While plastic season tickers are popular in the sporting industry, this was a first for the Australian performing arts industry.

The plastic season ticket is both a membership card and a loyalty card, and is an important element in the company's strategic marketing relationship with its season ticket holders. It is used by patrons to gain entry to the theatre and also entitles them to additional benefits as part of the company's loyalty program, such as free programs, entry to special events, and discounts from other businesses.

Each card is personalized with the patron's name and patron number, a bar code, and detailed information on the patron's season ticket purchase, including play titles, performance dates, and seat numbers.

This valuable marketing tool has practical benefits for the company, the patron, the ticketing agent, and the venue. Each year, instead of receiving an envelope containing a year's supply of tickets, the patron receives one ticket to keep in his or her wallet. This has resulted in a significant reduction in misplaced or lost tickets and missed performances.

The card acts as an important loyalty link for the company, and it allows ticketing and venue staff to easily identify the user as a valued patron.

With increased use of bar code technology, integrated with software and "capture" hardware, future applications of the card will allow the Queensland Theatre Company to more easily monitor buyer patterns and the buying trends of its season ticket holders.

Source: Jennifer Radbourne, Head, School of Communication and Creative Arts, Deakin University, Australia, and Bronwyn Klepp, Marketing Manager, Queensland Theatre Company, Brisbane, Australia.

organizations – for example, government departments, agencies, institutes, associations, and various government bureaus. Many polling firms and periodicals also publish study results.

These two sources of secondary data have their strengths and weaknesses, as shown in Table 10.1. In practice, the two sources complement each other.

Table 10.1 The Strong and Weak Points of Public and Private Data		
	Public data	**Private data**
Scientific methodology	+	−
Standardization of data	+	−
Possibility of studies being conducted over time	+	−
Accessibility	+	±
Aggregation	−	+
Currency	−	+

To compare the strengths and weaknesses of each, we will use the example of Statistics Canada, which has an enviable international reputation in the field of data collection and processing. However, the characteristics discussed generally apply to other national statistical bureaus as well.

Scientific Method

Statistics Canada serves the needs of a broad range of people, such as politicians, students, analysts, and executives, who often base important decisions on Statistics Canada data. As a publicly funded government organization, Statistics Canada must take methodological precautions to ensure the validity of all the data it publishes. In fact, Stats Can, as it is popularly known, describes the research procedure for each study in a clear and detailed fashion. This is not always the case for private secondary data. Often, the authors of a privately published report do not specify the research method used; hence, the reader cannot detect their bias. Sometimes, such studies are in fact seriously biased. In short, it is easier to check the method employed in public studies than that employed in private studies.

Standardization of Data

Statistics Canada data are categorized in a standard fashion, which greatly facilitates searches and comparisons from one year to the next. This is not the norm, for private data, since the studies they are part of are usually carried out on behalf of a particular client seeking specific information. In most cases, it is impossible to compare data from two studies performed by a private-sector firm, since the objective of the study and type of information gathered may vary tremendously between any two studies. It may happen, however, that a study is repeated so that two sets of results can be compared.

Possibility of Time Series

The standardization in Statistics Canada data enables the researcher to create time series. Stats Can classifies information gathered in categories that remain the same from one year to the next. Periodically, minor adjustments are made to reflect changes in the social environment. For example, the videocassette recorder (VCR) did not exist in the pre-1980 category of "Leisure Equipment for Home Use," since the product was not yet available to the public at large. The VCR was recently added to reflect the new reality. By correlating data from one particular category over time, researchers can monitor the demand for a product. Information gathered by private firms does not allow for this type of tracking or follow-up.

Accessibility

Statistics Canada data can easily be located and consulted, at little or no cost, in large libraries or directly on the organization's Web site. Private data are distributed but remain confidential and inaccessible. Moreover, the cost of buying private data can be rather high, or even prohibitive. All in all, accessibility to private data should be considered variable – somewhat like the weather!

Aggregation of Data

A research report published by a private firm usually summarizes a vast amount and variety of data. This is one of the main advantages of private data, since the synthesis of data makes the market analyst's task much simpler. For example, in a report produced by a research firm, the product market over 15 years may appear in one graph or table, whereas the researcher would have to look through several Statistics Canada catalogues to construct the same demand curve. Hence the aggregative aspect of the information presented in a private report is a definite advantage.

Currency of Information

The complexity of Statistics Canada studies and the precautions it takes usually translate to a two- or three-year lag from research to publication stage. Research reports published by private firms, however, usually focus on recent events and the orders given by the client organization. Consequently, upon publication the data are still recent.

10.2.3 Public Data

National Statistical Agencies

The main source of secondary data for any given country – and the most reliable and accessible – is unquestionably the national statistical bureau (NSB) of that country. NSBs publish a great deal of documentation on diverse topics. No matter what the framework or issue, the NSB has most likely published something pertinent.

NSBs publish, on a broad range of subjects, both general documents – for example, census data – and highly specific material – for example, studies on the performing arts. The marketing manager or researcher seeking documents on a particular country should first consult the general catalogue listing of the NSB publications to locate the most appropriate studies (see, for example, in the United States, www.census.gov; in Canada, www.statcan.ca; in Australia, abs.gov.au; and in France, www.insee.fr).

Of particular interest in Canada is the enormous survey that Statistics Canada conducts every two years on family expenditures in Canada (category 62-555). The results of this survey reveal, for example, average household spending and the percentage of families declaring expenditures on movies shown in theatres, on stage shows, and on admission fees to cultural establishments such as museums and galleries.

Other Governmental Agencies

Publications from various ministries and agencies are further sources of public secondary data.

In Canada, excellent sources of data are the Canada Council for the Arts Research Department (www.canadacouncil.ca), the Department of Canadian Heritage (www.pch.gc.ca), and the Department of Foreign Affairs and International Trade (www.dfait-marci.gc.ca), as well as the arts councils and cultural departments of the different provinces.

The National Endowment for the Arts in the United States (www.nea.gov), the Australia Council for the Arts (www.ozco.gov.au), the Arts Council of England (www.artscouncil.org.uk), and the Ministry of Culture in France (www.culture.gouv.fr) also publish several studies each year. The Council of Europe (www.coe.int) represents another major source of data.

Other government organizations or departments in different countries also publish study results and documents of potential interest to those in the cultural milieu.

10.2.4 Private Data

Databases and Indexes

There are also various databases on the market that may be consulted free of charge. Until very recently, these databases provided only printed documentation. Now they are computerized and may be available on paper, microfiche, CD-ROM, and, of course, the Internet.

Publications by Private Organizations

The manager of a cultural or artistic enterprise can obtain useful information from private organizations,[1] whether or not arts is their main focus. The Council for Business and the Arts in Canada (www.businessforarts.org) and the Ford Foundation in the United States (www.fordfound.org) are indirectly involved in culture or the arts and publish reference material pertinent to arts management.

A proliferation of Web sites ensures companies easy access to a wealth of basic information on particular industries. For example, all professional associations in the arts and culture sector have their own Web sites, many of which offer links to the Web sites of their member organizations.

International organizations are a valuable source of foreign data. The majority of disciplines are represented by an international association that provides information on activities in the discipline in other countries. In this regard, UNESCO is a particularly rich source of information, chiefly through its International Council of Museums (www.icom.museum).

The marketing manager may also want to look at management journals such as the *Journal of Marketing*, or journals devoted to cultural affairs such as the *International Journal of Arts Management* (www.hec.ca/ijam), the *Journal of Cultural Economics*, the *International Journal of Cultural Policy Research*, or the *Journal of Arts Management, Law and Society*.

10.3 PRIMARY DATA

Primary data may be obtained by consulting the target market directly through data-collection techniques called "market study," "survey," or "poll."

Data may be collated by the marketing manager, or a specialized firm may be hired to do the work. The procedure involves collecting data pertinent to a previously stated problem, analyzing the data, and then interpreting the data with a view to making decisions.

The cost of collecting primary data should always reflect the value of the information sought. In other words, the manager in charge must calculate whether the study is worth the effort. It would be useless to spend $5,000 on a survey if the information obtained does not enable the company to save, or gain, at least $5,000. If the financial outcome of the decision were any lower, the entire project might not be worth the trouble.

There are three types of research for primary data: exploratory research, descriptive research, and causal research.

10.3.1 Exploratory Research

Exploratory research basically supplies qualitative data. It is not based on hypotheses or preconceived ideas and should be used only when little or no prior information is available. As a method, it is flexible, unstructured, and qualitative.

This type of research may serve several purposes. It may be useful for defining a problem, suggesting hypotheses to be tested, generating ideas for new products, capturing consumers' first reactions to a new concept, pretesting a questionnaire, or determining which criteria play a role in the choice of one show or film over another.

Exploratory research can reveal the consumer's vocabulary and areas of interest, thus helping the researcher and marketer to become familiar with what may seem a virtual terra incognita. It can also be used to assess the level of customer service within an organization. This is the principle behind the use of "mystery visitors" in museums, whereby trained investigators visit one or more museums and then report their observations; the findings are then analyzed and can lead to important improvements.[2]

Several techniques are available. These include discussion groups, in-depth interviews, case studies, observation, and projection. The population sample used is usually a convenience sample.

10.3.2 Descriptive Research

Descriptive research seeks specific information on a given topic. It usually starts from a hypothesis, which is tested and confirmed or disproved. This type of research is used only when the situation is fairly clear, with specific and well-defined information needs, frame of reference, and variables. Exploratory research often precedes descriptive research so that the research hypothesis and parameters involved can be defined more clearly.

While exploratory research is qualitative and uses a small number of respondents, descriptive research provides results that enable the researcher to proceed to a quantitative analysis from representative samplings of the population studied.

Descriptive research may, for instance, determine which factors intervene in the decision-making process for the purchase of a theatre ticket within a specific population. It may also provide a sociodemographic profile of museum visitors or outline the characteristics of popular music fans in a given area.

Data-Collection Techniques

There are three key data-gathering techniques used in descriptive research: mail, telephone, and personal interviewing. The choice of one technique over another depends on the purpose or objective of the study and the resources available. The breadth and precision of the data collected, the time and effort required, the type of questions asked (open-ended versus closed), the cost associated with different techniques, and the administration required are all influential factors. While other methods of data collection can also be employed (observation, projective techniques, etc.), this chapter focuses on mail, telephone, and personal interviewing because these are the three techniques most commonly used by polling firms.

Mail-in Surveys

Mail-in surveys have two main advantages: they are inexpensive for the large number of people they can reach in comparison with either of the other two techniques, and they respect the respondent's wish to remain anonymous, which enables researchers to obtain more personal information while reducing any potential bias in the interviewer or in the respondent vis-à-vis the interviewer. The main disadvantages are as follows: the inability to control the identity of the respondent, who may consult a third party in replying; the lack of control over the order in which questions are answered; and the possible misunderstanding of terms.

With mass-consumption products, the rate of response for mail-in surveys ranges from 2% to 5%. A study carried out on a cultural matter may obtain a response rate of anywhere between 25% and 40%. The rate may rise significantly for a study carried out among a sampling of consumers related somehow to an establishment; for instance, "friends of the museum" will fill out a questionnaire more readily if it comes from the establishment they support or patronize. The same pattern may be observed among the members of a professional association.

Telephone Surveys or Polls

The telephone survey is a quick way to reach a large number of people within a short period. By increasing the number of operators, a polling firm can reach several thousand people within a week.

The response rate is generally quite high, at approximately 80% to 90%. However, overuse of this technique in a region may lead to a high rate of refusal.

The telephone survey allows the interviewer to clarify a question in the event that the respondent does not understand. This technique also proves more productive on a daily basis, since the interviewer does not have to travel anywhere to conduct interviews. Although more expensive than mail-in surveys, telephone surveys are less expensive than one-on-one interviews.

One disadvantage of the telephone interview is, obviously, the lack of visual support. It is also difficult, if not impossible, to use multiple-choice questions. In fact, the questions asked must be relatively simple. Further, they must be asked quickly, since the respondent will not stay more than 15 minutes on the line unless the subject of the survey is of particular interest.

Personal Interviews

The personal interview is effective if the marketer wants to obtain fairly complex data. It enables the interviewer to use visual material and to clarify or repeat questions. This technique allows the respondent who has not understood a question to ask for additional information and lets the interviewer delve deeper into certain answers.

The personal interview costs much more in time and money than the other two techniques. It is also more complicated and more open to potential bias caused by the presence of the interviewer.

Sources of Error

Regardless of the technique used, every researcher must try to minimize bias and sources of error that can creep into the data-collection process. There are four main sources of error: refusal to answer, sampling errors, vague or inaccurate answers, and human error caused by the interviewer. The researcher must always keep these possible sources of error in mind and try to minimize their influence.

If some members of the sample refuse to answer, a serious source of error develops. The higher the refusal rate, the greater the possibility of the statistics giving a biased view of reality. Since the researcher does not know what these people think, the results of a survey may not be accurate. Although the rate of refusal can never be eliminated, it must be kept to a minimum through the use of adequate evaluation tools.

Sampling errors can also yield results that are not representative of the overall population being studied. These errors arise when the sampling method is inadequate or when the size of the sample is insufficient.

The third main source of error in descriptive research is obtaining vague or inexact answers. This error may be caused by sheer ignorance on the part of a respondent who wants to give any answer rather than appear stupid or who wants to answer according to perceived consensus on a particular issue. It may be linked to forgetfulness if the data collection takes place too long after the facts to be analyzed took place. Attitude may also play a role, since respondents can voluntarily bias their answers for a variety of personal reasons. Common reasons are lack of time, general fatigue, a feeling that their privacy is being invaded, a natural tendency to furnish socially acceptable answers (e.g., inflating annual book purchases if the activity is perceived as valued), and even a desire to please the interviewer. Some respondents may politely agree with the interviewer although they actually disagree completely.

The last source of error is the interviewer, who may unwittingly, through body language or speaking style, influence the respondent. Good interviewer training can reduce this potential bias to a minimum.

10.3.3 Causal Research

The third technique is causal in that it analyzes the effects of one variable on another. An example of this technique would be a study on the impact of distributing free tickets on the future consumption of a theatre troupe's product.

Relatively rigid and specialized, this type of research analyzes only one aspect of reality. Causal research is based on the principle that knowledge of a product is extensive and that several influential variables have already been defined and are relatively well known. This type of research seeks to find the cause-and-effect relationship that may exist between pairs of variables. It takes one or several hypotheses and then tests each one.

10.4 THE STEPS INVOLVED IN DESCRIPTIVE RESEARCH

Descriptive research attempts to meet objectives set out after the research problem has been defined. These objectives are to be met as inexpensively, accurately (low margin of error), and rapidly as possible. A marketing manager may decide to run a series of projects covering a part of the objectives rather than have a full study of all aspects of a problem.

Table 10.2 lists a series of 14 steps that should be the basis of any research activity.

Table 10.2
The 14 Steps of Any Research Project

Step 1	Defining the problem
Step 2	Defining research objectives
Step 3	Deciding on the human and financial resources required
Step 4	Setting a schedule
Step 5	Choosing the appropriate tools and techniques
Step 6	Deciding on the sample
Step 7	Designing the questionnaire
Step 8	Testing the questionnaire
Step 9	Coding responses
Step 10	Gathering data
Step 11	Monitoring interviewers
Step 12	Compiling data
Step 13	Analyzing the results
Step 14	Writing the report

We can divide this 14-step series into two sections. The first four steps are common to all research. Only by answering the questions they pose can a manager or researcher select the appropriate technique or method to resolve the problem and choose the most appropriate form of data collection. The other 10 steps, although given here within the framework of descriptive research, may be applied to both exploratory and causal research, depending on the situation. The content of some steps, however, may be different or not even applicable.

Step 1: Defining the Problem

Before beginning any form of data collection, the researcher or marketing manager must be sure that the problem to be studied has been properly defined. If the definition is specific, decisions throughout the subsequent steps are easier to make.

Since cultural enterprises usually have limited funds, market studies are not frequent. The risk, therefore, is that the company trying to squeeze every penny out of the study overloads its questionnaire and in the end respondents find it too long or complicated to answer.

A good definition of the problem being studied is one that lets the manager or researcher know just how helpful internal data or secondary data already available could be in solving all or part of the problem. In any event, it is wise to begin checking before the collection stage to ensure that the information does not already exist elsewhere.

The following situations may initiate the research process:

- The number of subscribers has dropped considerably over the previous year's figures.
- A corporate executive wonders about consumer reaction to a product price change.
- The company wants to enter an unknown market.

Step 2: Defining Research Objectives

An analyst can use the problem to be solved as a starting point to define research objectives. For instance, a theatre may want to find out why subscribers are not renewing their subscriptions, or know the percentage of consumers likely to react negatively to a price change, or define the consumption habits for residents of a specific area.

Step 3: Deciding on the Human and Financial Resources Required

The marketing manager must also calculate the staff and budget available for research purposes. Obviously, the subsequent decision will depend on study procedure and complexity, as well as on the way in which the research will be carried out – for example, by an outside firm or an in-house team. The budget allotted to the collection of primary data will be greater than that needed for gathering secondary data.

Analyzing the budget required for a market study provides an excellent opportunity to examine the value of the information sought in relation to the inherent cost of collecting it. The value of information provided by a market study is often difficult to estimate beforehand. Nonetheless, the marketing manager or researcher must try to answer this question so as not to waste time or money.

Step 4: Setting a Schedule

Time is an important element in drawing up any study plan. The manager and company must know when the data will be available. A tight schedule in descriptive research might necessitate the use of telephone interviews, which may be carried out quickly but generate a limited amount of data.

Step 5: Choosing the Appropriate Tools and Techniques

Once the objectives have been set out, the marketing manager or researcher must choose, from among the three methods (exploratory, descriptive, causal), the one that will provide the necessary information at the lowest cost in terms of both time and money. The manager can then select the data-collection technique to be used; in descriptive research, for example, there are mail-in surveys, telephone surveys, and personal interviews. The choice of one technique over another depends on budget and schedule.

Step 6: Deciding on the Sample

Once the "descriptive" technique has been chosen, the researcher decides on the parameters of the sample. The sample must include a sufficient number of respondents chosen at random who represent the population studied in order to generate significant statistics. In some cases, such as if the population is fairly limited and heterogeneous, the marketing researcher will study the entire population.

Regardless of population size, the sample must include a minimum of 30 respondents. According to statistical laws, a sample is considered statistically significant once there are 30 respondents chosen at random. The accuracy and reliability of the results increase along with the size of the sample. The same rule applies when drawing conclusions about a subgroup of individuals within the main sample population: researchers must always have at least 30 respondents in any particular cell. Of course, it is possible to analyze the results of a study or the subgroups of a sample with fewer than 30 respondents. In this case, non-parametric statistical methods are used, which do not allow a researcher to generalize the results as if they were the same for an entire population. (Readers interested in these methods should consult *Non-Parametric Statistics* by Siegel.[3])

The size of the population studied does not determine the number of respondents needed to make up a representative sample. However, the size of the sample does determine the degree of accuracy. The more homogeneous the population, the more limited the sample will be. The laws of statistics prove that whether an opinion poll is conducted in a town of 5,000 or a city of 5 million, the same sample size provides the same degree of accuracy.

The size of a sample is calculated according to the number of people who respond to the questionnaire, not the number of people who receive it. For example, if a sample of 400 respondents is needed and the rate of response is usually 40% for this particular type of survey, 1,000 questionnaires should be sent out. It should be kept in mind that the larger the sample size, the higher the cost of the study and the longer the data-processing and analysis stages. The rate is also a function of the length of the questionnaire, the respondent's interest in the subject, and the motivation created by the questionnaire style. Various strategies can be used to increase motivation, such as a $1 included in each mailing or a postage-paid return envelope.

The size of the sample influences how much faith a manager should place in the information gathered (see Table 10.3). The market researcher who selects 269 people has a 90% probability of not being wrong (maximum level of reliability sought) by more than 5% in any estimates (5% is, therefore, the maximum acceptable margin of error). If the sample includes 382 people, the level of reliability rises to 95% with a maximum margin of error of 5%. For instance, if a survey based on a sample of 382 individuals shows that 30% of the respondents prefer a particular type of show, it actually proves that, with a probability of 95%, the percentage is between 28.5% and 32.5%.

Three methods are frequently used to develop a sample: the simple method, the systematic method, and the quota method.

Simple sampling consists of selecting at random, from the population studied, the individuals to be surveyed. In this method, each individual has the same probability of being chosen. If a company wants to send a questionnaire to a sampling of the residents of a town, the names and addresses of all those to be contacted are required. The strategy of asking passers-by at the intersection of two main downtown streets will not yield statistically significant

Table 10.3
Sampling Size According to Reliability Sought

Maximum margin of error (%)	Reliability sought		
	80%	90%	95%
± 1	4,100	6,715	9,594
± 3	455	746	1,066
± 5	164	269	382
± 10	41	67	96
± 15	18	30	43
± 20	10	17	24

results, since each individual within the population studied does not have the same chance (or probability) of being at that corner at a specific time.

The simple method cannot be used in all circumstances; hence the utility of the systematic sampling method. This method consists of taking a slice of the population studied – for example, one person per x number of names. If the population studied were symphony subscribers, the marketing manager or researcher could simply draw one person's name per block of, say, 10 names on the list until the sample has been completed. This method is particularly effective when the total population comprises a known and finite number.

Lastly, the quota method seeks to represent the entire population studied by retaining certain common characteristics, which must be found in the same percentage within the sample. These characteristics could be age, gender, income, level of education, or any other variable of interest. For example, in a telephone survey, if the company wants to reach a target of 51% female respondents, then interviewers could be instructed to interview no more women once that target has been met.

Step 7: Designing the Questionnaire

Designing a structured questionnaire is a delicate task. The questionnaire plays a key role not only in the quality of the information obtained, but also in the rate of response.

Questions must be worded so as not to bias the answers. The vocabulary must be readily understood by respondents.

The market researcher draws up a list of information to be gathered on the basis of the research objectives. This list is then transformed into a logically ordered series of questions, starting with the questions most likely to interest the respondent and ending with the most delicate or confidential questions, such as age and income.

Questions may be closed or open-ended. For closed questions, the respondent has a choice of answers and indicates this choice. Open-ended questions allow the respondent to answer freely. Closed questions are generally used in descriptive research in order to facilitate the analysis of results drawn from the long questionnaires used with a large sample.

For the highest possible response rate, the questionnaire writer must ensure that the final version is short and well laid out, with questions in a logical order. Closed questions are preferable. An introduction stressing the importance of the answers will encourage respondents to fill out the questionnaire.

Step 8: Testing the Questionnaire

The marketing manager or the head of the marketing-research team must have the questionnaire pretested before using it to collect data. This stage usually reveals any ambiguity in the questionnaire and allows for any necessary changes before the mailing begins. The pretest usually needs only a dozen respondents who fit as closely as possible the profile of the population studied.

One way of making a questionnaire even more efficient is to test it in a real situation. Researchers can survey a sample using a certain number of people, such as 100, who are asked to respond to the questionnaire. The analysis of these data after compilation allows for any relevant changes to be made. Testing a questionnaire in a real situation is all the more necessary if there are many questions and the accuracy of the respondents' answers is essential.

This step is a crucial one that enables a company to improve a questionnaire and avoid costly errors.

Step 9: Coding Responses

Once the researcher is ready to gather data and the questionnaire is in its definitive version, the responses should be coded. This step facilitates the eventual processing of the data.

Step 10: Gathering Data

Once the questionnaire has been prepared and coded, the researcher can start collecting data. Interviewers are trained and respondents are contacted by mail, telephone, or in person.

Step 11: Monitoring Interviewers

Even if the interviewers are trained professionals, the company must monitor their work to ensure that the respondents are being reached and that the interviewers are following instructions. Usually, the contacts made by the interviewers are checked. This ensures that the respondent was both reached and asked questions properly.

Step 12: Compiling Data

Compiling data is a mechanical step that can be manual or computerized. If using a computer, the analyst can use specialized software that makes analysis easier. This step must be performed carefully, since errors in transcription can lead to false interpretations.

Step 13: Analyzing the Results

Caution should always be exercised in analyzing survey results. The popular expression "numbers say what we want them to say" is sad but true. The analyst must strive for rigour and not simply look for the answers that the company executive wants to hear.

It is at this point that the market study takes on its full meaning. Now, the researcher must transform disparate data into relevant analysis. Here it is important to understand the meaning of the responses and the links between them in order to interpret the data collected. The use of graphs and diagrams may make this task easier.

Step 14: Writing the Report

The results of a survey are usually presented as a written report. Several excellent manuals on writing research reports are available in bookstores and libraries. The first rule is that the report be easy to consult. Since the report may be used later by the company or others to repeat the study, so as to compare or update results, it is wise to detail the methodology used and to include a copy of the questionnaire itself as an appendix.

SUMMARY

The MIS has three types of data: internal, secondary, and primary. Internal data are usually supplied by the company's accounting system. Other parties may contribute – for example, employees or even customers.

The two main sources of secondary data are public-sector and private-sector publications. The main source of public data is the national statistical agency of each country. Other government departments and agencies also publish documents of potential interest to managers and executives. Private data can be accessed through databases. Public and private data have their respective strengths and weaknesses. In fact, they more or less complement each other. The main strengths of public data are standardization of data, precautionary methodological measures, comparative studies over time, and ease of access. The strength of private data lies in the aggregation and currency of the information.

Primary data are gathered through surveys or market studies. The research may be exploratory, descriptive, or causal. In the first case, variables are sought which might fit even though no hypothesis has been outlined. In the second case, the researcher starts with a hypothesis and sets out to prove or disprove it. In the last case, the causal relationship between one variable and another is examined.

Several techniques are used in exploratory research (group interviews, individual interviews, case studies, observation, forecasts, and projection). The group interview is often used to test a new product or formulation.

In descriptive and causal research, the research plan usually includes 14 steps: defining the problem, defining the objectives, determining the financial and human resources, setting a schedule, choosing methods or tools, determining the size of the sample, writing the questionnaire, pretesting the questionnaire, coding, gathering data, monitoring interviewers, compiling data, analyzing results, and writing the report.

QUESTIONS

1. What are the three types of data used in an MIS?
2. What does "internal data" mean and what are the main sources of internal data?
3. Why is it wise to consult different sources of secondary data before commencing a market study?
4. What are the strengths and weaknesses of public data and private data? Why do we often say that the strength of one is the weakness of the other?
5. What are the main sources of public data? Private data?
6. Define the following three types of research: exploratory, descriptive, causal.
7. Give an example of each of type of research.
8. Why is it important to define the research problem before starting a market study?
9. What is a random sample?
10. Does the size of a sample vary according to the population studied? If so, why?
11. What is quota sampling?
12. What are the basic rules to follow in writing a questionnaire?
13. Why do research firms monitor a certain percentage of the interviews conducted by the interviewing team?

Notes

1. The Carmelle and Rémi Marcoux Chair in Arts Management Web site publishes bibliographies (some in PDF format) of interest to cultural managers, students, and academics: http://www.gestion-desarts.com

2. Kirschberg, V. 2000. "Mystery Visitors in Museums: An Underused and Underestimated Tool for Testing Visitor Services." *International Journal of Arts Management*, Vol. 3, nᵒ 1 (Fall), p. 32–39.

3. Siegel, S. 1956. *Non-Parametric Statistics.* New York: McGraw-Hill, Series in Psychology.

For Further Reference

Bennett, R., and R. Kottasz. 2001. "Lead User Influence on New Product Development Decisions of UK Theatre Conmpanies: An Empirical Study." *International Journal of Arts Management*, Vol. 3, n° 2 (Winter), p. 28–40.

Gilhespy, I. 1999. "Measuring the Performance of Cultural Organizations: A Model." *International Journal of Arts Management*, Vol. 2, n° 1 (Fall), p. 38–53.

Harrison, P., and R. Shaw. 2004. "Consumer Satisfaction and Post-purchase Intentions: An Exploratory Study of Museum Visitors." *International Journal of Arts Management*, Vol. 6, n° 2 (Winter), p. 23–33.

Appendix 1
Evaluation of an International Territory for Television or Film Sales

Before deciding to export to or enter a partnership in a foreign country, the firm should evaluate the possibilities, risks, and challenges that might lie ahead. This will allow it to make better choices, avoid costly mistakes, and ultimately take maximum advantage of any potential business opportunities.

Market Potential

The first step that any firm wishing to export should take is to evaluate the potential of the foreign market. Libraries and the Internet are good basic sources of information. National governments also publish pertinent statistics on the desired market. Most countries post data regarding their cultural industries on the Internet. The European Audiovisual Observatory (http://www.obs.coe.int/index.html.en) circulates information on the audiovisual industry in Europe. The Observatory is a public service body with 36 member states as well as the European Community, represented by the European Commission.

A number of trade magazines provide a wealth of data on various cultural industries, including trends within those industries. http://www.variety.com; http://www.hollywoodreporter.com; http://www.worldscreen.com

It is also useful to consult economic data in order to study the economic situation of the territory of interest (purchasing power, strength of currency, etc.). The weekly magazine *The Economist* is an excellent source of information. http://www.economist.com

Access

It is worth determining whether the target country has imposed restrictions on imports, a quota system, or entry barriers. Even restrictions on foreign currency could limit the company's access to the market.

Some consideration should be given to possible difficulties with piracy or the unauthorized use of intellectual property.

Finally, the firm should look into the matter of national subsidies. If the government of the target country provides subsidies, the firm might have difficulty competing in that domestic market.

Competition

An evaluation of the intensity and quality of the competitive environment should be carried out. Discussions with representatives of embassies or consulates can be a good starting point.

(continued)

Questions should be asked as to what products are offered by present and future competitors and consideration given to substitute products. If the identified market is already saturated, then the company should question the potential for success.

Product fit

The product or service that the firm intends to export must meet the expectations of potential consumers. The product or service might need to be adapted for the different markets, in which case the firm will have to determine the related costs. Shipping costs, import restrictions, and the cost of preparing the information will all have to be taken into account.

It is essential that the firm be familiar with consumer behaviour in the target market. For example, in the United States the four major broadcasters (CBS, NBC, ABC, and FOX) never air programs that are dubbed or subtitled.

A good understanding of the national culture is also crucial. A firm that is exporting to an Arab country, for instance, should be aware of the restrictions that the national broadcaster or the theatres might impose on the product. Some images or scenes might be shocking to a different culture and will have to be edited.

Service or consulting services after the sale

If the product requires some follow-up after the sale, then appropriate plans will have to be made. For example, when a television format is sold, production follow-up is usually required. It may be necessary to plan for travel to the country in question in order to set up proper consulting services.

International fairs and festivals

A good way to become acquainted with a particular industry worldwide is to attend an international fair or festival. Such events are held for most types of cultural product (MIDEM for music, the Cannes film festival for cinema, MIP-TV for television, the Frankfurt Book Fair for books, etc.).

A visit to the identified territory

A visit to the selected or identified country in order to meet local industry representatives is an excellent strategy. Although somewhat costly, this strategy, if well planned, could yield valuable information and greatly enhance the firm's chances of success.

PLAN

Chapter **11**

Planning and Controlling the Marketing Process

OBJECTIVES

- Describe how marketing contributes to the corporate mission
- Set out the strategic marketing process
- Discuss key strategic approaches
- Study the contents of a marketing plan
- Consider the importance of controlling marketing within the firm

INTRODUCTION

Throughout this book, we have looked at the various components of the marketing model. Together, these components comprise a process that enables a company to reach certain objectives. This process is called the "planning and control cycle."

Planning and control are closely linked, complementary functions. In fact, control occurs only after some form of planning has taken place, planning that includes setting measurable objectives that enable the executive to judge the company's activities by comparing concrete results to forecasts or target figures. Planning consists of defining the target to be reached, whereas control shows how successfully that target is being or has been reached. Control also assists the executive in future planning by indicating the effort required to obtain the expected results.

In this chapter, we examine the various components of the planning and control cycle in marketing. We start by defining the contribution of marketing to the overall mission of a company. We then look at the marketing planning process itself, which stems from the marketing plan and organizational structure. The marketing plan must be drawn up with a broader corporate strategy in mind, since any marketing strategy must contribute to the success of corporate strategies. Lastly, we focus on the key elements in controlling marketing activities.

11.1 HOW MARKETING CONTRIBUTES TO THE CORPORATE MISSION

A successful company usually assigns tasks and powers to its various departments or organizational units. Each unit contributes differently to the overall mission of the company. For example, the marketing department contributes to the corporate objectives for growth, development, profitability, and general operations in a specific way. The responsibilities of this department are different from those of the finance and production departments, although they share the same general objectives. Once again, the synergy already applied to the marketing mix also applies to the different functions or departments of the company. The combined effort of all departments must produce an effect that is greater than the sum of the efforts made separately.

Marketing must be linked to the corporate mission before planning or monitoring are even considered.[1] The company's mission leads to a series of overall objectives. In any managerial planning process, the hierarchy of objectives corresponds to a hierarchy of strategies (see Figure 11.1).

Figure 11.1
Hierarchy of Corporate Objectives and Strategies

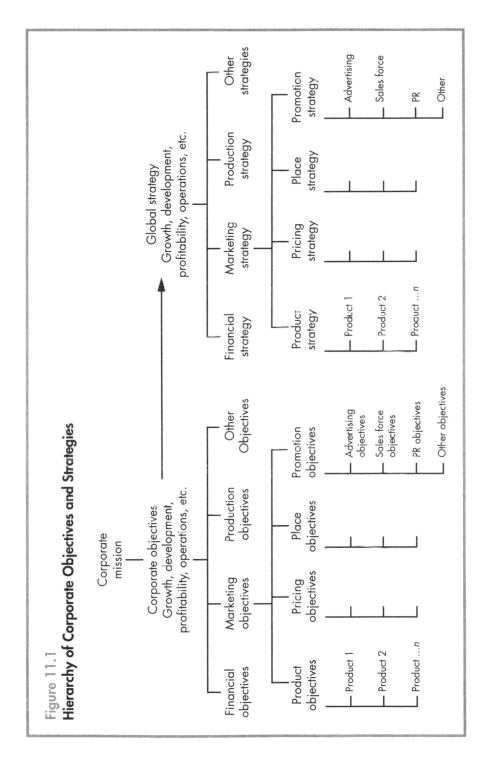

The marketing department must define its objectives within the framework of the overall corporate objectives. The marketing objectives are then translated into a series of objectives related to each variable in the marketing mix. Each variable may then lead to a chain of specific objectives. Similarly, the company may use its overall objectives to develop strategies, which support the marketing strategies which are in turn supported by the strategies for each variable in the marketing mix. Obviously, corporate planning includes the plans of each unit or department; consequently, marketing planning must fit into the overall corporate plan.

11.2 MARKETING PLANNING

11.2.1 The Process of Marketing Planning

Marketing planning (see Figure 11.2) implies a series of questions related to the components of the marketing model. By answering these five key questions, the marketing manager can ensure that the marketing plan is well grounded.

Example 11.1
The National Gallery of Victoria: The Link between Mission and Strategy

Telling stories is the raison d'être of a gallery. One of the best ways to tell stories is to consider the detail of activities and events in an institution and in its branding of events and activities. The events and activities with which the National Gallery of Victoria (NGV) in Melbourne, Australia, has pulled in tourists are the Melbourne International Arts Festival, the annual Winter Masterpieces Exhibition, and its own innovative Aboriginal art hang.

The NGV's current mission is to bring art and people together. In other words, it is the audience response to the gallery that is most important in determining its status. Thus over time the NGV has shifted its focus from the tangible collection to a balance between collection and name, logo, and visual features, plus intangible elements such as personality and symbolic benefits through events and activities that it has branded.

(continued)

Example 11.1 (continued)

The redeveloped NGV brand is distinctive in the public mind – the use of the NGV acronym is itself part of the branding process that took place during the redevelopment of the gallery in the new millennium. In mid-2001 *The Australian* newspaper published a two-page colour profile of the gallery. Links are made to the regeneration of the central district of the city. This focus is reinforced in the company's documents. For example, the 1999–2000 president's report stated that the NGV was "already changing the way we view the centre of our city" and that "slowly and steadily our ambitious visions for the Gallery's future are becoming a reality." Further, the NGV sees its role as engaging with contemporary art and life, so that "we can tell the Australian story in many different ways and engage constantly with art of its time."

As a result of telling stories in new ways, the number of visitors both to the gallery and to Melbourne for key events has grown. Visitors can choose packages for their visits, including gallery events, accommodation, travel, and food experiences.

The NGV's mission statement about people and art illustrates the transformation of museums – from temples for the muses to valuable spaces for exhibitions and other events of value to society. Museums are therefore combining their traditional functional role with their new purposive role. Functional definitions relate to activities performed in the museum and are object-based: to collect, preserve, and display objects. More recently, the shift in definitions relates purpose to the intent, vision, or mission of the museum, where the focus is on leadership and visitor services: to serve society and its development by means of study, education, and enjoyment. The NGV mission is a prime example of the shift in museum missions that has affected the museum marketing role.

Source: Ruth Rentschler, Executive Director, Centre for Leisure Management Research, Deakin University, Australia.

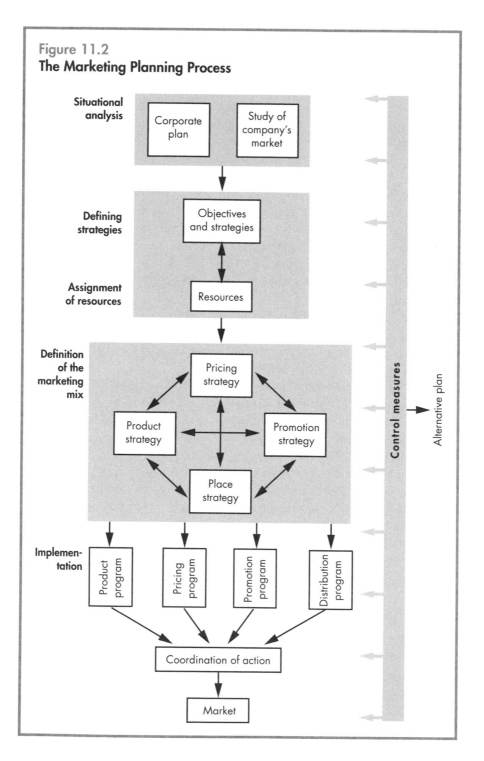

Figure 11.2
The Marketing Planning Process

Situational analysis
Corporate plan
Study of company's market

Defining strategies
Objectives and strategies

Assignment of resources
Resources

Definition of the marketing mix
Pricing strategy
Product strategy
Promotion strategy
Place strategy

Implementation
Product program
Pricing program
Promotion program
Distribution program

Coordination of action

Market

Control measures

Alternative plan

1) Where are we as a company and where are we going? (situational analysis)
2) Where do we want to go? (setting strategic objectives)
3) What effort are we going to put into marketing? (assigning resources)
4) How do we want to get there? (marketing mix)
5) How can we do it? (implementation)

The procedure suggested in these five questions involves looking at the past, the present, and the future. The way in which a company behaves today is largely due to its past actions. Similarly, the way in which a company behaves in the future will reflect today's actions. These five questions encourage the marketing manager to draw up a plan with continuity in mind, be it a short-term or a long-term plan. In fact, a long-term plan usually comprises a series of short-term plans.

11.2.2 The Marketing Plan

The marketing plan is the result of a process. If it is broad and involves the company as a whole, the plan becomes a transposition of the company's strategic vision. The plan may also be limited to a particular sector and thus focus on one market, range, or product. The marketing plan (see Table 11.1) is an analytical outline that may be applied to either situation.

Situational Analysis

The first part of a marketing plan requires that the manager analyze the situation. This analysis must answer two questions: Where are we now? Where are we going if we continue our current activities with no change in current objectives and strategies?

Markets

The various markets served by cultural enterprises evolve over time due to pressures from uncontrollable variables and the competition's actions. The marketing manager should check to see whether the consumer profile has changed, whether market segments have shifted, whether demand has evolved, and whether the intermediaries in the distribution network are still the same. The same checklist applies to the other three markets: private sector, partners, governments.

Competition and the Environment

Since competition and environmental variables affect the company and its markets, environmental trends – be they political, social, cultural, or technological – and changes in competitors' strategies should be studied.

Table 11.1
The Marketing Plan

1. Situational analysis (Where are we and where are we going?)	Markets
	    Consumers, demand, segments
	Competition and the environment
	Company
	    Mission and objectives
	    Strengths and weaknesses
	    Distinct advantage

2. Setting objectives and defining strategies (Where do we want to go?)	Marketing objectives
	    Sales, market share, contribution to profits
	Marketing strategies
	    Target segments, positioning desired

3. Assignment of resources (How much effort do we want to expend?)	Budget Human resources
4. Definition of the marketing mix (How do we want to get there?)	Objectives and strategies
5. Implementation (How can we do it?)	Program of activities for each variable of the marketing mix Definition of the responsibilities of each member of the marketing team Coordination of operations Schedule of activities Alternative plan Description of control measures

The Company

In a marketing plan, the big picture, or overall view of the company, is important, since the marketing department must strive for essentially the same objectives as the company. The marketing manager should look for consistency in the marketing objectives, the corporate mission, and the company objectives, and then weigh their strengths and weaknesses. Lastly, the situation ought to be seen in terms of a competitive advantage. The following questions should be asked: Is there such an advantage? Should it be redefined? How?

This rather sweeping overview enables the senior manager to place the company within the internal and broader external environments and take stock of the situation. This is also an opportunity to ponder the future direction of the company if no changes are made. The overarching question, given the evolution of the environment and the competition, becomes, "Are our current marketing strategies leading us where we want to go?"

Setting Objectives and Creating Development Strategies

Setting objectives means answering the following question: Where do we want to go?

The marketing department reviews its objectives, changes them as needed, sets sales targets, and determines market share or contribution to corporate profits to be achieved. Since these objectives are known, the manager can choose a marketing strategy that will assist the company in reaching them. This overall strategy actually describes which segments are to be reached and the desired positioning in each of the company's markets.

Assigning Resources

Market objectives require human and financial resources, both of which are normally limited. The answer to the question "How much effort can we put into it?" determines the means used to reach the objectives already set and also influences the viability of the strategies envisaged. In other words, objectives and strategies cannot be set or developed in a vacuum. Objectives, strategies, variables in the marketing mix, and available resources must all be considered. The result may be the adjustment of certain objectives and strategies.

Determining the Marketing Mix

Once the marketing department has found its orientation, it must answer the question "How do we want to get there?" The time has come to make decisions for each one of the variables of the marketing mix.

While traditional marketing ponders which features a product should have, cultural marketing tries to identify product features, since they are predetermined. In both cases, pricing policy and distribution possibilities are decided and a balance of all four components of the promotion variable (advertising, PR/publicity, promotion, and personal selling) is struck.

Implementation

The last section of the marketing plan lists the operational aspects that will help the company reach its objectives.

The plan should be a detailed statement of the activities projected for each component of the marketing mix, including the responsibilities of each member of the marketing team, coordination of activities, and a schedule clearly indicating all deadlines.

A marketing plan should also include a fall-back or alternative plan. The marketing manager must go through a "future or anticipatory audit" and forecast all possible scenarios that might disrupt the schedule or objectives. Potential reaction by the competition is a key element of this exercise.

The answer to the last question, "How to proceed?", must include some description of the control system selected to measure the company's efforts in achieving its objectives.

In any company, the marketing plan is an essential tool that enables the marketing manager to plan, coordinate, implement, and monitor corporate marketing activities.

11.2.3 Organizational Structure

If a company adopts a marketing plan, the organizational structure of the company enables it to meet the objectives set out. Organizational structure may take many forms, depending on the size of the firm, the product range, and the variety of markets.

In small companies, the marketing team can be quite limited in size. In fact, it may comprise the promoter or entrepreneur working alone. In other cases, marketing activities are carried out by one manager with a small support staff. For instance, presenters who have a season that includes a few productions over eight to ten months may perform all managerial and marketing tasks. On the other hand, production companies in the performing arts and film, as well as record companies and publishing houses, normally have one employee in charge of PR/publicity or sales for the entire distribution market.

Many companies in the arts sector rely on volunteers to support a small team of full-time employees. While some volunteers choose to devote all their time to a single organization, others donate their time to several organizations.[2]

Managers must treat these volunteers as employees and make every effort to integrate them into the organization, motivate them, keep them informed, and even, if necessary, dismiss them. The more that volunteers are made to feel part of the team, the more useful and effective they will be.

Large companies marketing many products and serving several very distinct markets require a more complex organizational structure, in which the major corporate functions are assigned to upper-level executives (e.g., marketing vice-president) who coordinate the activities of several managers from different specialized departments. Figure 11.3 provides an example of an organizational structure that large companies might use. This is, of course, only one of many possible structures.

11.3 STRATEGIES

11.3.1 General Considerations

First, a distinction must be made between a strategy and a tactic. A strategy starts from a broad overview of the means to be used in reaching a final objective – for example, securing a specific market share. A tactic is a timely adjustment of an element in a strategy – for example, inviting critics to the third night rather than the opening night of a production. The marketing manager

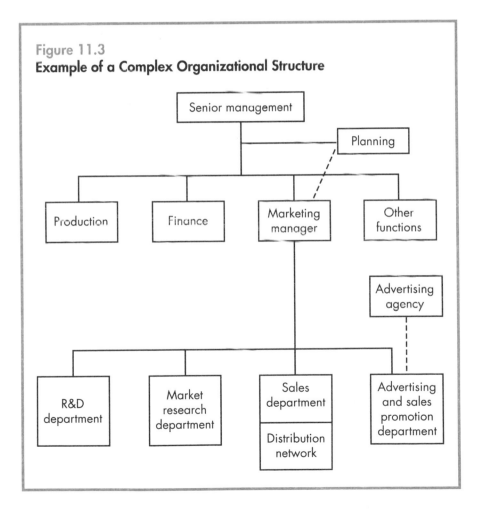

Figure 11.3
Example of a Complex Organizational Structure

Example 11.2
Queensland Arts Council: "Inverted Pyramid" Organizational Chart Impacts on Marketing Arts and Cultural Services

The mission statement of the Queensland Arts Council (QAC) is "arts access statewide." Through three different programs, this organization provides communities throughout Queensland with access to various art forms. QAC's in-schools program is the largest in the world, reaching close to 600,000 students a year, its by-request program gives communities the opportunity to book artists and workshops, and its on-stage program tours leading state and national performers to the regions.

Marketing to such a wide area, when QAC is based in Brisbane, would not be possible without the 62 Local Arts Councils (LACs) spread throughout the state. The relationship between QAC and these volunteer organizations plays a large part in ensuring grassroots support and word-of-mouth publicity for upcoming productions. The LACs are involved from an early stage and are encouraged to promote the shows through member discounts and a commission on ticket sales.

Prior to each tour, the relevant LAC is contacted to discuss what it sees, "on the ground," as the main promotional and advertising opportunities. In many cases these opportunities include small-circulation gazettes not listed in any media guide.

Using the LAC's suggestions, QAC plans a mixed-marketing strategy consisting of some small-scale print or radio advertising, posters and leaflets for the LAC to distribute, and distribution of an eFlyer and information on its Web site (www.qac.org.au). This mixes in with group booking and information distributed to LAC members throughout the year via a quarterly newsletter that gives audience members a chance to learn about the performers and various LAC activities.

The LAC supplies an audience comment book at every performance and then sends QAC a feedback form with thoughts and suggestions on different elements of the production.

As is clear from QAC's mission statement – "arts access statewide" – ticket sales are less important to the organization than ensuring that small communities have an opportunity to see and experience dance, music, drama, and other art forms.

Source: Jane Frank, Lecturer, Queensland University of Technology, Brisbane, Australia.

can use various tactics to reach the desired outcome of a strategy, without modifying the strategy itself.

We have already underscored the fact that in any company there is a hierarchy of strategies, ranging from the overall corporate strategy and marketing strategy to strategies specific to each component of the marketing mix. Moreover, the overall corporate strategy and the marketing strategy are easily confused. Often, the corporate strategy is defined in terms of the marketing mix. In the next section two corporate strategies are presented – competitive strategies and development strategies. Both are closely related to marketing strategy.

11.3.2 Corporate Strategy

Every company must adopt an approach that takes into account the power ratio between itself and other companies in the same sector. This ratio is a function of the size of the company, its rivals, and the importance of its competitive advantage. That competitive advantage or edge may be linked to unique product features as perceived by the consumer. This power ratio shapes both the competitive strategy and the development strategy of the company.

Competitive Strategy

There are four types of competitive strategy: leader, challenger, follower, and specialist.[3]

The Leader Strategy

The leader company dominates a market. This fact is recognized by the competition. The leader is often a point of reference or a target to attack, a model to imitate, or an enemy to avoid. The leader sets the tone of the market and is constantly observed by the competition. The market leader has a host of strategies from which to choose, since it is in a strong position and dominates the market in terms of either size, market share, number of foreign territories where it has a presence, and economies of scale.

In the arts, however, a leader is not necessarily large, since artistic enterprises are usually modest in size. As a result, none can benefit from advantages of size. Leadership in the arts is generally defined in terms of the product itself – that is, the capacity of the production to draw a large audience or to achieve peer recognition. Nevertheless, the leader in the arts does enjoy a choice of strategies.

The Challenger

The challenger is the company considered the main rival of the leader. Obviously, the challenger wants to be the leader. The challenger relies essentially on offensive strategies centred on one goal – taking the lead position in the marketplace. The challenger can confront the leader directly by using the same strategies as the leader. For example, the challenger can run an aggressive ad campaign, develop an impressive product, or offer highly competitive prices.

The challenger may attempt to become top dog by taking advantage of the leader's weaknesses. It could try to infiltrate an underdeveloped network, offer the same product at a more advantageous price, give better service, or penetrate a region or segment that the leader has only partially covered. Obviously, the challenging company cannot simply throw caution to the wind in its choice of strategy. It must try to predict and judge the leader's reactions.

The Follower

The follower is a competitor with a fairly small market segment. It adapts all corporate action to the competition rather than trying for first place. The follower develops strategies to retain the company's market share without trying to increase it very much. These strategies are found primarily in oligopolies, where there are few companies and no one really needs to upset the pecking order.

This type of strategy is not, however, synonymous with laziness or laissez-faire. The follower does what the name says: it follows the competitors' actions very closely and adjusts its own conduct accordingly. These are active strategies based on the reality of the market and all the firms that are active in that market.

The Specialist (or Nicher)

The specialist focuses on a fairly distinct market segment. It carves out a niche that sets the company apart from the competition. The company then concentrates exclusively on that niche.

Specialization may stem from the originality of the product, knowledge of certain foreign territories, the use of some unique technique, or a production capacity that, in turn, lowers retail prices. Any of these may prove a distinct advantage. This type of strategy may be adopted by a small company in the cultural sector that must compete against established giants.[4] For example, Scéno Plus, a Canadian company, has developed solid niche expertise in the theatre design and construction market, becoming a world leader in the sector. This company is responsible for designing all of Cirque du Soleil's theatres as well as the Las Vegas theatre where Céline Dion performs.

Capsule 11.1
History of Scéno Plus

Founded in 1985, Scéno Plus specializes in the design and construction of cultural and recreational facilities based on innovative solutions. The Scéno Plus team combines the passion and expertise of architects, technicians, stage designers, graphic designers, stage and audiovisual equipment designers, and project managers to carry out its highly ambitious projects.

Services

Upon its inception, Scéno Plus offered theatre design and planning services (layout and equipment). In 1985, however, recognizing the need for better coordination of all the steps involved in developing its projects in order to offer the highest standard of performance at both the functional and the aesthetic level, the company added project management to its range of integrated services.

Awards

In 1995, Cirque du Soleil commissioned Scéno Plus to design its second theatre in Las Vegas. The Bellagio Theatre is a unique performance space featuring a stage that is actually a deep pool containing six million litres of water. This remarkable project earned Scéno Plus and Cirque du Soleil the prestigious 1998 *Eddy Entertainment Design Award*, bestowed in New York, the 1999 *Award for Technical Merit* of the Canadian Institute for Theatre Technology, and the 1998 *Las Vegas Showroom of the Year Award*.

Source: Scéno Plus. http://www.sceno-plus.com/

Development Strategies

Most companies want to increase sales, profits, market share, organizational size, or international visibility. These are all examples of development objectives. The manager seeking to reach these objectives can use different strategies based on market-product pairing. Ansoff[5] outlines four strategies: market penetration, market development, product development, and diversification (see Table 11.2).

Through the first strategy, market penetration, a company attempts to increase product sales in existing markets by using different techniques. The company could, for example, create a more dynamic distribution network,

Table 11.2
The Ansoff Model

	Current market	**New market**
Current product	Market penetration	Market development
New product	Product development	Diversification

launch a new promotional campaign, or set more advantageous prices. In any event, the company remains in the same niche with the same product.

Market development enables a company to increase sales by introducing its corporate products into new markets without changing the market segment already held. The company thus expands its clientele by offering the same product to new customers. A touring company that convinces presenters in other regions to buy its show and a promoter trying to break into the international market with a particular artist exemplify this strategy, as does the movie producer who develops international contacts in order to facilitate future co-productions with foreign companies.

The product-development strategy enables a company to increase sales by offering completely new or modified products to currently held markets. The sale of spin-off products is part of this strategy.

The diversification strategy allows a company to improve its sales figures by offering a new product for new markets. This strategy is riskier than the other three, since it involves two new unknowns: the product and the market. This is the strategy used by large corporate conglomerates that own companies in several cultural sectors – for example, film production, publishing, and electronic games.

Table 11.3 lists several examples of possible action for each of the strategies discussed above.

Ansoff's grid enables a company to classify different scenarios according to the risk associated with a particular choice of strategy. The business risk rises with the newness of the product or market. Diversification as a strategy is therefore the riskiest, since new products are developed for new and unfamiliar markets. The penetration strategy is the least risky, since the company remains in terra cognita. The other two strategies represent interim situations.

This analytical tool may be used in various market contexts. For example, the agents in a specific region may use the grid to compare the strategic

Table 11.3

Possible Courses of Action for Ansoff's Four Strategies

1. Market penetration (increase current product use in existing markets)	Increase the customer's current rate of use • Increase the purchase unit • Increase the product's rate of obsolescence • Advertise other product uses • Offer bonuses for increased use
	Attract the competition's clientele • Improve brand differentiation • Increase promotion
	Attract non-customers • Use samples, bonuses, and the like to encourage consumers to try the product • Adjust prices up or down • Advertise new product uses
2. Market development (sell current products in new markets)	Open up new geographic markets • Regional expansion • National expansion • International expansion
	Attract other market sectors • Develop different versions of the product for other sectors • Penetrate other distribution channels • Advertise in other media
3. Product development (create new products for existing markets)	Develop new product features • Adapt (to other ideas, other improvements) • Modify (colour, movement, sound, scent, shape, line) • Amplify (stronger, longer, thicker, greater value) • Miniaturize (smaller, shorter, lighter) • Substitute (different ingredients, new processes, other possibilities) • Change the look (new design, new layout, new order, new component) • Turn around completely (invert) • Combine (mix, match, pair up elements, blend parts, objects, attributes, and ideas)
	Develop different degrees of quality
	Create new models and formats (proliferation of products)
4. Diversification (create new products for new markets)	Any new product developed by the company is earmarked for a new market

Source: Adapted from Kotler, P., and B. Dubois. 1973. *Marketing management, analyse, planification et contrôle*, 2nd ed. Paris: Publi-Union, p. 287.

choices open to them in their bid to develop tourism. Table 11.4 illustrates a hypothetical situation for a region that wants to lead a coordinated offensive campaign to attract tourists. The possible choices are given in terms of the risk involved.

The strategy involving the least risk consists of trying to extend the tourist's visit and increase the tourist's expenditures through coordinated promotion of the activities that already exist in the region (square 1). This objective can be reached by modifying the other three components of the marketing mix (price, distribution, and promotion), by organizing a promotional campaign that vaunts the various cultural products to the existing clientele, or by offering reduced prices to those who combine several activities.

A second strategy (square 2), which both extends the tourist's stay and increases the tourist's expenditures, consists of offering a new activity (new product) to the current clientele. For example, a region that already attracts sports lovers for hunting and fishing might consider opening a nature-interpretation centre that would reach the same clientele.

Marketers can also try to attract people not reached by current strategies, through a promotional campaign abroad or package deals offered to special categories of customers, such as seniors, who are not part of the current clientele (square 3).

Finally, there is the possibility of developing a new offering likely to interest another market segment, such as a summer theatre or festival (square 4).

11.3.3 Marketing Strategies

Strategic Choices

Table 11.4
Use of Ansoff's Grid to Increase Regional Tourist Traffic

	Current market	**New market**
Current product	1 Penetration Intensive promotion	3 Market development Promotion abroad or packages
New product	2 Development of new products Opening of a nature-interpretation centre	4 Diversification Establishment of a summer theatre or other type of festival

Example 11.3
Theatre Bay Area Marketing Strategy: Stunningly Audacious and Captivatingly Simple (A Penetration Strategy)

Founded in 1976, Theatre Bay Area (TBA) is a not-for-profit service organization with a mission to unite, strengthen, and promote theatre in the San Francisco Bay Area. Since 1998, TBA has participated in "social marketing" programs designed to influence the voluntary behaviour of target audiences, given the view that the performing arts are an essential public good. In this context, TBA organized a Free Night of Theatre (FNOT) in October 2005 – part of a pilot project developed with Theatre Communications Group, a national service organization. Philadelphia, Pennsylvania, and Austin, Texas, also participated in the project.

The marketing objective was to increase attendance at and exposure to live theatre. In response, 93 theatre companies agreed to give away a segment of tickets for their performances clustering on or near the designated date. The primary target was new audience members, including non-traditional theatre-goers. A diverse committee of leaders from the theatre community, representing both large and small producers, led the FNOT campaign, which was fully funded by local corporations and foundations. Elements of the campaign included print, e-card, radio, and TV advertising and banners in mass transit stations throughout the region.

A high-visibility launch event featuring live performances and civic dignitaries was paired with the opening of an exclusive TBA-hosted TIX Bay Area Web site section for reservations, which immediately received over 100,000 hits. The first 4,000 tickets were "sold" within a week, with a final total of 7,500 tickets distributed for 122 performances. By all measures, the event was extremely successful: 80% of the attendees had never been to the theatre attended, 70% were under the age of 50, a substantial majority were women, and 40% were people of colour.

Results from a post-event e-mail survey conducted by a nationally recognized research firm showed that these FNOT patrons returned to the theatre. More than a third of the respondents returned to their FNOT host theatre as a paying customer, and a third reported attending theatre more often than before, with 85% of those directly attributing their increased patronage to FNOT; 98% indicated interest in attending future FNOT events. In 2006 FNOT expanded to 15 cities nationwide, using TBA's campaign model.

Source: Anne W. Smith, DPA, Arts Management and Education Services, San Francisco, USA.

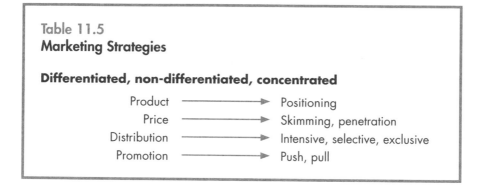

Table 11.5
Marketing Strategies

Differentiated, non-differentiated, concentrated

Product	⟶	Positioning
Price	⟶	Skimming, penetration
Distribution	⟶	Intensive, selective, exclusive
Promotion	⟶	Push, pull

The main strategies available to a marketing department have been outlined in previous chapters (see also Table 11.5).

These strategies can be combined to provide a firm with an array of strategic options. For example, the firm seeking positioning could opt for price skimming, selective distribution, and a push strategy. Another firm might use penetration pricing, intensive distribution, and a pull strategy.

Analysis of Potential Marketing Strategies within a Market

Choosing from the arsenal of marketing strategies described requires some analysis of the strategic position of the company's product(s). The strategic position may be defined using the BCG model, developed by the Boston Consulting Group.[6] This model takes into consideration the position of the company or one of its products based on the market share relative to the market leader's share, and the rate of growth for that market. For instance, if one company has a market share of 20% while the leader holds 60% – a ratio of 1:3 – the situation is different from one in which the main competitor also holds 20% – a ratio of 1:1. In the first case there is a leader that can impose its will on the market, whereas in the second case there are equal opponents competing for the consumer's patronage. Similarly, the strategic significance of these market shares would be different in a high-growth market, where a firm can increase its sales by attracting new customers, and a stagnant market, where firms lock horns over market-share percentiles.

This analysis of a product market produces the BCG matrix, with four squares defining four probable situations. They are: 1) fairly large market share in a high-growth market, 2) fairly small share in a high-growth market, 3) fairly large share in a low-growth market, 4) fairly small share in a low-growth market (see Table 11.6).

Table 11.6
The BCG Model

		Relative market share	
		Large	Small
Market growth	High	Stars	Problem children
	Low	Cash cows	Dogs

Stars

A company's star products are those that represent a large market share in a growth market. These products require a large injection of funds to finance growth. They are profitable when demand drops and could eventually become cash cows in a mature market.

Problem Children

A company must withdraw the "problem child" products that it does not intend to improve in terms of market share. Simply maintaining these products in their market position drains away capital that cannot be recovered. Other products in this category should be financed as necessary to improve their position vis-à-vis competing products.

Cash Cows

If the market is experiencing sluggish growth, a company may reap substantial profits from its products with a large market share. These profits should serve to fund star products and improve the competitive situation for "problem child" products.

Dogs

No company can afford to use its capital to increase its market share in a market with little potential for growth. The company has the choice of cutting its marketing costs to the bare bones for the dog product, knowing that this decision will lead to withdrawal of the product.

Product analysis based on the BCG matrix promotes the making of strategic decisions, such as supporting star products, investing selectively in problem children, maximizing profits from cash cows, and cutting out dogs. The matrix also enables a company to gauge future financial needs, the potential profitability of products, and the balance required in its portfolio of products.

This type of analysis applies particularly to large corporations whose objective is profitability – for example, in the cultural industries. The conceptual framework may also be used to analyze the market for small firms in the arts, since it allows for greater understanding of market dynamics and possible market changes or trends.

11.4 CONTROL

Control consists of examining all or part of the results of a marketing move in order to judge the impact of the tactic or strategy, and then making any necessary changes should there be a gap between projections and reality. The marketing manager using the marketing plan illustrated in Figure 11.2 could monitor one, several, or all of the components. It is considered a marketing audit if all components are controlled.

11.4.1 Control by Cycle

Marketing activities should be monitored or evaluated in a continuous and regular fashion using specific tools. Control is part of this cycle, which includes planning and implementing corrective measures. Naturally, only if planning has occurred can there be any form of control.

The objectives of the marketing unit and of each variable or component of the marketing mix translate to a series of actions or programs. These objectives and courses of action must correspond to norms and criteria that measure the gap between projection and reality. Analysis of the causes of any differences should lead to the adoption of corrective measures affecting the objectives, the action taken, or both (see Figure 11.4).

11.4.2 Control Tools and Measures

All managers know that they must control their firm's operations in order to ensure that its objectives are met. This aspect takes on added importance in cases where the government takes into account the extent of an organization's control of its business.[7]

Tools used in marketing control vary according to what is actually analyzed and the light shed upon it through analysis, the objectives of the marketing department, the objectives of each variable in the marketing mix, the budget presented, and so on. Each one of these may be monitored and may require specific tools.

The objectives of the marketing department usually translate to sales figures, number of visitors, market share, or profit forecasts. The tools used are therefore tailored to these parameters. The marketing manager wants to

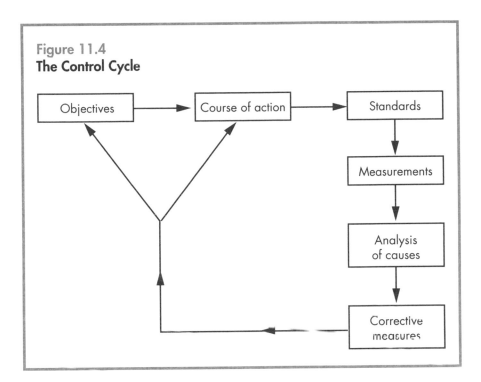

Figure 11.4
The Control Cycle

```
┌─────────────┐      ┌──────────────────┐      ┌──────────────┐
│ Objectives  │ ───► │ Course of action │ ───► │  Standards   │
└─────────────┘      └──────────────────┘      └──────────────┘
                                                       │
                                                       ▼
                                               ┌──────────────┐
                                               │ Measurements │
                                               └──────────────┘
                                                       │
                                                       ▼
                                               ┌──────────────┐
                                               │   Analysis   │
                                               │  of causes   │
                                               └──────────────┘
                                                       │
                                                       ▼
                                               ┌──────────────┐
                                               │  Corrective  │
                                               │  measures    │
                                               └──────────────┘
```

know if the sales volume targeted was actually reached. This can be ascertained by comparing data obtained from sales reports, as detailed in the marketing plan, on an objective-by-objective basis. Similarly, the market share can be checked by comparing sales to demand according to the objective expressed in the marketing plan. Profitability can be reviewed by looking over the financial statement and comparing it to the objectives in the plan.

The next step is to check not only whether the objectives were reached, but also whether they were reached efficiently, for each component of the marketing mix (product, price, place, and promotion). The marketing manager or executive can check sales figures per product over time and scrutinize profitability per product or territory. The price levels of the company in comparison to those of the competition can be studied, as can the effectiveness of promotional tools currently or previously used.

The internal data and secondary data gathered from the company's MIS are vital to this exercise. Control may also involve the use of primary data, in which case the marketing manager can measure to see whether product positioning is what it should be, whether product awareness created through a promotional campaign corresponds to the objectives set, and whether members of the distribution network are satisfied.

The marketing manager or executive should develop specific criteria to monitor operations and periodically compare results, ensuring that the same criteria are being used. Dissimilar criteria are useless because they do not permit a real comparison of the results obtained. Similarly, inaccurate measures can lead to questionable or wrong decisions.[8]

One tool that the marketing manager can develop to monitor the performance of marketing activities is the balanced scorecard. This is an analytical document that incorporates a set of selected performance indicators in order to keep track of progress. Introduced by Kaplan and Norton in 1992, the balanced scorecard is an effective performance management tool that allows managers to include all the indicators necessary to implement an organizational strategy. It is a widely used tool that requires careful deliberation on the part of marketing managers when choosing the indicators to include.

The balanced scorecard must reflect the firm's marketing objectives and strategies. In addition, the manager must understand the causal link and use financial as well as non-financial measures originating both internally and externally. This instrument serves not only to monitor the firm's activities, but also as a tool of communication between marketing managers and company management.

11.4.3 The Marketing Audit

The marketing audit is an in-depth, systematic, periodic critical study of a company's marketing orientation within its specific environment. This audit should enable a company to solve current problems, reinforce its competitive strengths, and raise the level of efficiency and profitability in its marketing activities.

The marketing audit reviews the objectives, policy, organization, procedures, and staff of a company. The audit should be carried out regularly, not only during a crisis. It should cover all corporate marketing activities, not only those experiencing difficulties. An independent firm or another department that the board of directors or company executive considers credible should perform the audit, to ensure objectivity.

Table 11.7 is a checklist for a marketing audit. It includes all the questions that an organization should ask during an audit.

Table 11.7
Key Questions to Ask in a Marketing Audit

A. Situational analysis

Market and environment

- Which market(s) does the company already reach?
- Who are its customers?
- How are the market segments defined?
- What is the current and the potential demand?
- Who are the competitors? How big are they? What strategies do they use?
- Which environmental elements are likely to affect the company? How have they evolved and how might they evolve?

Company

- What is the company's mission?
- What are the company's corporate objectives?
- What are the company's overall strategies?
- What are the company's strengths and weaknesses?
- Does the company have a distinct advantage? What is it?
- Does the company have a long-term plan? A short-term plan?

B. Analysis of the marketing plan

Objectives and strategies

- What are the marketing objectives?
- What results have been achieved through these objectives?
- What marketing strategies does the company use? Which market segments have been targeted? What is the company's positioning?
- Do these strategies correspond to the overall corporate strategy?
- Which control measures has the company put in place to evaluate the marketing objectives and efficiency of corporate strategies?

Marketing mix

- Which objectives have been defined for the variables of the marketing mix?
- What is the product strategy?
- What is the positioning sought for each product?
- Is the product mix consistent?
- Is the service offered adequate?
- How does the product itself help the company reach its marketing objectives?
- What is the pricing strategy?
- Which factors have been considered in setting the product price?

(continued)

Table 11.7 (continued)

- How does the price compare to that of the competition?
- How does the pricing strategy work toward achieving the corporate marketing objectives?
- Which distribution strategy has been adopted?
- Are the distribution networks adequate? Effective?
- Are relations positive among the members of the distribution channel?
- How does the distribution strategy work toward achieving the corporate marketing objectives?
- What is the promotional strategy?
- What is the role of each component of the promotional mix?
- Has the promotional mix been tested? How, and with what result?
- How does the promotional strategy work toward achieving the corporate marketing objectives?
- Do the strategies of each variable in the marketing mix correspond to the overall marketing strategy?

C. Analysis of the marketing program
- Is there a written plan of the activities (programs) for each variable of the marketing mix?
- What role does each member of the marketing department play in the success of the marketing plan? Have the tasks been assigned clearly?
- Is there a schedule? Is it followed?
- How are the various functions coordinated?
- Is there an alternative marketing plan? Is it realistic?

D. Forecasts
- How are the environment and competition developing?
- What effect have they had on the organization?
- Is the company ready to handle changes foreseen in the environment?
- What interesting business opportunities are available to the company?
- What are the keys to success for the company? How can the company acquire the new skills or knowledge it needs?

E. Suggestions
- What changes should the company make in its objectives and strategies?
- How can the company effect these changes?
- What will the cost be?
- What additional information is needed to make relevant decisions?

SUMMARY

Marketing planning and control are two complementary parts of the same process. Planning —the setting of operational objectives and drafting of specific policies — must necessarily precede any monitoring of marketing activities. Only with reference to objectives and policies can the marketing manager assess the results of marketing activities.

Marketing planning depends on two things: the creation of a marketing strategy and the drafting of a marketing plan. Planning relies on the answers to the following five questions:

- Where are we and where are we going?
- Where do we want to go?
- What effort are we going to expend?
- How do we want to get there?
- How can we do it?

Before choosing a marketing strategy, the marketing manager may want to define the company's strategic position in the marketplace. The BCG model may prove useful, as it positions competitors' products according to the market share of each competitor or according to market growth. The company can choose between two types of strategies: competitive and development.

Competitive strategies take into account the power ratio that already exists among firms active in the sector. The strategies based on the respective position of each firm are called the leader, the challenger, the follower, and the specialist.

The development strategies categorized in Ansoff's grid set out parameters based on the product and the market. Depending on degree of novelty, or newness, a company may decide to concentrate on its current market with an existing product, launch its product in a new market, or introduce a new product into a new market.

A marketing plan consists of five steps: situational analysis; definition of marketing strategy (marketing objectives, target markets, positioning, and other strategies); assigning of financial and human resources (budget); decision on the marketing mix; and implementation (alternative plan, control mechanisms).

Marketing control consists of tracking and evaluating how well objectives are being met based on qualitative and quantitative standards. It should be seen as a cycle. Beyond the results provided by sales figures and market share, the marketing manager usually controls the results for each variable of the marketing mix. The manager may also want to fully and systematically review all marketing operations – in other words, proceed with a marketing audit.

QUESTIONS

1. What is the planning and monitoring cycle?

2. Where does the "distinct advantage" fit into a marketing strategy?

3. How does the strategic planning process in a cultural enterprise differ from that of a traditional business?

4. Describe the four competitive strategies.

5. Why is the diversification strategy riskier than the penetration strategy, according to Ansoff's grid?

6. What are the main elements of a marketing plan?

7. Provide examples of the elements that a manager can control for each variable of the marketing mix.

8. What is a marketing audit?

Notes

1. Voss Giraud, Z., and G.B. Voss. 2000. "Exploring the Impact of Organizational Values and Strategic Orientation on Performance in Not-for-Profit Professional Theatre." *International Journal of Arts Management*, Vol. 3, n° 1 (Fall), p. 62–78.

2. Wymer, W.W. Jr., and J.L. Brudney. 2000. "Marketing Management in Arts Organizations: Differentiating Arts and Culture Volunteers from Other Volunteers." *International Journal of Arts Management*, Vol. 2, n° 3 (Spring), p. 40–54.

3. Lambin, J.-J. 1998. *Le marketing stratégique*, 4th ed. Paris: Ediscience International.

4. Valentin, M. 1993. "Le marché du disque : un oligopole avec frange concurrentielle." In *Proceedings of the Second International Conference on Arts and Cultural Management*. Jouy-en-Josas, France: Groupe HEC.

5. Ansoff, I. 1957. "Strategies for Diversification." *Harvard Business Review* (September/October).

6. Lambin, J.-J. 1998. *Le marketing stratégique*, 4th ed. Paris: Ediscience International.

7. See, for example, Paulus, O. 2003. "Measuring Museum Performance: A Study of Museums in France and the United States." *International Journal of Arts Management*, Vol. 6, n° 1 (Fall), p. 50–64; Chatelain-Ponroy, S. 2001. "Management Control and Museums." *International Journal of Arts Management*, Vol. 4, n° 1 (Fall), p. 38–48.

8. Silderberg, T. 2005. "The Importance of Accuracy in Attendance Reporting." *International Journal of Arts Management*, Vol. 8, n° 1 (Fall), p. 4–8.

For Further Reference

Einola, K., and N. Turgeon. 2000. "International Marketing of Canadian Television Programs: Industry Players, Export Successes and Strategic Challenges." *International Journal of Arts Management*, Vol. 3, n° 1 (Fall), p. 46–62.

Mejon, J.C., E.C. Fransi and A.T. Johansson. 2004. "Marketing Management in Cultural Organizations: A Case Study of Catalan Museums." *International Journal of Arts Management*, Vol. 6, n° 2 (Winter), p. 11–23.

Conclusion

The marketing model presented in this book provides the manager of a cultural or artistic enterprise with a framework and an analytical outline. It ties together the different aspects involved in any marketing process. Of course, readers have realized by now that marketing is not an exact science but, rather, a blend of science and art. It is a science in that problems can be rigorously analyzed using recognized models, and an art in that marketing concepts and strategies are rarely applied under textbook or clear-cut circumstances. The marketing manager must therefore make decisions without all the necessary information, in a situation that is in perpetual flux, and must therefore know how to trust his or her intuition.

Our knowledge of the cultural consumer remains quite limited. The models developed to explain consumer behaviour in other purchasing situations are useful only in the sense that they enable us to understand phenomena related to all purchasing situations, including those involving cultural products. Research on the special behaviour of cultural consumers must continue, since this information will help the marketing manager support the artistic mission of the company. Naturally, further research in cultural marketing is needed, and just as traditional marketing evolved from other sciences by developing its own models, cultural marketing must borrow relevant traditional concepts while still acquiring its own specific body of knowledge.

Anyone considering a marketing career in an artistic or cultural enterprise should have the same qualities as any other good marketer – intuition, imagination, empathy, analytical skills, and the ability to summarize material and deal with uncertainty. The ideal marketing manager will be able to understand and explain a cultural product and, above all, enjoy taking risks and making miracles happen on a shoestring budget. Lastly, like an artist, the marketing manager needs talent to succeed – tools may be acquired, but not talent.

The following, final, figure summarizes the marketing model for culture and the arts, including the main concepts touched upon in this book. We ask readers to consider the model as a starting point for their own marketing career in the cultural milieu.

The Marketing Model for Culture and the Arts

Enterprise

Company	Product
Mission	Artistic product
Objectives	Spin-off product
Resources	Customer service
• human	Experience
• financial	Benefits
• technical	Dimension
Image	• referential
Competitive advantage	• technical
Marketing plan	• circumstantial
Organization	Complexity
Strategies	Life cycle
• corporate (competitive/development)	Marketing plan
• marketing	New-product development
Control	• R&D
• cycle	• risk
• marketing audit	Line and range
	Brand

Market information system

Internal data
Secondary data
Primary data

- public
- private
- exploratory, descriptive, and causal research
- 14 steps

Residual marketing mix

Price
$ – Related expenses
– Time – Risk
– Effort expended
Skimming – Penetration

Place
Channels – Physical distribution –
Location
Intensive distribution –
Selective distribution –
Exclusive distribution

Promotion
Tools
- advertising
- personal selling
- PR
- sales promotion

Respective role of each tool
Communications plan
Push – pull

Markets

Consumers	Private sector
Demand	Arts patrons
Behaviours	Foundations
Segmentation –	Sponsors
Positioning	
Differentiation –	
Non-cifferentiation –	
Concentration	

Governments	Partners
Federal	Distribution intermediairies
Provincial	Co-production
Municipal	Distribution partners
	Media

Time
Specificity of the company

Competition
Leisure industry
Fragmentation
Globalization

Macro-environment
- economic
- political-legal
- demographic
- cultural

Index